What readers

Reading these pages is like walking along the dusty roads of the Gedarenes, or the hills by the Sea of Galilee, with Jesus and his disciples as he lifted the veil on the world they thought they understood. In *Toolbox for Discipleship and Growth* the dynamics of the supernatural realm are translated for a new generation of disciples into a whole new culture with all the same old human problems. In most practical and non-sensational ways, Jan entrusts a lifetime of Spirit-given revelation and the experiences gleaned from an anointed ministry to the modern spiritual warrior. He delivers an armoury of spiritual weapons to the Body of Christ. If you are serious about ministry, if you want to help people to be free, fruitful, and full of the abundant life Jesus came to give us, read this book and apply it to your own life. Then, as the Holy Spirit leads and empowers you, take what you have freely received, and freely give. What makes this work even more impactful to me is that I know the faith, the prayer, the ministry and the personal price Jan has paid to fulfill this ministry calling and now to deliver his life's work to the Church. It is a precious and powerful gift from a true servant of Christ.

—Reverend Glenn Breitkreuz
Lead Pastor, Christian Fellowship Assembly
Grande Prairie, AB

Phyllis and I have known Jan and Brenda for many years, both as participants in Jan's seminars and as co-ministers with them. This book, *Toolbox for Discipleship and Growth*, is packed full of great teaching, amazing stories and practical lessons. The "tools" section at the end of the book features practical helps, providing a useful guide for pastors, leaders and counsellors. We highly recommend this book to pastors, teachers, and those who need ministry.

—Revs. David and Phyllis Roch
Founding Pastors of Dawson Creek Community Church
and Heart to Change the World
Ministers in the Prophetic
Conference Speakers

Sold out commitment and unswerving devotion to God describe both Jan and his ministry to the people God has led into his life. This book serves as a legacy of how God works in the life of an obedient servant of His. I have had the privilege of being alongside Jan over the many years he has counselled the oppressed, and brought them to the throne room of God for healing and freedom. Jan has captured the heart of God in this book, and given us a treasure house of wisdom for practical ministry to others. The tools and advice Jan provides us are down to earth, tested and true. Jan is a man of integrity, and what he shares in his book is an extension of his love and calling to help people "break free" into their destiny as sons and daughters of Christ. I truly recommend it to anyone who desires to live and serve God with all their heart.

—Elmer Spilchen

President/Chair, Break Free Ministries

Life Care Pastor, Grande Prairie Alliance Church

TOOLBOX
for Discipleship and Growth

Practical Teaching for Helping Yourself and Others Break Free

Jan Van Haga

TOOLBOX FOR DISCIPLESHIP AND GROWTH
Copyright © 2019 by Jan Van Haga

This book is intended to provide helpful information on the subjects discussed, and is not a substitution for medical advice. As in all matters of health, please consult a physician before undertaking any changes to diet, exercise, and medication.

The views and opinions expressed in this publication belong solely to the author, and do not reflect those of Word Alive Press or any of its employees.

Printed in Canada

ISBN: 978-1-4866-1740-1

Word Alive Press
119 De Baets Street, Winnipeg, MB R2J 3R9
www.wordalivepress.ca

MIX
Paper from responsible sources
FSC® C016245

Cataloguing in Publication may be obtained through Library and Archives Canada

CONTENTS

ACKNOWLEDGEMENTS

First and foremost, I would like to thank my Father God for never giving up on me completing this book. Without His help it would have never been finished. All praise goes to Him. I would also like to thank the many people who assisted in typing, researching and editing my words. Your help was invaluable. You all know who you are. I do want to say a special thanks to two amazing women who were with me from the beginning of this journey. Rhonda Hewko and Vanessa Klassen, you were both steadfast and sure in your commitment to seeing this book published. Thank you for your faith in me and your patience to endure to the end. God bless all of you for your faithfulness to God and to me.

GOD'S CALL ON YOUR LIFE

Part I

Chapter One

INTRODUCTION

THIS BOOK/MANUAL HAS BEEN ON MY LIST OF THINGS TO DO FOR A LONG time. Writing a book was not something that I had ever wanted or planned to do. The call to write a book, and its specific format, came out of a time of prayer in the mid 1990s. While seeking God's direction for my life, I was shown two books lying on a tabletop. One was large, and looked to me to be a participant's manual for a seminar. The other, which I presumed to be the leader's handbook for the seminar, was much smaller. My strong impression was that I was to create the material I had been shown. With this revelation and understanding in mind, I immediately went to work. Six to eight months later, I had a somewhat rough but completed seminar outline and was ready for a trial run. I gathered about a dozen participants and held a one-day seminar. It was awesome, resulting in some real fruit and benefit to those attending. Its obvious effectiveness definitely had me looking forward to the day when I could introduce my seminar to local pastors.

But life moved quickly on. Before I could get my seminar up and going, I was introduced to Pastor Craig Hill from Denver, Colorado, as well as a series of seminars he'd developed, which at that time were called *From Curses to Blessing*. I laid aside my own materials and took advantage of the opportunity to become a coordinator for Pastor Craig's seminars. Coordinating these seminars involved me travelling for a few years, presenting and promoting the various Family Foundations seminars that are still in use today in many locations around the world. (Information about them is available online at www.familyfoundations.com.)

While I was leading one of these seminars, a woman who had her own full-time counselling ministry joined our team as a small group ministry facilitator. She approached me at the seminar and said, "Jan, I think the Lord is telling me you are to write a book."

Another team member responded, "Well, isn't that interesting. Jan, just this morning as you were talking to participants, I thought to myself, 'These things that Jan talks about during break times need to be in a book.'"

I heard what they said, but paid little attention and, before long, forgot about it. Subsequently, over the years, various people—some that did not even know me—also said, "You are to write a book." Once again, I paid little, if any, attention to them; I was just not interested.

Then, while coordinating a seminar in a distant small town where I knew none of the participants, a man came running toward me from the other side of the room. He introduced himself as the principal of the public school and stated, "Jan, the things we're hearing from you need to be in a book. I'm not talking about the words spoken on the DVDs. I'm talking about those things that you share during break times; they need to be in a book!" As soon as he had said that, his mouth literally fell open, and he said, "Oh, you're already writing a book, are you?" Well, I wasn't. But those words, for the first time, really got my attention. Certainly it was on my mind, and I was thinking much about it. In fact, because of the number of individuals that had, over the years, raised this question, I had been, in a sense, drawn to mentally consider what a book would look like if I were to write one. I finally surrendered to the repeated reminders by simply saying, "Okay, Lord."

Still, I did not just jump into it. Many things stood in the way of writing. The largest impediment was my commitment to Break Free Ministries, a full-time counselling and deliverance ministry (which I had founded a few years earlier). I was so busy with it that it did not leave time and energy for book writing.

Then, in 2003, I was diagnosed with burnout. I had been suffering from increasing and severe head pains and seizures in the brain. This unforeseen disability removed me from the office for about a year, with instructions to rest my brain. There was really no other option at that time; something as simple as reading my Bible was overload for my brain. Over the next few years, the pain gradually subsided and I slowly began working full-time again.

Then in 2008, I had another breakdown; the head pain and other symptoms were considerably more severe than previously. This caused my psychologist and consulting medical specialists to arrange another head scan.

The three or four scans taken during the previous breakdown had failed to reveal any physical problems in the brain. However, this latest scan—the most in-depth available—gave evidence of something not previously visible. The doctor described a picture of a "black rut" that cut through the white matter of the cortex from side to side! What could have happened to cause such a severe brain injury? As I looked back over my life history, I recalled an incident on a job site that I had not thought of for many, many years.

At the age of seventeen, I had fallen from the second storey of a three-storey commercial building, landing head-first on a pile of concrete blocks. This latest scan left me with no doubt that there had been severe damage to my brain at the time of that fall. The apparent reason for the severe head pain was what one of the medical experts called "mini seizures," akin to tiny needles being driven through the brain. One of my doctors said, "Jan, we know of these seizures, but at this time we have no means by which to deal with them. We cannot help you. My instructions for you are to go home, sleep and just rest. Do very little reading, even from your Bible. Go ahead and do a little work in your garage. Who knows? Maybe someday you'll even write a book."

With no help available from the medical field, I lived on with continuing pain and ever-decreasing ability. I eventually lost the ability to do simple, everyday things, at times not able to even find my own bedroom. Then one night, about midnight, I awoke. I was in much pain and deeply discouraged, fearing my working days were over. And then, the Lord spoke!

"Jan, write the book!"

I plainly heard the instruction, but had no idea how to proceed. Despite my best efforts, even after months of trying, I was unable to produce anything on paper. Then one morning I awoke and found myself wondering if there may be some useable material in the previously prepared seminar manual, the one I had written years ago and shelved before completion. I searched for and found the unfinished manual. I was ecstatic! It certainly needed some work, but it became the foundation for the first five chapters of this book, a perfect fit that could only have been foreseen and shaped by God Himself.

Just by reading this far into the book, you, the reader, will have realized that God has been at my side, helping and encouraging, directing and enabling every step of the way. Most of us, as born-again believers, are familiar with the Scripture that says, *"I live in a high and holy place, but also with the one who is contrite and lowly in spirit, to revive the spirit of the lowly and to revive the heart of the contrite"* (Isaiah 57:15). I have certainly experienced that this promise is true. The Lord Himself has revived both my heart and spirit, making it possible for me to continue this book to completion.

We may sometimes question how personally involved God wants to be with us. From my own experience, I assure you that we can put our doubts and uncertainties aside and confidently believe His promises. God desires to be intimately close to me and to you. Know that He desires to be a part of our every thought and action, without control and manipulation, but instead with divine protection and supernatural direction. His desire is that we would grow into the very image of His son, Jesus; and in that image, with the authority given us in the name of Jesus, that we would be able to do the same things that Jesus did.

Biblical references and application will be enountered in almost every chapter, relative to the teaching and Biblical principles presented there. Some readers may at times find the book repetitious; you may find the same examples or Scriptures cited in different chapters. I have purposely done this at times, simply to emphasize an important point or significant revelation. The book is not intended for just a once-through read, although that is a good start. It is designed to be much more. It is written very specifically as a reference resource for the spiritual equipping and growth of God's saints. The material included has been tested, tried and proven effective during more than twenty-five years of ministering to hundreds of people who have come seeking understanding, help and freedom. The overarching purpose for this book is first to encourage every reader to become a disciple of Jesus. From there, in obedience to the command of Jesus, let us go forth, making more disciples. Being and making disciples is a central theme emphasized throughout the whole of this book. As disciples of Jesus, we have both the mandate and authority to set people free from all manner of problems and afflictions.

My desire and intent is for you, the reader and potential practitioner, to use this book while you minister to others. A large part of the book is written and laid out in an "instruction manual" format. This allows you to draw directly from the book as a ready tool during a ministry session. The manual-like format intentionally groups related teachings, making it easy for you to find topics or teachings while in session. As you can see in the Table of Contents, one chapter is entitled the "Toolbox." Subjects in the "Toolbox" are linked to and expand on topics found elsewhere in the book. This keeps useful ministry tools and answers to important questions easily accessible during study, preparation and ministry time. For example: there are tools designed to assist in uncovering and dealing with sin issues. Also, you will find step-by-step means to walk individuals through a deliverance session. If you are ministering to someone afflicted with dissociative identity disorder (DID) or multiple personality disorder (MPD), you will find appropriate tools provided to equip you to help set them free!

The foundation: the platform and power of this book are based on the commands, principles and authority Jesus imparted to His followers just before leaving this earth. In Matthew 28:18–20, Jesus said, *"All authority in heaven and on earth has been given to me. Therefore go and make disciples of all nations, baptizing them in the name of the Father and of the Son and of the Holy Spirit, and teaching them to obey everything I have commanded you. And surely I am with you always, to the very end of the age."*

Thus, I present to you my manual on how to set the captives free by delivering them from the clutches of Satan, and in the midst of this, raising up disciples that raise up more disciples.

Chapter Two

GOD'S CALL REVEALED AND DEFINED

2.1. God has a Call on Your Life and Mine

THIS CHAPTER IS WRITTEN PRIMARILY SO THAT YOU WILL REALIZE AND respond to the fact that God has a call on your life. But it is not just any call. It is a calling and purpose that is specifically designed for you, and you alone! I strongly encourage you to read through this chapter with the following question at the forefront of your mind: *"God, I know you will have me doing many different things during my time here on earth, but what is the unique gifting you planted in my person? What is to be the heartbeat that gives life to the call you have on my person?"*

As you read, open your heart to the understanding that God created you with an individual purpose and unique destiny. The completeness of identity, purpose, and destiny can only be found by discovering all that God has created us to accomplish. This encompasses all we are, who we can become, and all that we have potential to do.

As Oswald Chambers reminds us,

> The call of God is not just for a select few, it is for everyone. Whether we hear God's call or not depends on the condition of my ears, and exactly what I hear depends upon my spiritual attitude. "Many are called but few are chosen." That is, few prove that they are the chosen ones. The chosen ones are those that have come into relationship with God through Jesus Christ, and they have had their spiritual condition changed and their ears opened. Then they hear "the voice of the Lord" continually asking, "…who will go for Us?"[1]

---

1   Chambers, p. 10.

2.2. Your "Call" and the Command Jesus Gave to All Believers

There is a significant difference between your unique, personal "call" or "destiny" and the "Great Commission" command of Jesus Christ to make disciples: What I have termed the call is a specialized equipping for ministry or making disciples. It comprises the various and unique giftings within us, personal and unique to our own individual, peculiar call. For example, apostles Peter and Paul both obeyed the "Great Commission." Peter was uniquely gifted and sent to preach to the Jews. Paul, however, was set apart and uniquely equipped to preach mostly to the Gentiles. Both were successful and made many disciples; each laboured in and fulfilled his individual calling. The command to make disciples is for each and every child of God, regardless of our gifting or our call. Discipleship involves us in other peoples' lives. And through that process of being involved, God is purposely stretching us, so that we can be more effective in our personal call, which becomes more and more evident as we grow in Christ.

Discipleship gets us involved in other peoples' lives... so that we can be more effective in our personal call.

2.3. Calling is Real! No One is Exempt!

You may be thinking, "This might be for some people, but you don't know about me!" Let me reassure you: not one of us is here on earth by accident; you are here because God created you. He intended you. He loves you, and you are here for a purpose. It doesn't matter how you were conceived and raised. Were you expected with joy and raised in a loving home? Or, were you unwanted by your parents and did you spend your early years in very difficult circumstances? You may have had people call you a "surprise" or "mistake," because your arrival to this world was unexpected or inconvenient for your parents.

It makes no difference! Whether you had the most wonderful childhood or very bad life experiences, no matter how people may have treated you, remember: our loving, Heavenly Father planned you and treasures you! He has specific purposes prepared just for you. He lovingly counts the number of hairs on your head. Surely, He listens for your voice and desires that you know each other, "heart to heart." Then He can bring you into the joys of His specific calling, prepared just for you. No matter what your personal history and life experience may tell you, God's plan for you remains. If you choose to press on, to truly know and obey God, the past cannot stop you from discovering the present and future joys of walking in God's calling for you.

Principle #1: The past cannot stop you from discovering the present and future joys of walking in God's care for you.

Many people live out their lives by simply following an easy or logical path. They discover, develop, and use the natural, physical and mental abilities God has given them. Our natural abilities and gifts indeed may indicate the type of Holy Spirit-filled purpose for which we are created. Please grab and hold onto the revelation that there is more! We are not to settle for only our natural potential. Seek and find the greater and better; press beyond the natural into God's supernatural potential for you.

What is your "higher calling"? Everyone's supernatural calling is unique. It is interesting that our higher purposes, sometimes unseen by us, are often obvious to those close to us. Ask God and ask those who know you well what greater potential they see or sense in you. What call does God reveal to you and those who know you? Below is an example of one person's developed natural abilities resulting in self-doubt and internal questioning, or a sense of unfulfilled purpose. Though her training and work "fit" her natural abilities, she still sensed something missing. She was looking for her calling and destiny in God's call.

Shelly, at the age of fourteen, applied for a job for two hours, three times a week at her local hospital. She knew she would enjoy helping the nurses get their patients ready and into bed at night. Just a few years later, we find Shelly, trained and working as a nurse's aide. She absolutely loves her work and would happily do it forever. But more recently, from time to time, she has found herself unsettled and asking herself, "Did I choose the wrong career? Did I miss my call?" This is the point where many bail out, but I would say to you, "Be encouraged!" For this is a part of the growing pains of moving upward in your call. My answer to Shelly was, "Ask God and dream big!" Dutch Sheets writes, "Dreams and destiny are connected. If you don't dream you'll never achieve your destiny. A desire to discover and fulfill one's purpose is one of the strongest forces driving us."[2]

There is a risk here that applies to each and every one of us: it is the danger of falling short of our God-given destiny. Do not settle for only the obvious natural abilities present in you due to your physical skills, mental ability or personality type. While it is good and right to intentionally develop and effectively use these obvious abilities and giftings, we all lose when people assume that this is as good as it gets and so fail to attain the true and deepest fulfillment in their lives. Let us not fall short of the fullest life God has intended for us. Using developed natural abilities plus God's imparted supernatural abilities brings results above and beyond the natural.

Principle #2: Press beyond the natural into God's supernatural potential for you.

For example, my wife, Brenda, has a very obvious, natural ability to be a school teacher. She loves to both learn and teach. She is intelligent and articulate. She communicates in ways others can understand and remember. Both she and her students have fun while she teaches. All these attributes naturally point toward the gift of being a good teacher. However, over and above all these abilities, Brenda has a very distinct and active gifting at work. This gifting is something beyond her natural talents; it enables her to display the love of God to those she teaches. She not only teaches her students, but she imparts to them that God loves them and implants in them the truth that each one of them has a unique call of God on their life. Because she operates in her God-given calling, both natural and supernatural abilities, the students

---

2   Sheets, p. 47.

are not only taught, they have the opportunity to accept Holy Spirit inspiration and seek God's calling for their own lives.

If Brenda chose to use only her natural giftings and abilities, her students would still graduate and pass to the next grade level. However, they would miss out on something vastly more important: the eternal truth of their full value and purpose in God. Fulfilling our call requires the use of all our gifts and abilities, natural and supernatural. It results in others finding and fulfilling their own unique purpose and destiny in God. This is abundant and eternally enduring fruit.

We can become very proficient at wrestling the Word of God down into our human perception of how God works and what He expects of His children. For many, this mindset is a façade or a well-rehearsed set of excuses they hide behind, fearful that God may call them into something they simply do not want to do. I know this to be true because, after years and years of counselling people, I have heard their individual stories of how they hide from God. They think if they dare to give God some of themselves, He will send them off to India or China or somewhere they would not want to go. For others, they fear they may be expected to give money or pay a tithe to God's work and are unwilling to do that.

Well, God has given us free will, and we can choose the road we wish to travel. For some who have never given their life to Jesus, that means they will forfeit Heaven. If you have chosen Jesus but have never considered there could be a call on your life, consider it now. Otherwise you could forfeit the incredible opportunity you still have: living out your remaining years fulfilling that which God would have you do. Remember always: Jesus has promised to complete us. He will work in and with us so we can understand, succeed and flourish in His purposes for us.

2.4. Discovering Your Calling

There are as many calls as there are people; no call is superior to any other. I find it very interesting that we can often spot a person's call developing in grade school and then increasing into the postsecondary years. By college, questions such as, "What do I want to do in my lifetime?" run through the mind as the search for ultimate meaning and purpose grows more insistent. When pondering over life's questions, do not underestimate the active involvement of Father God. These questions are, more often than not, the germination and then sprouting of the God-planted seed for your call. The call, discovered, accepted and activated, makes way for our giftings to come forth. Pressing forward in our unique and individual callings, we shall find ourselves fulfilling Jesus' universal call for every believer—the command to win the lost and make disciples. Living our destiny becomes a joyful and fruitful journey. Calling, gifting, and discipleship become one, with Jesus leading us onward!

Principle #3: Pressing forward in our unique callings finds us fulfilling Jesus' call to win the lost and make disciples.

Many have come to me over the years saying, "I could never do what you do!" Well, that might be true—not because you "can't," but because it wasn't your call to do so! I believe this manual has the potential to raise up many who will go forth in God's call, anointing, and Holy Spirit power. This occurs for each and every obedient, trained and willing servant, effectively advancing them into each divinely specific calling and purpose.

If this is the first time you have considered that God may have an individual call on your life, let me assure you—He certainly does. My prayer is that you will reach deep into your soul and spirit, by asking yourself and then the Holy Spirit, "What gifts lay dormant within my person, undiscovered or unused? What can I discover that relates to God's call on my life?" Do not resist the wonderful reality that there is a unique call from God on your life. Make a decision, right now! Give Father God full permission to bring you understanding and acceptance of your calling and gifting. He will reveal it to you in His perfect time and for His perfect purpose.

As you intentionally seek and accept God's purpose and equipping for your life, deal thoroughly with the fears and doubts you hold onto. They will only hinder you as the Father works to uncover, develop and authenticate your unique abilities, both to yourself and those around you. *Only believe! Of course He has a call on your life, as He has on the lives of all His children!*

2.5. How Can I Possibly Do It? Abundant Grace!

Many times I have marvelled, and subsequently been deeply humbled, that God would allow individuals like me to be part of the shaping and growing of His people. Please hear what I am saying. It is only by His grace that we are able to work side-by-side with Jesus Christ as He shapes and grows His people. We get to share in God's preparation for their initiation into His ultimate purpose. Before we had any idea of God's special purpose for us, He was busy behind the scenes, directing, arranging and working to bring us into what He knows to be the very best place for us. Why? To give us a precious gift: *"… that they may have life, and have it to the full"* (John 10:10).

Knowing that we are called is absolutely essential for experiencing the fullness and abundance of our Christian life. Once we understand our identity and purpose, we can begin to intentionally and successfully live out God's plan for us at its fullest. As we acknowledge and take the steps to engage in our call, little by little we begin to recognize God's hand in our particular gifting, as our hearts move us toward our unique call. Many times I have experienced great joy while living out my calling to "release the captives" through counselling or deliverance, and by setting someone free from years of multiple personality disorder (MPD) or dissociation. Certainly, I did not start out at that level of understanding, complexity, and success. It required hard work and perseverance. Start where you are! Follow your heart relative to your call, and Jesus will ensure success.

2.6. How Does God Help Me Do This?

In Exodus 28:3 and 31:3, God supernaturally gave his followers the ability, knowledge, and skills to work with all the materials needed to build the tabernacle of worship. *The men that did the highly skilled work and completed very intricate tasks had not been trained or sent to school to learn the skills!*

... and I have filled him with the Spirit of God, with wisdom, with understanding, with knowledge *and with all kinds of skills—to make artistic designs for work in gold, silver and bronze, to cut and set stones, to work in wood, and to engage in all kinds of crafts. Moreover, I have appointed Oholiab son of Ahisamak, of the tribe of Dan, to help him. Also* I have given ability to all the skilled workers to make everything *I have commanded you...*

—Exodus 31:3-6 (emphasis added)

From Old Testament times to our present day, God has empowered and enabled willing servants to do the specific works He calls us to. If we obey the call, the giftings needed will be supplied, enabling us to complete our calling. The knowledge, skills, insights, and abilities come from God. The Holy Spirit, who has lived with and in us from the day of our salvation, empowers and enables us for tasks far beyond our natural abilities. Day by day, the decision to obey and make ourselves available to Him remains our responsibility.

2.7. "Working Out" Your Calling

You will have both successes and difficult times! What I am about to say can possibly save you much frustration, heartache, and maybe even from bailing out of your call. In the early stages of working with people, the smallest success becomes very exciting. In our immaturity, we go forth in that new excitement, thinking that we have arrived at our destiny. God certainly allows those times of early success as a means of encouragement to help us move forward in our call. But as we move along ministering to others, we may see our success waning. This is typical. Don't bail out now!

If we obey the calling, the giftings needed will be supplied.

The fact is, even after years of effective ministering, we can all experience the transition from being very excited and comfortable with our call to suddenly finding ourselves in a place where this is no longer the case. It seems that no matter how much faith we have, what proven technique or principle of Scripture we use, nothing brings satisfying results. We can find ourselves thinking that the level of ministry we previously experienced is now unattainable. This is a normal part of growing in our call. No one is exempt from the experience of struggles and disillusionment. You and I, those we minister to, and even those who have spent their lives in service to others are susceptible. We must accept this reality and by faith press through and persevere, despite our difficulties.

In truth, no life or ministry is without ups and downs, successes and failures. We must live out our call and Christian life realistically. Though we may start out with favour and quick success, there will come a time when bearing fruit in ministry to others seems rare or even impossible. It may feel as though we've hit a brick wall, and there is no apparent progress regardless of the time invested and tools used. Don't be discouraged! Remember, no plant bears fruit in every season—and we will all, at times, find ourselves in this situation. Jesus promised that as we remain in Him, we will bear fruit. Stay connected to the vine (see John 15:5). Hang in there through the cold, heat, wind, and rain; harvest season is coming again.

If you find yourself in the place of no progress or apparent failure, be practical and realistic. It may be time for a break or change of direction. Sometimes, when you seem unable to help someone, the simple answer is to be a friend, genuinely and effectively loving God and people.

2.8. Is it Time for a Change or Redirection?

The best thing we can do for ourselves in times of hardship, trials, or even confusion is to ask God to reveal His crossroad for us. It could very well be time for a Jeremiah 6:16 experience. There God calls us to *"Stand at the crossroads and look; ask for the ancient paths, ask where the good way is, and walk in it, and you will find rest for your souls."* This crossroad is not only a gift from God. It is a meeting place with God for all who seek His will and ways. It is a place we can run to in times of confusion, hardship, or trouble. The crossroad is a place of reflection, regaining perspective and seeking God for the best way forward. There, God has opportunity to correct and reconnect with us. He purposely brings us to a place of personal evaluation and decision making. This often brings about a redirection of our lives, our homes, and our ministry. Loss of enthusiasm or apparent lack of progress can bring difficulties, but be encouraged—God has a purpose. It causes us to dig deep into our souls to assess the condition of our relationship with our Heavenly Father. This is a good place to be.

Why do we sometimes have troubles and setbacks for which we cannot find a reason? Negative or troubling experiences, very hard times, loss of family or finances, etc. are not always your fault, or someone else's, or even Satan's, for that matter. This could very well be a God-directed inner strengthening, with God using Satan as a tool for maturing us and increasing our effectiveness as we minister to His people. *"See, it is I who created the blacksmith who fans the coals into flame and forges a weapon fit for its work."* (Isaiah 54:16).

God allows hard times. It is imperative that we understand this! If we do not understand this truth, we will find ourselves forever angry at God for not protecting us. In the Bible, we see that God sometimes allows hardship and offers no explanation or justification for it. These are times when our faith, love, and trust in our Heavenly Father must carry us. We trust that ultimately the "Judge of All the Earth" will be faithful. As we read in Hebrews 12:7, *"Endure hardship as discipline; God is treating you as as his children."*

2.8.1. Losing Touch with Our Source: Soulish Ministry

Success and recognition are necessary and enjoyable parts of ministry. They also hold a snare or temptation that needs to be avoided. After many great spiritual successes and regularly working hand-in-hand with the Holy Spirit, we can slip back into living and ministering out of our soul rather than our spirit, or what some call our "spirit man." If we find ourselves in this particular situation—courageous, full of confidence and carried onward by momentum of past successes—we may rush expectantly onward in our own natural giftings and strength. We presume what needs to be accomplished and, thinking we can fix it, off we go. Thus, we eventually find ourselves in a place of all work and no fruit.

At this point, if we just take a moment to look back, we will likely see Jesus, still standing at the crossroad where we left Him. As I write, my heart is in sorrow, remembering the times I have walked away from Jesus' direction, walking my way, in my own strength. Yet, I'm rejoicing for those of you reading this chapter. If you take what you have just read seriously, it will help you avoid the confusion and heartache that takes place when you make a left turn at a crossroad when you should have taken a right. The right turn will consistently position you in a working relationship with Jesus Christ.

We can so easily slide from our dependence on the Holy Spirit. As Paul wrote to Timothy, *"Watch your life and doctrine closely. Persevere in them, because if you do, you will save both yourself and your hearers"* (1 Timothy 4:16).

2.8.2. Essentials of Ministry Success

Very often, the inability to bear fruit in ministry is because we have attempted to do things on our own. We cannot carry out ministry without making room for the Holy Spirit, who is our indwelling Counsellor, and Jesus, who walks with us step-by-step. What I am about to say will be said in other places in the book. *If there is to be success in ministry, we must intentionally and literally make room for Jesus and the Spirit* by asking Them to open every session, to be part of everything that is said and done, and to ensure that nothing is left undone. I find myself in constant communication with Jesus as I work out my peculiar call, and so should you, as you work out the call on your life. For He is the One that makes ministry successful.

Principle #4: If there is to be success in ministry, we must intentionally and literally make room for Jesus and the Spirit.

The great reward of ministry is that Jesus shares with us His joy and excitement as the captives are set free and healed. I have experienced untold joy by doing ministry hand-in-hand with Jesus Christ. And so can you, as you step out and do whatever needs to be done! Never forget that, at your conception, whether you realized it or not, God planted the seeds of your calling and gifting. He has been working throughout your growing years, ensuring that your gifting is developing according to His purpose and His impending call into active service with King Jesus.

As you walk out your calling, know that you are gathering jewels (the fruit of your call) for Jesus. It's my hope to walk through Heaven's Gate on that final day with at least one or two jewels for the Crown of Christ Jesus, my Saviour and reigning King. So should you! As born-again believers, and therefore disciples of Jesus Christ, it is incumbent upon us to do as Jesus did when He said,

> *All authority in heaven and on earth has been given to me. Therefore go and make disciples of all nations, baptizing them in the name of the Father and of the Son and of the Holy Spirit, and teaching them to obey everything I have commanded you. And surely I am with you always, to the very end of the age.*
>
> —Matthew 28:18-20

2.8.3. Discovering My Call

I was forty-three years old when I gave my life to Jesus Christ, and I was two years old in Christ when those close to me began encouraging me to obtain some training. They saw within me a gift of prayer, particularly praying for hurting and needy people. At that time, I had no idea of people's spiritual needs, let alone their need for prayer. Nor was I looking for the opportunity to work with people. I knew little about God and His ways, let alone "The Call of God." This phrase was totally unfamiliar to me. As a child, I had gone to church for a year or so, but that certainly did not equip me in any way whatsoever for what I was about to see.

As I was stepping out in faith to pray for others, I was seeing some "weird" stuff. For instance, some people would have seizures while I prayed for them, while others would growl like a dog. I had no idea what to do. This prompted me to meet with a pastor acquaintance from a large church in a nearby community. I shared my experience and to my surprise, he said, "Praise God, the enemy was exposed. '*However, do not rejoice that the spirits submit to you, but rejoice that your names are written in heaven*'" (Luke 10:20).

That was that—he said nothing else. We then shook hands and parted. Those few minutes with the pastor helped me turn the corner to acknowledge a real demonic realm, active in present times. I then understood that Satan and his demons could come against mankind and even indwell people where sin issues were not properly dealt with. Sometime before meeting with that pastor, I had purchased a few books on the topic of demons and their activity, but they were mostly unread. At that point I couldn't accept the concept of demonization. I had previously thought that something similar to this may have happened in the dark ages, but certainly not today. After that very brief meeting with the pastor, my understanding of the supernatural realm was radically changed. I retrieved the books I had bought on this topic from the garbage. Through study over time, I came to realize that if your theology does not match your experience, maybe you need to change it.

Each one of us, as a Christian, has a mandate to be prepared to deal with the demonic, for the Word says, "*And these signs will accompany those who believe: In my name they will drive out demons; they will speak in new tongues*" (Mark 16:17).

There! It is written in the Word! Maybe you have never witnessed or experienced demonic activity. Or maybe your perception all along has been, yes, it does exist, but lay people are not called to deal with the demonic—that job is just for pastors, or missionaries, etc.

It is true that some Christians may never deal directly with the demonic. However, we need to be prepared according to the verse just referred to which says, "*… signs will accompany those who believe.*" This authority and ministry is for all of God's people, and therefore it is inseparable from our personal calls. Setting captives free is not just a job for pastors, but also for "pew-warmers"—a task for sheep as well as shepherds.

For some of you, deliverance ministry, counselling, or working with multiple personality disorder (MPD) individuals will be your personal call. While praying with individuals, I have often "bumped" into demons; this naturally triggered my curiosity about this subject. So I asked the question, "Is this something I am to be involved in?" What followed was an encounter I had with the Father and the Son when I was about two years old in the Lord. I was reading,

> *Therefore, brothers, since we have confidence to enter the Most Holy Place by the blood of Jesus, by a new and living way opened for us through the curtain, that is, his body, and since we have a great priest over the house of God, let us draw near to God with a sincere heart in full assurance of faith, having our hearts sprinkled to cleanse us from a guilty conscience and having our bodies washed with pure water. Let us hold unswervingly to the hope we profess, for he who promised is faithful.*
> —Hebrews 10:19-23

I had been in the Word a great deal in those early years, and had gained the understanding that under the Old Covenant, the priesthood offered up to God the same sacrifices day after day on behalf of their people. But these sacrifices could never take away their sins. I had also come to the understanding that Jesus, by His death and resurrection, had made an everlasting, final way to deal with all of mankind's sins—the same Jesus who is now our High Priest, forever. This had me asking the question, "I wonder if Jesus, as High Priest, ever prayed for me?"

Instantly, I was looking at Jesus, who was completely alive inside a picture frame. He was on His knees before the Father, a flood of tears running down his face, and I heard Him say to Father God on my behalf, "He [Jan] cannot climb this mountain alone; I love him too much to lose him now." That was a holy moment that I will never forget! I felt as though I was on the mountaintop with the Father and the Son. I wept and wept, and even now as I put this story on paper, the tears have returned. It was such a holy and sacred time that I was unable to share this with anyone for a year or two.

A few weeks after I had seen the picture, I was reading through Psalm 91 when I came to verse 12 or so. I found myself crying, (yes, you're right; I cry often when the Spirit moves, seeming to be overcome). At this time, I had no idea why I was so emotional. There had been nothing that I that was aware of as I read Psalm 91 that would cause this response, but these feelings continued and intensified until finally I cried out, "Jesus, what is happening?"

Jesus responded, saying, "Jan, this Scripture is your Heavenly Father's answer to My prayer for you."

As I read through Psalm 91:1-13 again, I saw it! It was my "call" with the Word itself, speaking directly to me:

You will tread upon the lion and the cobra; you will trample the great lion and the serpent.

—Psalm 91:13

It was in that moment I received the revelation that this was the heart of my lifelong call, *"to trample the great lion and the serpent"*! God longs for a deep and intimate relationship with us so that He may be a part of all and everything we do. *He has placed in each and every one of us a destiny.*

Principle #5: Each of us has a destiny within us.

2.8.4. Understanding Your Realm of Authority

When I was about three years old in the Lord, with little or no prayer experience, my wife and I received a call from a pastor of a church about 250 km away. I had no idea who he was or even how he got our names, but he was asking if we would come and work with some of his people. Well, Brenda and I had never done that before, but we really felt God was telling us to go. So we went, shaking in our boots and not knowing what we had gotten ourselves into.

We arrived in the little town, and were about a block away from the church when the Lord gave my wife Scripture that says, *"I will give you every place where you set your foot…"* (Joshua 1:3). That was some twenty years ago, at the start of my ministry.

Much later, when I was more established, I had become very busy and involved in numerous aspects of ministry. I felt pulled in many directions and needed to seek God for a more specific direction relative to my call. I asked

Him, "Out of all the many ministry things I am doing at this stage of my life, what would You have me do?"

He responded immediately, saying, "Jan, years ago when I told you I would give you every place you put your foot, you didn't understand. If I hadn't first given you territory, you would not have had a place to put your foot."

From there, the Lord brought to my attention Isaiah 57:14, which reads as follows, *"Build up, build up, prepare the road! Remove the obstacles out of the way of my people."* That is my God-given and very specific call—"removing the obstacles out of the way of God's people." Obstacles are sin issues that hinder our ongoing growth and relationship with the the Father. What God spoke to me here should be like a ringing bell to all of us. We all have a call, we all have a territory, and God requires that we fulfill the obligation of His call on us.

For this is what the high and lofty One says—he who lives forever, whose name is holy: "I live in a high and holy place, but also with him who is contrite and lowly in spirit, to revive the spirit of the lowly and to revive the heart of the contrite."

—Isaiah 57:15

The Scriptural mandate is that we strive for holiness, living righteously because He is a "High and Holy God."

God closed that time of prayer with these words, "Jan, this is your call; I want you to be working throughout all of your territory, not just the places you are comfortable and happy to be, but in all areas of my peoples' lives." The realm of my authority was to go and remove obstacles out of the way of God's people. God had given me the territory and I needed not only to let go of aspects of my ministry that were not part of my call, but also to claim and work in the entirety of the area given to me.

2.8.5. Stewarding the Territory

Enlarge the place of your tent, stretch your tent curtains wide, do not hold back; lengthen your cords, strengthen your stakes. For you will spread out to the right and to the left; your descendants will dispossess nations and settle in their desolate cities.

—Isaiah 54:2-3

We understand this command was spoken by Isaiah for the whole nation of God's people. As God's Word is timeless, it is just as relevant to us today as it was in the Old Testament. Therefore the principle of "stewarding" applies to our lives today as it did in the Old Testament. As you seek and ask God, He will begin to reveal the scope of your call. Once you have accepted your call and have begun stewarding it, God will provide the means and authority to work out your call as you expand your territory. Step into your calling by honouring God, faithfully stewarding the territory He has given you. This last Scripture is provided to help you as you begin to work out your boundaries, obligations and opportunities for your territory.

2.9. Conclusion

Before the beginning of time, God saw each one of us individually and put within us a purpose, with all the attributes and all the gifting necessary for us to fulfill our destiny in the days He has numbered for us. When God looks at you or me, He also sees us generationally. He sees our ancestors. He knows that if we make a wrong decision or a bad choice it can affect many, many of our generations to come. In a nutshell, this is only one of many reasons why God wishes to be in an intimate relationship with us. He knows our future, and He calls to each one of us to stand at the crossroad and then choose to walk in His will (see the teaching on the crossroads in Toolbox, Chapter 12).

As our small part is played out, it will fit into His bigger agenda, an agenda we cannot see with the natural eye. I love the teaching of 2 Peter; the message is of our complete oneness with Him. In my Bible, the caption preceding chapter 1, verse 3 is "Making One's Calling and Election Sure." Then verse 3 follows, with *"His divine power has given us everything we need for a godly life through our knowledge of him who called us by his own glory and goodness."* I can hardly restrain myself, because this verse speaks volumes. I remember so well when I received a revelation of these words, *"through our knowledge of him."* I was so excited that I could do something very tangible that could affect my growth. The more I know Him, the more I grow. I realize that this is not rocket science, but if we are to individually attain all that God has for us, we must learn how to "mine" the Word of God. Carrying on with the concept that God wants an intimate, working relationship with us, we move forward in the chapter to where it states:

> *Above all, you must understand that no prophecy of Scripture came about by the prophet's own interpretation of things. For prophecy never had its origin in the will of man, but men spoke from God as they were carried along by the Holy Spirit.*
> —2 Peter 1:20-21

This Scripture did not come about by the mind of man. One of God's purposes during the Apostolic Age was that His Word would be written, and Peter tells us that God used man to see His purpose fulfilled. God's bigger purpose today is that none shall perish: *"The Lord is not slow in keeping his promise, as some understand slowness. He is patient with you, not wanting anyone to perish, but everyone to come to repentance"* (2 Peter 3:9). And once again, God will use man, "carried along by the Holy Spirit."

I know I am getting dangerously close to repeating myself as I emphasize that God does have a call on the life of absolutely every born-again believer! It is not a matter of physical life and death if we choose to disbelieve the call, or know it and turn away from it. However, it is significant to the spiritual life or death of the call.

Choosing to reject the call or, at the very least, failing to inquire of God for His ongoing direction is akin to making plans to cross the Sahara Desert and back again in a pickup truck without sufficient fuel and only half a dozen bottles of drinking water. It's very obvious that you aren't going to get very far. If there is no intervention, you will surely die. We can liken this scenario to our Christian lives. If we begin ministering into the souls of others without first engaging Christ for the application and ongoing direction of the gifting for the call, we won't get very far! If Christ is not invited to intervene as we seek to save the lost, set the captives free, and raise up disciples that will also go forth and raise up disciples themselves, then we will surely die.

God never intended for us to feel that we must save the world on our own for Jesus Christ. Jesus specifically tells us that without Him we can do nothing! What He does ask of us is to purposely move forward with Him, fulfilling our very own specific and personal call. Nothing more, and nothing less. When we each work hand-in-hand with Jesus, setting captives free of their arthritic pain, or delivering those bound up by the demonic, or seeing those healed of seizures as in Matt 17:15, we find ourselves in a place of inexplicable joy!

And surely I am with you always, to the very end of the age.
—Matthew 28:20

THE FUNDAMENTALS

Part II

Chapter Three

FORGIVENESS

THIS CHAPTER ON FORGIVENESS IS IN NO WAY THE ALPHA AND OMEGA ON the subject. My intention is first to present material in a very practical and usable platform, based on Biblical truths and principles. Along with that, I will identify some of the consequences of living in unforgiveness towards others, as well as towards oneself. Secondly, I will help you apply forgiveness in real life situations from a Biblical perspective. Thirdly, I will share examples from my experience of many years as a practitioner as I lived out my call to "set the captives free."

3.1. What is Forgiveness?

Forgiveness is a central theme woven throughout the whole of the Old and the New Testaments. It is the very heart of the two greatest commandments: *"Love the Lord your God with all your heart and with all your soul and with all your mind and with all your strength,"* and *"Love your neighbor as yourself"* (Mark 12:30–31). For every one of us, the fulfillment of these two commands is attained only when we live moment by moment, day by day, in complete forgiveness. We cannot love if we cannot forgive.

The inescapable consequence if we choose not to forgive is stated by Jesus: *"For if you forgive other people when they sin against you, your heavenly Father will also forgive you. But if you do not forgive others their sins, your Father will not forgive your sins"* (Matthew 6:14-15). This is not a spiritual condition that any one of us would like to be in.

Our conscious, intentional, and effective forgiveness of others is absolutely essential to our relationship with God and people. Jesus powerfully emphasized and illustrated the paramount importance of forgiving others in this parable:

Therefore, the kingdom of heaven is like a king who wanted to settle accounts with his servants. As he began the settlement, a man who owed him ten thousand bags of gold was brought to him. Since he was not able to pay, the master ordered that he and his wife and his children and all that he had be sold to repay the debt.

At this the servant fell on his knees before him. "Be patient with me," he begged, "and I will pay back everything." The servant's master took pity on him, canceled the debt and let him go.

But when the servant went out, he found one of his fellow servants who owed him a hundred silver coins. He grabbed him and began to choke him. "Pay back what you owe me!" he demanded.

His fellow servant fell to his knees and begged him, "Be patient with me, and I will pay you back."

But he refused. Instead, he went off and had the man thrown into prison until he could pay the debt. When the other servants saw what had happened, they were outraged and went and told their master everything that had happened.

Then the master called the servant in. "You wicked servant," he said, "I canceled all that debt of yours because you begged me to. Shouldn't you have had mercy on your fellow servant just as I had on you?" In anger his master turned him over to the jailers to be tortured, until he should pay back all he owed.

This is how my heavenly Father will treat each of you unless you forgive your brother or sister from your heart.

—Matthew 18:23–35

In the words of David Augsburger, "Forgiveness is acceptance with no exception. It accepts not only the hurt you have received, it accepts the one who did the hurting, and it accepts the loss caused by the hurtful actions or words. Seven times a day. In fact, seventy times seven."[3]

---

3   Augsburger, 1988, p. 29.

3.1.1. How Does the Cross Fit In?

Why does serious talk about forgiveness require us to talk about God on a cross? Because God accepted the Cross to make forgiveness possible and to demonstrate forgiveness to an unforgiving world.

Principle #6: Forgiveness accepts the hurt received, the one who did the hurting, and the loss caused by the hurtful actions.

The Christ of the Cross is our great example. *"Christ suffered for you, leaving you an example, that you should follow in his steps"* (1 Peter 2:21). In Jesus we see compassionate, undeserved forgiveness modelled. We see forgiving love embodied. We see faithfulness to truth in relationships carried to its ultimate expression. We see human possibilities that we are called to own and experience. We see the face of God, and it is a face of forgiving love. Augsburger says,

> That face offers us the ultimate example to live by, and the love shining from that face offers us the power to live in new ways. Just as admiring beauty will not make us beautiful, so respecting an example of goodness will not improve our character. All lasting change comes within relationships—and the final relationship that can set us free is encountering this God, knowing God at whatever level we are mature enough to experience; and yearning to incorporate—not just imitate—His example, to truly become and be like Him. This transforming relationship is at the heart of forgiveness.[4]

Again, why does serious talk about forgiveness require us talk about God on a cross? Simply because, *"Salvation is found in no one else, for there is no other name under heaven given to mankind by which we must be saved"* (Acts 4:12). The rock, in which the cross of Jesus was anchored, is the granite-hard

---

4   Augsburger, 2000, pp. 30–31.

rock of forgiveness—unmovable, unchangeable, put in place by God before the beginning of time.

God's plan for a Saviour came closer to fruition when an angel from God delivered a message to Joseph, who at that moment was working though a plan to divorce his pregnant wife.

> *But after he had considered this, an angel of the Lord appeared to him in a dream and said, "Joseph son of David, do not be afraid to take Mary home as your wife, because what is conceived in her is from the Holy Spirit. She will give birth to a son, and you are to give him the name Jesus, because* he will save his people from their sins.
> —Matthew 1:20-21 (emphasis added)

3.1.2. Jesus' Work of Salvation

I believe it is imperative that we individually establish our own Biblical foundation, relative to the cross of Jesus Christ, by which He made eternal salvation available for all of mankind. Our reasoning on Biblical forgiveness, first mentally "understood" and then personally "received" into our reality, becomes the perceptual platform from which you and I realize and receive all of our forgiveness from God and from people, as well as forgiveness or unforgiveness towards ourselves and others.

Jesus did not come to simply be a good example or a good teacher, though He was both of those things. He did not come to save us *in* our sins, as some have said. He came to save us *from* our sins. To save us in our sins is to save us from the punishment of our sins, but without offering help to overcome them. To save us from our sins, at the very least, is to help us overcome the entrapping power of sin.

Jesus came as both Saviour and Redeemer. *"After he had provided purification for sins, he sat down at the right hand of the Majesty in heaven"* (Hebrews 1:3b). His work of salvation for all mankind was complete.

Through the Sacrificial Lamb, Jesus, man can be reconciled to God. This rock of forgiveness, post-salvation, has become the rock on which our relational sins are exposed, dealt with, and forgiven, making a way for intimate relationships with God and mankind. Forgiveness, or the lack of it, plays a major role in our individual lives, whether it is a simple lie or a blatant, obvious sin. As Jim Logan says,

> If I had to sum up the message of the Scriptures in one word, it would be the word forgiveness. The Bible is the story of how God forgives. It begins in Genesis and continues through Revelation. Along the way we see God reaching out to people to forgive them.
>
> Now if forgiveness is one of the central themes of the Bible— perhaps the central theme—where do you suppose the enemy might attack you and me as God's children? Through unforgiveness. How can I go and tell other men and women the good news that they can be forgiven by God when I am harboring unforgiveness in my own heart? In fact, when unforgiveness and bitterness rule in my heart, I'm moving backward in my relationships with people and God, and I'm opening myself up to Satan's attacks.[5]

I completely agree with Logan's concept of forgiveness. Where does this leave the average born-again believer after some sort of altercation with a brother or sister in the Lord, or a husband and wife in a marital breakdown?

3.2. Unforgiveness – The Jailhouse

Many of those that come into my office are unknowingly in the "jailhouse." I have worked with many who have attended Christian churches most of their lives, yet have no understanding of the ramifications of living in unforgiveness. The Kingdom of Heaven and the kingdom of earth work very much the same when it comes to settling accounts.

Let us look again at the parable of the unmerciful servant. Jesus begins with a king on earth wanting to settle an account with a servant; this particular servant owed a debt which he was utterly unable to pay. "*The servant's master took pity on him, canceled the debt and let him go*" (Matthew 18:27). This, of course, parallels the sin debt Jesus paid for each one of us—a debt we could never, ever repay.

---

5   Logan, p. 60.

Now this forgiven servant, as he left the presence of the king, met a peer servant who owed him just a few dollars. The first servant demanded immediate payment that the second servant could not pay. Instead of granting forgiveness or reasonable terms of repayment to his fellow servant, the forgiven but unforgiving servant had his debtor arrested. The master was informed of this and took immediate action by throwing the first servant in the jailhouse until he could pay all he owed, and *"In anger his master turned him over to the jailers to be tortured, until he should pay back all he owed"* (Matthew 18:34). Jesus, in verse 35, took this situation out of the earthly realm and put it into the spiritual realm by saying, *"This is how my heavenly Father will treat each of you unless you forgive your brother or sister from your heart."*

Principle #7: Unforgiveness confines us in the jailhouse, where we become a prisoner to our strongholds.

We do jail time today just as they did in the time of Jesus. Verse 34 is a real stumbling block for many of God's people. They read the following statement, *"turned over to the jailer to be tortured,"* and their response is, "No way, that cannot be. God wouldn't do that to His people; this has to be a mistake!" They continue by saying, "There must have been a mistake in the translation from the original version of the Bible." Off they go with no personal application from this absolutely essential truth.

There is an incredible cost to pay for living in unforgiveness, as illustrated in the following personal story.

I had been scheduled a month or two in advance to bring the Sunday morning message at my church. As it turned out, my construction work was taking me about two hundred miles from home, working seven days a week and twelve-hour days. I was the only manager on site; thus, I was tied to the work site. I had to put something together, but no matter how hard I tried, whatever Scripture I chose, it seemed absolutely impossible to get a message on paper.

I arrived at home Saturday evening empty-handed. I tried again to put something together, but gave up within the hour. I told my wife, "Maybe God will wake me up at six with a message!" About 3:00 am, God woke me with the following Scripture on my mind. *"For if you forgive other people when they sin against you, your heavenly Father will also forgive you. But if you do not forgive others their sins, your Father will not forgive your sins"* (Matthew 6:14-15). He also gave me a picture of an endless ocean full of people. I could see that they were all praying. I saw the words come out of their mouths, rise up to about mid-forehead, and then fall to the ground. It was so real, so intense that I broke and cried out loud.

The Lord spoke and said, "I cannot hear them because of unforgiveness in their hearts." Then the Lord showed me a scenario He'd created involving a family of three: a dad, a mom, and a daughter. The daughter had run away from home and had been gone for some time; her parents did not know where she was. It's very hard to put words to what I experienced that day, but it was like I entered into the hearts of her mom and dad. God showed me their thoughts and let me feel their emotions and their heart pain directly. They both had a long, deep relationship with Father God, and as they cried out to Him with a flood of tears running down their faces, I felt and knew their level of faith. They knew without a doubt that the God they had served faithfully all their lives would respond to their prayers and bring their daughter home. God said to me, "I cannot hear their prayers because of unforgiveness in their hearts." The cost of their unforgiveness was separation from God.

Forgiveness is the hard, granite rock of our Christian life. We see the Biblical anchor for forgiveness in the following: *"'Which is easier: to say, "Your sins are forgiven," or to say, "Get up and walk"? But I want you to know that the Son of Man has authority on earth to forgive sins.' So he said to the paralyzed man, 'Get up, take your mat and go home'"* (Matthew 9:5-6). For us today, coupled with that authority, it is the "shed blood" of the Son of God that is the key component for our forgiveness.

We learn in the Old Testament, *"For the life of a creature is in the blood, and I have given it to you to make atonement for yourselves on the altar; it is the blood that makes atonement for one's life"* (Leviticus 17:11). However, Paul states, *"It is impossible for the blood of bulls and goats to take away sins"* (Hebrews 10:4).

Day after day every priest stands and performs his religious duties;
again and again he offers the same sacrifices, which can never take away
sins. But when this priest had offered for all time one sacrifice for sins,
he sat down at the right hand of God, and since that time he waits for
his enemies to be made his footstool. For by one sacrifice he has made
perfect forever those who are being made holy.

—Hebrews 10:11-14

It is the shed blood of Jesus Christ that takes away sin and unlocks the jailhouse. It is what allows us not just to say "My sins are forgiven!" but to get up and walk free. *"God presented Christ as a sacrifice of atonement, through the shedding of his blood"* (Romans 3:25). *"Repent, then, and turn to God, so that your sins may be wiped out…"* (Acts 3:19). This would bring to the minds of early readers the method used for record keeping, which was performed with wax tablets. When you incurred a debt, it was written on a wax tablet. When this debt was paid, it was wiped out; all record of previous owing was removed, and the slate was wiped clean. There was no permanent record.

3.3. Our Position

Paul presents a similar explanation. *"Therefore, since we have been justified through faith, we have peace with God through our Lord Jesus Christ…"* (Romans 5:1). From this verse, we can see that:

- We are *justified.*
- We are at *peace* with Christ. This also brings the possibility of an intimate relationship with Father God. *"Since we have now been justified by his blood, how much more shall we be saved from God's wrath through him!"* (Romans 5:9). *"The Spirit himself testifies with our spirit that we are God's children."* (Romans 8:16).
- We are *positioned* with Christ. We now find ourselves seated in the heavenlies with Christ Jesus. *"And God raised us up with Christ and seated us with him in the heavenly realms in Christ Jesus…"* (Ephesians 2:6).

3.3.1. Based on Authority

This, of course, enrages Satan, no doubt bringing him to a hot boil and precipitating a level of warfare that we will fight until Jesus returns.

As for you, you were dead in your transgressions and sins, in which you used to live when you followed the ways of this world and of the ruler of the kingdom of the air, the spirit who is now at work in those who are disobedient. All of us also lived among them at one time, gratifying the cravings of our flesh and following its desires and thoughts. Like the rest, we were by nature objects of wrath. But because of his great love for us, God, who is rich in mercy, made us alive with Christ even when we were dead in transgressions—it is by grace you have been saved. And God raised us up with Christ and seated us with him in the heavenly realms in Christ Jesus, in order that in the coming ages he might show the incomparable riches of his grace, expressed in his kindness to us in Christ Jesus.

—Ephesians 2:1–7

We were dead in our transgressions and followed the ways of Satan. But now, once we have partaken of Christ's free gift of salvation, we reign in the heavenly realms with Him. For as He rose from the dead, He stripped Satan of his authority over the world and mankind, and then positioned mankind in the place of authority over not only the world, but Satan and his demons as well.

Jesus says, *"I have given you authority to trample on snakes and scorpions and to overcome all the power of the enemy; nothing will harm you"* (Luke 10:19). I have had people in my office who have taken the words "snakes and scorpions" literally. But that is not what Jesus is saying. In Genesis chapter 3, Satan was the snake in the garden, who brought about the fall of man by deception, removing him from God's presence. *"But the Lord God called to the man, 'Where are you?'"* (Genesis 3:9). God is still calling out today: Adam, Tom, Joe, Sally, Elizabeth, Paul, Simon, Timothy, where are you? Satan, along with his minions, is still doing all he can to steal, kill and destroy. The use of deception has always been, and always will be, his most successful tool against mankind.

3.3.2. Satan's Resistance

The biggest satanic scam in our Western world today is that many believe once we are saved we don't need to give Satan a second thought. Some of the church still believes that because of the finished work of Christ on the cross, Satan was defeated and therefore can no longer touch us born-again believers. For instance, just recently, a very popular female preacher stated on television, "Do not give Satan a second thought. If you are born again, you have been sealed by the blood of Jesus, and Satan cannot get at you."

That teaching is contrary to the Bible, as well as my own experience of working with God's people. Ephesians 4:26–27 says, *"'In your anger do not sin': Do not let the sun go down while you are still angry, and do not give the devil a foothold."* If we go to bed angry, it means we have not forgiven someone, and oftentimes that someone is ourselves. Either way, we are in a place of unforgiveness, which furnishes Satan a foothold. On different occasions, I have received calls from pastors or other counselling firms in our community, asking if I would do some deliverance with a client of theirs, which I often do.

Principle #8: Unforgiveness furnishes Satan a foothold.

I remember one situation in particular. A counsellor was to bring a man and his wife in for ministry. The Lord gave me a verse for the client, *"... choose for yourselves this day whom you will serve... "* (Joshua 24:15). I had been told that both husband and wife were born-again believers. They had been a part of their church community for some time, but recently the husband had become violent on occasion, kicking out some house doors. He and his wife were not doing well at all, so I agreed to meet with them, and the next day they both came in. The wife was anticipating the possibility of some positive change in their situation, but the husband was in a different mindset than his wife. He was somewhat disengaged, and noncompliant.

While working with couples in ministry, I always try to deal with at least some current sin or pain issues first; obtaining a small amount of repentance and forgiveness between the two hurting individuals makes it much easier to move on with whatever the deeper issues may be. I tried that with this couple, but the husband was not interested. I shared the verse that God had given me for the couple, and then asked the husband if he would pray so that we could get started. But that was not going to take place! Next I questioned the husband about the surety of his salvation, because by this time I was beginning to doubt it. I shared this with him, and of course it unsettled him; he then opened his wallet and handed me a card that said, "I was born again at X place on X day, month, and year," along with the name of the crusade that he had attended; it also stated that he had prayed the sinner's prayer. I reminded the couple that the verse God had given them was a strong call to get right with God. After some persuasion, the husband agreed to be led through the salvation prayer; however, after we had prayed, he was still in the very same state of heart and mind.

Now, I was getting just a little bit concerned at this point. I was very aware that I didn't have a large amount of experience (this was early in my ministry), but I also had a strong sense that my God was leading! I shot up a silent prayer asking for help—"Where did I go wrong?" The Lord responded by saying, "His faith is in the card he carries in his wallet. He has confessed with his mouth, but the truth has not been able to penetrate his heart."

I understood that the teaching says, *"For it is with your heart that you believe and are justified, and it is with your mouth that you profess your faith and are saved"* (Romans 10:10). I explained this to him and said, "If it is okay with you, I am going to pray for you and pull down the barriers or strongholds that block the truth from reaching your heart."

As I prayed, I could see his countenance changing. When I had finished praying, my prayer partner, who was present, said, "Let me tell you what I saw as you prayed! As soon as you began to pull down the barrier in his heart, I saw two huge angels. They were so tall that they had to bend down to get under the ceiling to enter the room. One angel stood at the man's left side, and one stood at his right side. As you continued to pray, I saw one angel reach into the man's soul, grab a demon and throw it out; as one angel was reaching in, the other was throwing out. And so it went until the last demon was cast out." She then saw the man's spirit, which had been pushed down by the indwelling demonic entities, rise up and in her words, "torpedo into the heavenlies" and sit at the right hand of Jesus. This is in line with *"If you declare with your mouth, 'Jesus is Lord,' and believe in your heart that God raised him from the dead, you will be saved"* (Romans 10:9).

When I met and prayed with this couple, I wasn't aware that the husband had been unable to work for some time due to a long-term back problem. A few days after meeting and praying with this couple, they moved away from our city and I never heard from them again. A year or so later, some of their friends went to visit with them and returned with this story: Apparently, a few days after they arrived at their new place, the back problem had disappeared; he then gained employment and had been working ever since.

The point to be made here is that this man, a born-again believer, was taken captive by the powers of darkness because of unconfessed sins and ongoing anger in his heart. Certainly he had protection through the blood of Christ, as we all have. But if we continue to sin, Satan does gain a foothold. At the very moment of our salvation, the battle against darkness begins. *"For our struggle is not against flesh and blood, but against the rulers, against the authorities, against the powers of this dark world and against the spiritual forces of evil in the heavenly realms"* (Ephesians 6:12).

Most of what we do from salvation onward will be met with resistance from Satan and his minions. Certainly our names are taken out of Satan's book of death and written in God's Book of Life. I have never seen or read about a book of death anywhere in Scriptures, and I am sure neither have you. But Satan imitates everything God does as much as possible. Therefore, he likely has a book in hell which had my name in it for a season. But not anymore; it has been blotted out by the shed blood of Jesus! I now have been marked with a seal, the promised Holy Spirit. I have the breastplate of righteousness, and my position in Christ is secure. *"And you also were included in Christ when you heard the word of truth, the gospel of your salvation. When you believed, you were marked in him with a seal, the promised Holy Spirit... "* (Ephesians 1:13). Most of us have discovered that after we entered into our salvation experience, our problems began to escalate. Why is that? I will attempt to shed a little light in this area, but one thing's for sure: Satan does not let go easily.

3.4. Forgiveness as the Foundation

If we pack a few bags of garbage into our new life, rats will follow. For most of us, we have come to Christ, battle-scarred and beaten up, primarily because of our pre-Christ sinful lifestyle. Although saved, we continue to beat ourselves up daily because of our past. We have not understood the need to forgive ourselves for our past sinful deeds (watch for a discussion of forgiving oneself towards the end of this chapter). *"The purposes of a man's heart are deep waters, but one who has insight draws them out"* (Proverbs 20:5). That implies that we need to dig deep into our soul and uncover those things that are still hidden such as our hurts, shame, anger, bitterness, and unforgiveness.

We need to forgive ourselves.

Deep down in our souls, we can hide those battle scars. These things need to be "drawn out" and they do not, as a rule, come easily; we are only free from them to the degree we forgive the offender and ourselves. This subsequently allows us to receive God's forgiveness for the part we played as the perpetrator throughout our life's battles. The Bible is very clear on this principle. God will not forgive my sins and cleanse my heart if I refuse to forgive my brother. *"And when you stand praying, if you hold anything against anyone, forgive them, so that your Father in heaven may forgive you your sins"* (Mark 11:25).

The *Believer's Bible Commentary* states,

But one of the basic requirements for answered prayer is a forgiving spirit. If we nurse a harsh, vindictive attitude toward others, we cannot expect God to hear and answer us. We must forgive if we are to be forgiven. This does not refer to the judicial forgiveness of sins at the time of conversion; that is strictly a matter of grace through faith. This refers to God's parental dealings with His children. An unforgiving spirit in a believer breaks fellowship with the *Father in heaven* and hinders the flow of blessing.[6]

This once again illustrates to us that forgiveness is the bedrock of our Christian life! This is confirmed by Paul, when he states, *"And do not grieve the Holy Spirit of God, with whom you were sealed for the day of redemption. Get rid of all bitterness, rage and anger, brawling and slander, along with every form of malice. Be kind and compassionate to one another, forgiving each other, just as in Christ God forgave you"* (Ephesians 4:30-32). Grieve in the Greek means to "(be) sorrow (-ful)."[7] This means that when we sin, it causes the heart of God to be broken or sorrowful.

3.4.1. God, Our Discerner

Now, just in case we thought maybe we could continue in some of our pre-Christian thinking and wanting , we are reminded,

> *For the word of God is living and active. Sharper than any double-edged sword, it penetrates even to dividing soul and spirit, joints and marrow; it judges the thoughts and attitudes of the heart. Nothing in all creation is hidden from God's sight. Everything is uncovered and laid bare before the eyes of him to whom we must give account.*
>
> —Hebrews 4:12–13

I simply cannot mine all the gold in the Scripture quoted above; if I were to do that it would require me to include at least another chapter. I am going to focus only on the words, *"judges the thoughts and attitudes of our heart."* These words at the very least, have made many people anxious. For others, the thought that God sees everything they think, say, and do even angers them. It is true: God does see everything we think, say, and do! But it is not to judge or condemn us; it is for our benefit. As He is judging our thoughts and attitudes, He is also working in our hearts to bring our attention to those

---

6   MacDonald, p. 1351, emphasis added.

7   Strong, p. 45.

thoughts and attitudes that are about to push us off the road into the ditch of sin and heartache of some kind.

God's judging of our thoughts and attitudes is akin to a loving, earthly father who is teaching his five-year-old child how to ride a bike down a gravel road. The father, of course, is doing everything he can, outside of literally holding the bike upright to prevent his child from falling and bleeding. Our Heavenly Father dearly wants to walk hand-in-hand with us so we do not end up broken and shattered in some spiritual ditch. In His love, He wants to set us free from our past hurts and sinful old memories—memories that are fodder for the enemy and allow him to have a continued hold on us. Although this is a very small hold, it does allow the enemy to keep the past current by reminding us of sins that have been left undealt with. Shame, anger, hatred, and unforgiveness are so often still attached to those old memories.

3.4.2. Setting Us Free

Some years back, a very close friend of mine went home to be with the Lord. We had spent a great deal of time together just digging into the Word of God and enjoying every moment of it. We would often jump into one of our vehicles and drive around for a few hours, just to pray for whatever the Lord would put on our hearts. I was busy counselling in those days, and every once in awhile, my friend would come into my office to see me, asking if I would help him work through some spiritual pain that he had. We went back and forth in that way, helping each other come to an understanding of something or dealing with a prayer need.

My friend was born and raised in Holland, and for some years had fought against the Germans in the Second World War. Years later, after the war, he moved to Canada. I believe that he had hidden from everyone, even his wife, his intense hatred towards the Nazis. I had no idea of the murderous fire that raged in his soul until one time I was just talking casually about the need to search our soul and to ask the Spirit to uncover anything that we may have hidden there. In the midst of sharing my thoughts, he began to talk about the war. As he continued, what came out of him shocked me. It was like red, hot anger toward the Nazis spewing out of him. He also shared about dreams that had haunted him and had rocked his sleep night after night, and

41

even continued through the day. We were able to pray through it all, with him repenting and forgiving. He was wonderfully set free.

If we do not deal with these issues of the heart by repenting for our own sins and forgiving others for their sins against us, the soul becomes a deep, hot, dark, murky cesspool, with Satan stirring it up at every opportunity he gets. Of course we ask, "How can Satan do that? He has no right! We have the blood of Jesus!" The simple answer is that Satan has a legal right where there is unconfessed sin in our heart. Forgiveness is defined as: "To release, let go free, set at liberty, such as a debtor (Matt. 18:27)."[8] We would all agree that the New Testament is consistent in its teaching that when God forgives, justification is automatic. We readily accept that for salvation, but we are not so clear on the subject of "Satan's footholds." Once again, the principle is, if we are holding onto hatred, jealousy, etc. we are, step by little step, moving ourselves outside God's protective devices. This of course is being watched closely by the persecutor Satan. Because of unforgiveness, little by little, he is building a foothold in our lives. If we do not understand that, or choose to continue on in our sin of unforgiveness, our enemy soon has the upper hand over us.

We, His people, are very prone to become lazy. Because of God's abundant forgiveness and provision for us, our prayer life cools down and the next thing that drifts away is our time in the Word. If you are not hearing the preaching of the Word or receiving while reading the Word, maybe it is simply because you are living in some sin.

The Bible is chock-full of times where God, by His grace, poured out His love upon His people, lavishly meeting all their needs. In the Book of Amos, God sent a famine of hearing the words of the Lord because of continued sin (see Amos 8:11).

What immediately follows is the lack of application of the Word of God in our lives. It is not that we put God's Word on the shelf; oh no, we still make sure it is with us wherever we go. We know the Word well; we have memorized so much of it that we can throw a verse or two at almost every question that comes our way. It can look and sound virtuous, but often the reality is that it is only memorized head knowledge. As Christians, we need to be on

8   Zodhiates, p. 233.

our knees and in the Word, with a determination to live in obedience to what God has told us there.

3.5. We Do Not Have to Carry the Guilt

Forgiveness justifies us! We are not guilty! We are set free—no jailer, no jail time! Keep in mind that should we choose not to forgive our brothers and sisters, the Judge of all mankind cannot forgive us. We will find ourselves guilty! Satan, the jailer, has been given a legal right to torture us. How then, do we make relationships work? How do we love each other as ourselves? Where we retain unforgiveness, we cannot love as God loves.

Principle #9: Forgiveness removes guilt!

3.5.1. Forgiving Ourselves

If I cannot forgive and accept myself, I certainly cannot forgive and accept others. I must extend genuine forgiving grace to myself so to be able to extend it to others. *"No man sins more unreservedly than he who sins in desperation, believing that there is no pardon for him from God."*[9] As a rule, we find it much easier to forgive others than we do to forgive ourselves. Over my years counselling, a common question I asked people that were still living in pain and shame from past sin issues was, "Have you been to Father God, repented, and asked for forgiveness"? Their reply was often, "Yes, I have, and I felt His forgiveness when I asked Him, but I still carry the pain and shame." So I ask them if they have forgiven themselves. The common answer is, "No, I asked God to forgive me, and He forgave me, so why would I have to forgive myself?"

Here, the person is in a place where they know they are forgiven, because when they said or thought the words "God forgive me," they felt the release and received it in their heart. As Satan tried to be like God, so do we when we withhold forgiveness from ourselves. We recognize that sin deserves

---

9   Carter, p. 81.

punishment and proceed to punish ourselves until we think it is enough. In this case, it is as though we are saying, "God, I know better than you; I will not forgive myself. I will pay my own debts and suffer for my own failings." The instant consequence of your decision not to forgive yourself is the arrival of the jailer with chain and padlock. Following that, a moment or two later, comes the clanging of the metal doors, with you on the inside looking out.

The very same Law of Forgiveness found in Matthew chapter 18 that says we are to forgive our brothers from our heart should be applied on a personal basis. Most of us are harder on ourselves than others when, really, we should be our own closest friend.

3.5.2. Teaching on Forgiving Oneself

The following is a definition of wholly forgiving ourselves.

> I must now define what I mean by totally forgiving ourselves. It is accepting God's forgiveness of all our past sins and failures so completely that we equally let ourselves off the hook for our pasts as God Himself has done. It also means that since I must forgive others totally, I must equally forgive myself totally. This is an example of what it means to love our neighbours as we love ourselves (Matt. 22:39). To put it another way, Jesus commanded us not to judge others:

> > *Do not judge, and you will not be judged. Do not condemn, and*
> > *you will not be condemned. Forgive, and you will be forgiven.*
> > —Luke 6:37

> If I am not to judge or condemn others, it follows I should not judge or condemn myself (since God promised not to condemn me). If I am to forgive others, I must also forgive myself (since God has forgiven me). If then I do judge or condemn others, I will be judged and condemned (Matt.7:1–2). And if I don't forgive others, I forfeit the blessing of being forgiven (Matt. 6:14–15). So if I condemn myself for my past and refuse to forgive myself, I likewise

forfeit the wonderful benefit that is promised to those who enjoy God's forgiveness.

Why should God require me to accept His forgiveness and command me to forgive others but close His eyes as to whether I have forgiven myself? He doesn't.

I'm sorry, but this matter of forgiving ourselves is not an optional extra in God's plan for us; it is something we are required to do as obedient children of our heavenly Father.[10]

We need to learn to accept ourselves in our weaknesses and failures. It is not a matter of whether we go through our Christian lives without blowing it. Everything taught throughout this chapter relative to forgiving others is also applicable on a personal basis. We are to forgive ourselves as we forgive others.

We have the promise: *"If we confess our sins, he is faithful and just and will forgive us our sins and purify us from all unrighteousness"* (1 John 1:9). From here, we are to be channels of mercy and righteousness, and according to 2 Corinthians 5:16, 18–20,

> *... from now on we regard no one from a worldly point of view. Though we once regarded Christ in this way, we do so no longer... All this is from God, who reconciled us to himself through Christ and gave us the ministry of reconciliation: that God was reconciling the world to himself in Christ, not counting people's sins against them. And he has committed to us the message of reconciliation. We are therefore Christ's ambassadors; as though God were making his appeal through us. We implore you on Christ's behalf: Be reconciled to God.*

How can we be reconciled to God? Only as we forgive others. *"... Forgive us our debts, as we also have forgiven our debtors"* (Matthew 6:12). *"Therefore, if you are offering your gift at the altar and there remember that your brother or sister has something against you, leave your gift there in front of the altar. First go and be reconciled to them; then come and offer your gift"* (Matthew 5:23–24). *"Bear with each other and forgive whatever grievances you may have against one*

---

10   Kendall, p. 6.

another. Forgive as the Lord forgave you" (Colossians 3:13). We could read the previous verse as "forgive yourself as the Lord forgave you." This would be applying the Word of God to oneself. It means to have a clean slate, and at the end of the day all accounts, including our own, are settled with God. If we do not do this daily, down the road we end up with a week or two of unconfessed sins. Any unconfessed sin is a hindrance and danger for believers, and a potential opportunity for the enemy of your soul.

3.6. Useful Tools

The following are material and prayers for personal application as well as using while ministering to others. Instead of forgiving we may:

Behaviour	Example
Ignore the situation	"It will go away"
Make excuses	Instead of instant confession/ forgiveness
Rationalize	"It's not as bad as …"
Compensate or barter	"God, at least I go to church; at least I pray"
Punish others	We want to hurt the one that hurt us
Rely on ourselves	"I will put this behind me; I will try harder next time, I won't fail again!"
Make a promise	"I will never do it again, God!"
Shift blame and play the victim	"It's not my fault; someone else is responsible this time."
Give up	"What's the use?"
Display false humility	"Oh, I am no good; oh, I fail all the time; God can't bless me."

3.6.1. Why We Don't Confess One to Another

Feeling	Explanation
Insecurity	Feeling threatened; just afraid to open up
Enjoying grudges	There is a certain joy in holding a grudge of hatred. I don't want to love; I want the joy of hating them as they hate me.
Judgement	I don't agree with their lifestyle
Jealousy	Maybe the position they have over us; power they have; looks, money, etc.
Fear	I will be hurt again (mainly in close relationships)
Self-pity	The Martyr Complex—Do you know what so and so did to me after all I have done for them; why can't they forgive me?
Self-justification	I was right and I'm not moving until he acknowledges that
Fear of not being reciprocated	I won't move on this until he does
Deep hurts	I've been used before, but never again
Can't forget	We love to keep up-to-date records of past wrongs; to forgive is to intentionally *not* keep a scorecard; I only hurt you once—you got me eight times; we need to stop getting mileage out of past hurts

No Biblical perspective	Ignorance of the necessity to forgive others in order to receive forgiveness from God; what a difference this could make in our homes and in all our personal relationships, or within the framework of our church bodies

Reader, hear this: I do not believe there are many of us who understand correctly the Biblical concept of forgiveness. If we do understand it, we certainly seldom see it practised. Unrepented sin gives the devil an advantage. Sometimes the problem is not so much that we fail to forgive—it's that we fail to recognize the sin. So many of the boundaries between sinful actions and godly actions have become hopelessly blurred; many of us are no longer capable of recognizing sin. Let us just for a moment look at our marital relationships as Paul advised: *"Get rid of all bitterness, rage and anger, brawling and slander, along with every form of malice. Be kind and compassionate to one another, forgiving each other, just as in Christ God forgave you"* (Ephesians 4:31–32). We look at words like bitterness, anger, and slander and say, "Well, sometimes anger gets the best of me. But you'll never hear me slander my spouse."

Let's do a little word study on these three words: bitterness, anger, and slander.

Bitterness	• It is hard to accept (i.e. it doesn't come with grace) • Piercing or stinging • Resentful or cynical – the work cynical means "scornful of motives, virtue, or integrity of others" • Characterized by hostility

| Anger | • A strong feeling of displeasure
• Or to just be in a huff, easily offended |
| Slander | • A false statement injurious to a person's reputation; the word here means a specific character-istic or trait ascribed to a person |

Do we see ourselves getting tangled up in some of these sins? I think we all can. In my experience with forgiveness, we simply do not see many of our family relational problems as sin; *we just see them as problems.* We need to consider the seriousness of these problems, or sins, before God. At the most, we would label them as small sins, similar to "white lies."

Really, there is no such thing as a small sin—sin is sin. But let's just say there are small sins, and let's suppose ten small sins equal one average-sized sin—like rage or violence. Let's say two average-sized sins equal one large-sized sin like adultery or murder. With regard to murder, Jesus has some hard words. *"You have heard that it was said to the people long ago, 'Do not murder,' and anyone who murders will be subject to judgment. But I tell you that anyone who is angry with a brother or sister will be subject to judgment..."* (Matthew 5:21–22). The *Believer's Bible Commentary* says of this passage, "There is no mistaking the severity of the Saviour's words. He teaches that anger contains the seeds of murder, that abusive language contains the spirit of murder, and that cursing language implies the very desire to murder."[11]

If sins could be sized up comparatively—which we do, even though it is wrong—we might think it would take twenty of our small sins to equal one large sin. We would find ourselves owing a debt to our Heavenly Father equal to the debt owed by the one who committed adultery. How long would it take, in the relationship I have with my wife, or you with your spouse, to rack up a large sin debt by sinning one small sin at a time? For many of us, it would certainly be within the week.

---

11   MacDonald, p. 1220.

Now, this is only an example to get our attention, but there are many people who, for months on end, have neither forgiven, nor asked for forgiveness, of their spouses. Remember now, we are talking about people like you and me—people that claim to know better. Don't miss this: after a period of time without asking for forgiveness, we lose the ability to freely communicate and/or relate to one another. Our relationship comes to a frustrating and unmoveable halt. Why? Remember the slave that could not forgive in Matthew? Just like the unforgiving slave, our Heavenly Father has turned us over to the jailer. Where both husband and wife find themselves in a place of unforgiveness, it can result in them being in the jailhouse together. The torturers do their part by causing the husband and wife to torture each other. Have you ever been there?

Paul considered this important enough to spend most of the fourth chapter of Ephesians teaching us to *"Be completely humble and gentle; be patient, bearing with one another in love"* (Ephesians 4:2). He teaches that we are all joined together, and are to build each other up in love. He continues by saying that we must no longer live as the Gentiles do, but put off falsehood and speak truthfully to each other, *"for we are all members of one body. 'In your anger do not sin': Do not let the sun go down while you are still angry"* (Ephesians 4:25–26).

Remember that wax tablet we talked about some time earlier? This passage tells us that before the sun goes down, the slate must be clean. Sin is sin! Even when it is candy-coated, it is still sin. And wherever there is unrepented sin, in whatever disguise or form, the evil one can and will take advantage. We must remember that where there is no forgiveness, *the enemy has a legal right.* The bottom line is: Do not let the sun go down on your unforgiveness. Forgiveness is a choice, an act of our will. Emotions must be taught to fall in line.

3.6.2. Applying What We Have Been Taught

Make a list of the people you have hurt, or who have hurt you. Any persons with whom you may harbour hard feelings should be included on your list. Take your time and be thorough!

Forgiveness Prayer

Lord, I don't know how to make forgiveness happen! I can't cleanse my own heart or change my feelings! I don't know how to trust, and I'm afraid to hold my heart open. But today, I'm making a choice to forgive. I know for some of these hurts, I will have to choose again and again until You make forgiveness real and complete in me. Please God, give me the willingness and strength to persevere in choosing forgiveness until it is accomplished in me by Your power. Lord, I forgive all offences and painful experiences connected with (each name) because it made me feel _____.

I choose to forgive my father for _____

I choose to forgive my mother for _____

I choose to forgive (name) for _____

I choose to forgive (name) for _____

I choose to forgive (name) for _____

I choose to forgive (name) for _____

Forgive me, Heavenly Father, for all my sinful responses. Amen.

You can use this for a group prayer; or use it individually in the future. There may be other people that God will bring to mind at some later date. Deal with them using these prayers:

Today I choose to forgive all these people, not because I feel forgiveness or because they are right, but because I choose to be obedient to you, Father. I realize Your ways are higher than my ways, and I release these people, whom I have named, from my hurt, my disappointment, my resentment, my anger, my hatred, my unforgiveness, and my bitterness, especially my parents and family or anyone I have made a bitter root of judgement against. Thank you Lord, that I will no longer reap from those bitter roots that I have sown. Father, I let go of all resentments and bitterness stored in my heart. Wash me clean, Lord Jesus.

Here are the people I have hurt and the ones who have hurt me. I release them to you, and I forgive those who have despitefully used me. I pray for my enemies (those who have hurt me) as You have commanded, and I ask you to bless them and save them. Forgive me for the things I have done against them.

You tell me to give You my problems because You care for me. Thank you, Lord, that these people are no longer my problem; they are Yours. Thank you, Lord, for setting me free. Please heal me of my hurts in regards to these people. Please change my heart about them as only You can do. Forgive me for all condemning judgements I have made. Give me a new and right spirit that will enable me to hate sin but look with compassion and love upon the sinner. Heal the wounded heart of the child within me. Bring my childish ways and expectations to righteous maturity.

Fill me now, Father, in all the areas we have dealt with today and make them Yours forevermore. Lord, set a guard around my heart that I might function in love. Pour Your love in. Let Your light shine into all the hidden places of my heart. Enlighten the eyes of my heart, Lord, to see You and love You as You really are, and to walk in Your way. Amen.

Make a decision to forgive those who have hurt you. Today you have chosen to forgive all those hurts you remembered. In the future, God may bring others to mind; pray for them in the same way you prayed for these people today. Be alert to memories or pictures that seem to just "float" through your mind, or even dreams at night. This is a manner in which God very often brings to our mind issues that need to be dealt with.

We need to be aware of our enemy's tactics, as he will have us fishing for these forgiven sins if we let him. When and if feelings of bitterness, anger or other emotions connected with forgiven sins arise again, or if you have in any way allowed these feelings to grow, or stirred them up by allowing your thoughts to wander back into old forgiven issues, confess to the Lord the following:

On this date and time, _____, I forgive
_____ (person's name).

3.6.3. What it Means to "Forget"

Selwyn Hughes says this of recovering from painful memories:

> The question facing us now is this: How do we go about annihilating this giant which seeks to paralyse us by reviving memories of past sins that have been forgiven? But first let's be clear about what we are saying, as a wrong understanding can lead to unrealistic expectations and dampening disappointment.
>
> Some psychologists tell us it is impossible to forget anything. All our thoughts (they claim) are stored up inside us, and though they may be beyond the reach of recollection they are not outside our mental make-up. We may not be able to recall them at will, but they are not forgotten. Sometimes, of course, an accident or a trauma will produce what is known as amnesia (loss of memory), but with this condition memories are not so much lost as unable to be recalled. I do not believe it is part of God's purpose to expunge unpleasant memories from our memory banks. Instead, He takes the sharp edge off them and helps us avoid an emotional overload.
>
> As I sit here at my computer I can see on the top of my thumb an ugly scar. And I remember, albeit dimly, what caused it. Once, when I was using a sharp blade to cut some paper, it slipped and the blade penetrated my thumb. A few unpleasant hours followed, but now the memory of the accident is all but forgotten. The pain has gone and the memory is faint. There are things in our past that can be remembered as dimly as that. Give God the chance and He will make you forget anything that it would be harmful to remember. Not the event, but the acute recollection of it.[12]

---

12   Hughes, 1995.

Principle #10: Forgiveness requires one person; reconciliation requires two people.

Now, before I go any further, I wish to speak to those of you who have been deeply wounded by others. *Forgiveness is not completed until reconciliation has been achieved.* These words might cause the surfacing of some very painful memories. Perhaps your father sexually abused you from the age of 4–12 years, and still today will not acknowledge what he did to you. Or maybe you have been publicly betrayed by your longtime pastor. Maybe your thought was, "My heart will never heal." Don't give up; God has made a way for your heart to be healed!

3.6.4. Forgiveness Requires Only One Person

It takes a willful choice for one person to forgive the debt of another. It does not in any way require the involvement of the one who owes. This is a good thing, because sometimes situations arise where we literally do not have the ability to interact with the person in question, whether due to death, distance, or many other reasons. If forgiveness required both people, we would all be in big trouble. We forgive for the health of our own heart and to eliminate any possibility of unforgiveness that would create bitterness, resentment, or hard-heartedness within us.

There is a difference between forgiveness and reconciliation. Forgiveness requires only one person, whereas reconciliation requires two. Reconciliation is the willful choice to seek restoration of the relationship at hand. It is the choice to restore intimacy within marriage or any relationship.

I've found that the issue of trust is often used as a weapon when it comes to the choice not to reconcile, especially within a marriage. Trust is an all-or-nothing proposition. Often, I hear spouses say, "You don't trust me," demanding unconditional trust when there are gaping holes in certain areas of the marriage that, quite frankly, do not deserve trust until resolved. In the same way that John the Baptist chastised the Saducees and Pharisees coming to be baptized to *"bear fruit in keeping with repentance"* (Matthew 3:8, ESV),

Forgiveness

we must look for the same fruit in each other. Repentance literally means a "turning away," and we need to turn away from our old sinful ways and forge new godly ways under and through the Lord, as instructed by the Apostle Paul in Ephesians 4:17–32.

While we *do* need to forgive the issue at hand, we do *not* always have to reconcile the gaping hole until we see the fruit of changed ways. In this case, deciding not to reconcile is wise, as it prevents us from getting hurt over and over again with the same old issues because of a lack of real change (repentance). We are to "guard our hearts" until "fruit in keeping with repentance" is realized. Forgive? *Yes!* That we can do in our own hearts. Reconcile? Not until the heart has changed. There are some people who selfishly demand unconditional trust before anything else. This presents a real problem, since they demand trust and love but are not willing to change their heart and demonstrate that they are worthy of it.

Trust is a willful choice, just like forgiveness and love. Just as we willfully choose to love our mates, that willful choice then creates the feelings of being "in love" we long for, and the same applies with trust. We must make the willful choice to change our hearts and ways, and the trust we desire will be granted to us. People often demand the reverse. They wait around for the "in love" feelings to motivate them to love their mate or for their mate to trust them again, but the time never comes. In the meantime, more distance and isolation builds up as each mate creates their own "island of me" instead of an "island of we." Before long, emotional and physical divorce are not far behind. We have all heard the saying, "We just grew apart." Whenever I hear someone say that, my response is, "No, you just failed to grow together."

The Gospel message is much the same. God forgave all humankind through His work on the Cross, requiring only Him to do so. But each of us must reconcile with God through Christ in order to restore our relationship with Him due to sin. Reconciliation requires two: God and each person.

So, forgive for your own health and well-being. This does not necessarily mean to forget; we will probably never completely forget the memory of what happened. To reiterate, "I do not believe it is part of God's purpose to expunge unpleasant memories from our memory banks. Instead, He takes the sharp edge off them and helps us avoid an emotional overload. But if we

55

truly forgive, we no longer stew over what happened in our hearts."[13] The negative emotions that were wrapped up in memories then are no longer triggered and re-lived, since the issue has been handed over to God, and we trust that He will deal with our offender as He promises to in the Word. This last teaching is a conclusion from my twenty-five plus years of counselling, as well as what I have gleaned from different people's input and teaching. As I have compiled this together over the last several years, I am now not sure what has come from myself and what has come from others. If I have inadvertently used anyone's material, I ask for your forgiveness.

3.6.5. Receiving Forgiveness

Use this prayer as a closer for repentance and renunciation:

> *Thank You, Father, for Your complete forgiveness. Your forgiving love penetrates into the very depths of my being and sets me free from my past sins. It sets me free from fear and the mistakes of the past. Thank You for giving me Your grace and that it is flowing through me. Bitterness, guilt and condemnation have no control over me in the areas I have just renounced and received Your forgiveness for. As Christ has forgiven me, so I extend forgiveness to those who have wronged me. I enjoy the freedom of Your forgiveness and I enjoy being forgiven by others. I open the channels for your Holy Spirit to work. My prayers have life; Your image is clear, and You are using me to minister to others. Amen.*

---

13   Hughes, 1995.

Chapter Four

STRONGHOLDS

4.1. The Stronghold of God

As I endeavour to bring some understanding to the concept of strongholds, I shall begin with a quote from a must-read book, written by Francis Frangipane, called *The Stronghold of God*.

> The Bible tells us of a time when Satan shall be cast down to the earth. He will come, "having great wrath, knowing that he has only a short time" (Rev. 12:12). While some Christians question whether the church will be the victim of such hellish warfare, it is obvious even in our world today that the magnitude of evil has escalated. What is our response? Has God provided for us a Christian equivalent to the ark He provided Noah? Is there a spiritual Goshen where we can dwell in safety during God's judgments? We believe the answer to these questions is yes. God has provided spiritual protection for Christians, a stronghold where our souls can always find safe harbor. When we speak of a stronghold, we do not mean that we will escape suffering, persecution, or even death for Jesus' sake. For "all who desire to live godly in Christ Jesus will be persecuted" (2 Tim. 3:12). Nor do we expect to find a place where we are so 'spiritual' that the world finally loves us. If they hated Jesus, they will hate us as well (John 15:18–19). The stronghold of God is the shelter of God—that dwelling of eternal life the Lord has provided for our souls. Once we have found this place, nothing we encounter in life can defeat us; God Himself preserves us in all things. In every distress or devilish plot set against us, we emerge the better for it. It is the redemptive power of Christ reversing the

plans of Satan and annulling the effects of death in our lives. Although you may be in a place of fear, sin, or emotional defeat, your current condition is not a limitation to the Almighty. From where you are, you can reach the stronghold of God.[14]

Remember these following words, seal them in your heart and write them in your Bible. From where you are, you can reach the stronghold of God. God is never out of reach—never. The stronghold you have just been introduced to is made by God's hands for His people. It is a place of safety, a place of refuge, a place to run to in the time of overwhelming storm.

David was familiar with the stronghold of God as he wrote, *"The Lord is my rock, my fortress and my deliverer"* (Psalm 18:2). Frangipane says,

> The stronghold of God is not only a place to visit God but to dwell with Him. For those who dwell with God, His presence is not merely our refuge; it is a permanent address. When we are abiding in Christ, we become one with Him. It is His life, His virtue, His wisdom, and His Spirit that sustain us.[15]

How are we to live our lives such that we are assured of always living in His sustaining presence? Once again, Frangipane says,

> The primary means through which we are kept and preserved by God is through obedience to His Word. In the submission of our will to God, our soul finds protection from evil. Consider the Apostle John's words to the young men of the first century church. He said, I have written to you young men, because you are strong, and the Word of God abides in you, and you have overcome that evil one (John 2:14). Abiding in the Word of God brought spiritual strength to the young men in John's day, enabling them to overcome

---

14   Frangipane, 1998, p. vii–viii.
15   Frangipane, 1998, p. 63–64.

the evil one. Is this not the reason many of us are defeated by the devil—we do not abide in the Word?[16]

God has provided for us the ultimate haven of rest and protection. To avail ourselves of it, all He asks of us is to be faithful by always choosing, in every situation, to dwell in His presence. Such are the workings of the stronghold of God.

We have now had a good look at what the stronghold of God would look like. I will now provide some explanation on the stronghold of the enemy.

4.2. The Stronghold of the Enemy

From here, and for the rest of this chapter, I will discuss strongholds of a very different nature, strongholds that are embodied by the dark realm, the scheme of Satan as he wars against man and spews out his hatred of mankind—more specifically, his intense hatred toward God Himself.

As I endeavour to make strongholds a reality for you, the reader, the following story will help you to accept and understand the concept.

After two or three hours working with a client one afternoon, I had exposed a stronghold of fear. We dealt with the root sin issues and all connecting issues with this stronghold. I sent the demon to Jesus, and commanded, "You cannot ever return to this person."

I then moved on to some other sin issues. Unable to deal with all of them in the time we had, we met the following morning. However, we found ourselves dealing with a totally different topic. As I began to work with the issue at hand, I realized that I was dealing with the same demon I had dismissed yesterday.

"You are the same demon I was dealing with yesterday," I said.

The demon responded, "Yes I am."

"Why are you back again? I dealt with your stronghold, and I commanded you to leave, saying 'You cannot return.'"

---

16   Frangipane, 1998, p. 31.

"Yes, you told me that I could not return," the demon replied. "But I have a legal right to come back, because you did not remove the *structure* of the stronghold attached to the soul of this person."

4.2.1. What is a Stronghold?

What on earth is a stronghold? This question is asked by a very large percentage of new clients when I begin to discuss the need to search for possible strongholds in their lives. Because the majority of my counselling clientele are born-again, it appears that believers could spend much more time studying the Bible than we do. Perhaps daily reading is occuring, but there is a deficit in the application of the Word and understanding of what has been read. We Christians are notorious for just skipping over the hard-to-understand Scriptures, which is to our detriment. As it is written in Hosea 4:6, "... *my people are destroyed from lack of knowledge.*"

It is imperative that we ask the hard questions: What does the word "stronghold" in my daily devotional mean in my life and the life of my family? If we don't ask hard questions and apply the corresponding principles, we leave ourselves vulnerable to the enemy's scheming efforts to have us bound up by strongholds. We will have no idea that our inability to move on in particular areas of our lives may be due to a stronghold of hatred or anger or something else (the list goes on).

The concept of "strongholds" is introduced to us by the Apostle Paul.

> *The weapons we fight with are not the weapons of the world. On the contrary, they have divine power to demolish strongholds. We demolish arguments and every pretension that sets itself up against the knowledge of God, and we take captive every thought to make it obedient to Christ.*
> —2 Corinthians 10:4–5

Paul is particularly clear as he explains what type of battle he was fighting. He says, "*For though we live in the world, we do not wage war as the world does. The weapons we fight with are not the weapons of the world. On the contrary, they have divine power to demolish strongholds*" (2 Corinthians 10:3–4).

A discussion on verses 3 to 5 from the Expositors Bible Commentary is as follows:

> A clear distinction is drawn between existence "in the world" and worldly conducts and techniques. Paul does not deny his human weakness, yet he affirms that a spiritual warfare demands spiritual weapons (vv.3, 4a; cf. Eph 6:11-17). A successful campaign can be waged in the spiritual realm only as worldly weapons are abandoned and total reliance is placed on the spiritual weaponry, which is divinely potent for demolishing apparently impregnable fortresses where evil is entrenched and from which the gospel is attacked (v.4b).[17]

What are these impregnable fortresses that crumble before the weapons of the Spirit? Fanciful human sophistry and intellectual pretensions, or as Paul expresses it, *"the wisdom of this world"* (1 Corinthians 3:19). A different commentary has this perspective:

> This verse tells us what is meant by strongholds. In verse 4, Paul perceived himself as a soldier warring against the proud reasoning of man, arguments which oppose the truth. The true character of these arguments is used to describe the expression "against the knowledge of God." It could be applied to the reasoning of the scientists, evolutionists, philosophers, and religionists who have no room for God in their scheme of things. The apostle was in no mood to sign a truce with these. Rather, he still committed to bringing every thought into captivity to the obedience of Christ. All man's teaching and speculation must be judged in the light of the teaching of the Lord Jesus Christ; all would not condemn human reasoning as such, but would warn that we must not allow our intellects to be exercised in defiance of the Lord and in disobedience to Him.[18]

---

17   Harris, p. 380.

18   MacDonald, p. 1856.

The stronghold of the enemy is a viewpoint or way of thinking that is not in alignment with God's truth. It is a spiritual structure that is fortified and defensible, requiring spiritual weaponry to defeat.

4.3. Categories of Strongholds

Gary D. Kinnaman, in his book, *Overcoming the Dominion of Darkness* (pp. 54-58), says it well as he brings out the concept of strongholds as they apply to spiritual warfare and to us, the Body of Christ today.

Strongholds fall into three broad categories: ideological, personal, and territorial.

One: Ideological Strongholds
These have to do with world views and the corresponding lifestyles that are contrary to God's Word. These are ideas, philosophies and religious or nonreligious views that influence culture and society. Examples are political ideologies, like socialism or Communism; philosophical ideologies, like secular humanism or evolutionary materialism; and religious ideologies, like Unitarianism, Islam or New Age thinking.

These views may or may not be carefully defined, but they are ways of thinking that have a powerful and profound effect on society, and thus on individuals. The New Age, for example, has no commonly accepted doctrinal statement. It is not a conspiracy, as such, but there are certain aspects of the movement that are generally identifiable and that greatly influence the way people think and live.

Hollywood has not written a plot for the takeover of the American mind, yet every time you turn on your television you are risking the influence of whatever ideology lies beneath the surface of the program you watch. Our colleges and universities are cauldrons of persuasive ideologies. "See to it," Paul warns, "that no one takes you captive through hollow and deceptive philosophy, which depends on human tradition and the basic principles of this world rather than on Christ" (Colossians 2:8). It is true that not all of these ideologies are specifically demonic in origin, but all of them do have roots in Satan's master plan. They are what Paul calls "arguments and every pretension that sets itself up against the knowledge of God" (2 Corinthians 10:5). The important factor here is that we are dealing not merely with human ideas, but with human ideas that have an essential spiritual power. If we recognize their source, our resistance to these ideologies must be spiritual, not merely intellectual.

Two: Personal Strongholds

These have to do with you – your thoughts, your feelings, your attitudes, your behaviour patterns. Paul writes in 2 Corinthians 10:3, "For though we live in the world, we do not wage war as the world does." Life is full of spiritual influences, and spiritual power can be countered only with spiritual power.

Thus, "the weapons we fight with are not the weapons of the world. On the contrary, they have divine power to demolish strongholds…We take captive every thought to make it obedient to Christ" (verses 4–5). Your mind, your thought life is a battleground, not just between the old you and the new you, but with outside spiritual influences as well.

Resisting and overcoming the devil begins with recognition of the reality of the battle. Furthermore, success in spiritual warfare is grounded in a clear understanding of the wiles of the devil. My prayer, with the Apostle Paul, is that "Satan might not outwit us. For we are not unaware of his schemes. (2 Corinthians 2:11). It must be said again that those just read ideologies work against us always, individually as well as corporately, working with the hope of influencing us in some small way, causing us to question our foundational platform of Biblical knowledge, thought and practice from which we live our Christian lives. If our enemy can get the smallest little bent in our otherwise solid Christian theology, this just may be enough for him to cause a little doubt. This then causes us to question the inerrancy of God's Word. This can become the opportunity the enemy was looking for to begin the process of building a stronghold of doubt in a person's life.[19]

I will cover Kinnaman's third stronghold, the Territorial Stronghold, in Section 4.9. of this chapter.

4.4. The Process and Life of Strongholds

Strongholds are, for the most part, not on the mind or even in the vocabulary of most Christians, but they are very much alive and active. Whereas God's stronghold is a structure and place of refuge we can safely run to, Satan's stronghold of hate and destruction is a structure we need to resist. He and his helpers are sneaking around, always looking for places to breach our armour. It doesn't matter how small the hole may be—if he can get a little toehold, he's happy. He knows human nature and is counting on our lack of discipline; he is willing to take as much time as he needs. He has been watching us long before the fall of man. If we have sinned in a particular way once, there is a high probability that we will sin that way again. He knows it is only a matter of time before he will have an opportunity to expand his original breach. Just a little bit at a time for an average Christian, and he soon has a stronghold.

All this is done behind our backs. It isn't even suspected for reasons I've mentioned before: the church at large doesn't see strongholds as prevalent in our modern-day Christian life. Many of our spiritual insecurities, sin issues, and other maladies are recognized by ourselves, or those close to us, but not so with strongholds. They are often hidden from sight, simply because people are not aware of the possibility of Satan having a stronghold in their soul.

After working with thousands of individuals, there is no doubt in my mind that Satan works hard to keep strongholds hidden in the darkness of his presence, unseen by the untrained and unsuspecting eye. Along with that, we are disadvantaged by living in the natural (fleshly) realm. What follows is that we see, hear, think, and communicate in the natural, while a stronghold is lived out in the realm of the soul. We often look on the inside—we know

---

19   Kinnaman, p. 56–58.

something isn't right, but we aren't sure what we're looking for or even where to look.

4.4.1. The Jailhouse

We tend to have the same problem with the teaching on forgiveness in Mathew 18, with the potential for you and me to end up in a jailhouse. We simply cannot see ourselves being locked up in that place, but Scripture is clear about unforgiveness.

> *Then the master called the servant in. "You wicked servant," he said, "I canceled all that debt of yours because you begged me to. Shouldn't you have had mercy on your fellow servant just as I had on you?" In anger his master turned him over to the jailers to be tortured, until he should pay back all he owed. This is how my heavenly Father will treat each of you unless you forgive your brother or sister from your heart.*
> —Matthew 18:32–35

The jailhouse in Matthew represents a similar problem as strongholds do. Our question here is: how on earth can I be locked up in a spiritual jailhouse?

Jesus says, "… *the kingdom of heaven is like a king who wants to settle accounts with his servants*" (Matthew 18:23). What Jesus is saying is that some things are done similarly in Heaven and on earth. The principle of forgiveness in Heaven, then, is also to be applied on earth. Jump ahead to the situation where the servant of the king was unable to pay the debt he owed his master, and therefore, the servant, along with his wife and children, were about to be sold into slavery in order to pay the debt. But *"the servant's master took pity on him, canceled the debt and let him go"* (Matthew 18:27). The first servant, forgiven, then went out and met up with a fellow servant—one he had worked side by side with, a friend who had at one time borrowed just two or three small coins. The first servant now demanded payment from him, but he was unable to pay. The first servant, with no hesitation, had him put in jail.

We know the story, don't we? The master was soon informed of the first servant's wicked, unforgiving ways, and the first servant soon found himself looking out from inside the jailhouse. In the same way, this is how God will treat us unless we truly forgive each other from our hearts.

Jesus' last few words take this situation out of the earthly realm of kings and slaves and dropped it into the spiritual realm. Jesus was responding to Peter's question, and no doubt the question of dozens of others then listening to Him. Peter asked, "... 'Lord, how many times shall I forgive my brother or sister who sins against me? Up to seven times?' Jesus answered, 'I tell you, not seven times, but seventy-seven times"* (Matthew 18:21–22).

Jesus' warning about how his Father would treat the unforgiving was delivered later in this same discussion. If you don't forgive your brother from your heart, you will be turned over to the jailer to be tortured (Matthew 18:34). Whenever we continue to sin, the penalty is that we become locked up in a stronghold. As mentioned earlier, if we have sinned once in an area and never properly addressed it, we can develop a propensity to sin in that area again and again. Some time after, Satan can start to own portions of who we are.

4.5. Footholds and Strongholds

4.5.1. Footholds

Jailhouse? Me? Us? What on earth would that look like? We ask the same question of strongholds. Me? Us? Bound up in a spiritual stronghold of whatever the sin may be?

The same question should be asked of forgiveness: what on earth would that look like? I believe the answer is, *"'In your anger do not sin': Do not let the sun go down while you are still angry, and do not give the devil a foothold"* (Ephesians 4:26–27). A "foothold" in Greek means a place in your heart or in your soul. The main point being made in this passage is not so much about anger, it is what you or I are carrying overnight and then into the next day, and the next and the next... Any sin, even the smallest, that is not repented of, and for which reconciliation has not taken place between God, the offender, and the offended, will give Satan an opportunity to take the first steps in establishing a foothold.

> # Principle #11: The moment we agree, we have given our enemy the advantage; he has a foothold.

4.5.2. Strongholds

Strongholds carry forward very much in the same way as footholds. It is incumbent upon us to understand that God has established very definitive rules about forgiveness, unforgiveness, and strongholds. If we choose forgiveness, we can live in His presence. If we choose unforgiveness, instantly the door to God's presence closes. That is a given! God set it up that way, and there's no way around it.

The consequences for us are severe: we end up in Satan's jailhouse to be tortured by his demons. This is indicative of how much God hates unforgiveness and all the evil that it brings to us individually—within our families, in our work place, and around the world, where we see nation pitted against nation, simply because in their pride, they cannot forgive.

Unforgiveness, laced with anger and followed with hatred, is at the root of a very high percentage of relational breakdowns. From here, it is one small step for the enemy to snap the shackles on. We become captive in a stronghold of unforgiveness, anger and hatred.

Conversely, if we follow the Biblical practice of forgiveness and reconciliation before the sun goes down, then of course, we will be free—no shackles. From my experience, spiritual strongholds have a much broader reach into our lives than footholds and unforgiveness, which allows Satan to bind us up in his jailhouse. When it comes to strongholds, Satan has the freedom to worm his way into our lives, through the smallest of sin issues.

Sin that tarries will give the enemy an opportunity for a stronghold.

But in saying that, Satan and his cohorts are very definitely bound by parameters that God has established for them. God's Word tells us that Satan has come to kill, steal, and destroy, but God has also established parameters that Satan cannot cross. Satan and his cohorts cannot just walk into our lives because you or I just sinned. No, it is sin that tarries that gives him opportunity. Remember always: this is critical knowledge relative to spiritual warfare.

For the enemy to establish a foothold in our lives, we have to have carried sin overnight, according to Ephesians 4:26–27. It is our sin that allows Satan access to our soul. That is why the Word advises us to confess any sin we have committed before the sun sets; then Satan has no access. But if we choose not to forgive, Satan has a legal right to a foothold in the place of our sin. Again, it is sin *that tarries* that gives him opportunity. There is no other place in the Bible that expands on this concept, but God has established principles and guidelines consistent throughout the whole of the Bible, for humans as well as demons. God is a God of order!

Of course, once demonization is present, the evil one has made his way in through our armour and is attaching himself to our soul. This is a completely different level of spiritual warfare, with the demon getting itself settled on the inside; often it's not long until it begins challenging our mental and emotional stability. Remember, we are the ones that provided it with what it needed to get inside.

Deal immediately with the sin issue that gave entrance to the enemy. Repent and receive God's forgiveness; command the evil one to go, and tell it that it cannot return, and it will be gone, faster than it came in.

4.5.3. How Footholds Become Strongholds

Sins, and sometimes iniquities (the wickedness carried on down through the generations of the family line), are needed for Satan to begin chiseling his way through our armour. As for iniquities, all sins are birthed by our own personal sin, but there can be generational strongholds of propensities for whatever sin you may wish to name. Those sins come with a loaded gun, simply because of their longevity in the family line and the generational curses that become attached to the current generation. These generational "powerhouses" know exactly how to break down our poorly-built foundation of knowledge and faith.

If the powers of darkness can establish just the smallest bit of a foundation to work from, it isn't long until Satan and his cohorts begin to bring emotional, psychological, and physical confusion. Hence the need for us always to stay in step with the Spirit of God that indwells us. *"Since we live by the Spirit, let us keep in step with the Spirit"* (Galatians 5:25).

Giving the devil a foothold, as discussed in Ephesians 4:26–27 and the teaching on forgiveness, means to literally give him a place in your soul if you continue on in unforgiveness. Strongholds work in exactly the same way as footholds. This is *not* demon possession. Satan *cannot* possess a born-again believer, but he certainly can get a foothold or stronghold, and little by little, he will begin to promote his agenda from the soul. Any habitual sin, no matter how small and trivial it may seem, will be seized immediately by Satan to get just a little tochold, from which he will build a foothold. If the foothold is anger, he will do his best to create an atmosphere of anger within your person, and with those around you.

His intent, of course, is to eventually hold us in a stronghold—of anger, or whatever else. If we are living in unforgiveness, our enemy has a foothold in our soul. Satan then builds a stronghold, and if we continue to sin in this area or that area, we become boxed in by strongholds and footholds, with the evil ones actually making and directing our decisions. They are very discreet in doing so, primarily because their work is to control us for the advancement of their agenda. Thus, the strongholds of Satan form the dark side.

4.6. God's Counterpart to Satan's Weapons

God has a counterpart for each weapon of Satan's:

Satan's Weapon	Satan's Strategy	Satan's Role	God's Counterpart
Sin	Active	Tempter	Jesus' blood
Accusation	Passive	Accuser	Our testimony
Stonghold	Dormant	Deceiver	Dying to old self

Keep in mind that at the experiential level, none of Satan's weapons stand alone. If Satan has defeated us and caused us to sin, in all likelihood he is also accusing us, which he uses to build the stronghold that shouts loudly, "You will never be free of that sin!" However, we have God's counterpart:

> *The great dragon was hurled down—that ancient serpent called the devil, or Satan, who leads the whole world astray. He was hurled to the earth, and his angels with him. Then I heard a loud voice in heaven say:* "Now have come the salvation and the power and the kingdom of our God, and the authority of his Messiah. For the accuser of our brothers and sisters, who accuses them before our God day and night, has been hurled down. They triumphed over him by the blood of the Lamb and by the word of their testimony; they did not love their lives so much as to shrink from death. *Therefore rejoice, you heavens and you who dwell in them! But woe to the earth and the sea, because the devil has gone down to you! He is filled with fury, because he knows that his time is short.*"
>
> —Revelation 12:9–12 (emphasis added)

The Blood of Jesus is powerless for us in spiritual warfare until we can live out verses 10–11 (italicized above); only then do we begin to shake the gates of hell as we die to self. An understanding of God's counterparts will aid in avoiding the strongholds of Satan.

4.6.1. Jesus' Blood

Jesus bought back all humanity through His death, the spilling of His blood, and made salvation available for all that would come to Him. Along with His subsequent trip into the stronghold of Satan, Jesus stripped from him the title deed for both the world and mankind, making salvation a reality for all that would receive! Now in a right relationship with God, our position, even in times of warfare, is standing at the right hand of Jesus Christ, in the heavenly realms! For "… *God raised us up with Christ and seated us with Him in the heavenly realms in Christ Jesus*" (Ephesians 2:6); "…*we have been made holy through the sacrifice of the body of Jesus Christ once for all*" (Hebrews 10:10).

Truth begins to take root, for we *"... know that it was not with perishable things such as silver or gold that [we] were redeemed from this empty way of life handed down to [us] from [our] ancestors, but with the precious blood of Christ, a lamb without blemish or defect. He was chosen before the creation of the world."* (1 Peter 1:18–20). *"Therefore, if anyone is in Christ, the new creation has come: The old has gone, the new is here!"* (2 Corinthians 5:17).

4.6.2. Our Testimony

What really is our testimony? It becomes a reality for us as we understand that we have been given authority to trample upon snakes and scorpions and overcome all the power of the enemy. The position that we work from is in the heavenly realm, a place where nothing will harm us (Luke 10:19). This requires us to know who we are in Christ.

The truth is that all powers and authorities are under our feet. The truth is that we have authority over all the power of the enemy and nothing shall harm us. *"... do not rejoice that the spirits submit to you, but rejoice that your names are written in heaven"* (Luke 10:20). We need to think back to the power behind the Great Commission: *"All authority has been given Me in heaven and on earth"* (Matthew 28:18). It is with this authority that He has commissioned us to do His work.

4.6.3. Dying to Old Self

Dying to self means picking up your cross, denying your own pleasures and ways, and following God, even if it is uncomfortable and hard. There is help and life in none other than the Person of Christ, the one for whom we die to self.

In Matthew 16:24, Jesus says, *"Whoever wants to be my disciple must deny themselves and take up their cross and follow me."* This can be explained thus: "to deny self is not the same as self-denial; it means to yield to His control so completely that self has no rights whatsoever. To take up the cross means the willingness to endure shame, suffering, and perhaps martyrdom for His sake; to die to sin, self, and to the world."[20]

---

20   MacDonald, p. 1268.

"I have been crucified with Christ and I no longer live, but Christ lives in me" (Galatians 2:20). This is where the truth really begins to penetrate our whole person. Once we die to self and choose to live for Christ, all human speculations begin to disappear. Before Christ entered our life, we lived according to the beliefs and thoughts of the flesh and the attitudes of the world. Now, in Christ, we live by the truth of the Word, which causes those man-made assumptions to crumble before the throne of God, for the speculations of man cannot stand against the truth of the Word.

4.6.4. How Do We Destroy Satan's Three Weapons?

The Bible is very explicit in addressing how to counter the weapons of Satan. Colossians 3:1–17 instructs us how to live our lives so that we can claim daily the power of Christ's blood and live out the authority given to us by God. We must continually choose Christ over ourselves.

So if you're serious about living this new resurrection life with Christ, *act* like it. Pursue the things over which Christ presides. Don't shuffle along, eyes to the ground, absorbed with the things right in front of you. Look up, and be alert to what is going on around Christ— that's where the action is. See things from *his* perspective.

Your old life is dead. Your new life, which is your *real* life—even though invisible to spectators—is with Christ in God. *He* is your life. When Christ (your real life, remember) shows up on this earth, you'll show up too—the real you, the glorious you. Meanwhile, be content with obscurity, like Christ.

And that means killing off everything connected with that day of death: sexual promiscuity, impurity, lust, doing whatever you feel like whenever you feel like it, and grabbing whatever attracts your fancy. That's a life shaped by things and feelings instead of by God. It's because of this kind of thing that God is about to explode in anger. It wasn't long ago that you were doing all that stuff and not knowing any better. But you know better now, so make sure it's all gone for good: bad temper, irritability, meanness, profanity, dirty talk.

Principle #12: Hopelessness causes us to see our situation as unrepairable.

Don't lie to one another. You're done with that old life. It's like a filthy set of ill-fitting clothes you've stripped off and put in the fire. Now you're dressed in a new wardrobe. Every item of your new way of life is custom-made by the Creator, with his label on it. All the old fashions are now obsolete. Words like Jewish and non-Jewish, religious and irreligious, insider and outsider, uncivilized and uncouth, slave and free, mean nothing. From now on everyone is defined by Christ, everyone is included in Christ.

So, chosen by God for this new life of love, dress in the wardrobe God picked out for you: compassion, kindness, humility, quiet strength, discipline. Be even-tempered, content with second place, quick to forgive an offense. Forgive as quickly and completely as the Master forgave you. And regardless of what else you put on, wear love. It's your basic, all-purpose garment. Never be without it.

Let the peace of Christ keep you in tune with each other, in step with each other. None of this going off and doing your own thing. And cultivate thankfulness. Let the Word of Christ—the Message—have the run of the house. Give it plenty of room in your lives. Instruct and direct one another using good common sense. And sing, sing your hearts out to God! Let every detail in your lives—words, actions, whatever—be done in the name of the Master, Jesus, thanking God the Father every step of the way.

—Colossians 3:1-17, MSG. (Emphasis in the original.)

This is where sanctification really begins to work, and we are brought to our knees in confession, as the light exposes the darkness. And "... *he is faithful and just and will forgive us our sins and purify us from all unrighteousness*" (1 John 1:9). We destroy Satan's weapons as we walk in the Word.

4.7. Types of Strongholds

There are many many types of strongholds, some of which will be mentioned below. One definition comes from Ed Silvoso, founder of Harvest Evangelism: "A stronghold is a mindset impregnated with hopelessness that causes us to accept as unchangeable situations that we know are contrary to the will of God."[21] This "mindset impregnated with hoplessness" is also found as a part of a structure in many many different types of strongholds, as you will see.

4.7.1. Stronghold 1 – Hoplessness (in Marriage)

We see God's established standard for marriage in his Word. The Message Bible states,

> He answered, "Haven't you read in your Bible that the Creator original-ly made man and woman for each other, male and female? And because of this, a man leaves father and mother and is firmly bonded to his wife, becoming one flesh—no longer two bodies but one. Because God creat-ed this organic union of the two sexes, no one should desecrate his art by cutting them apart."
>
> They shot back in rebuttal, "If that's so, why did Moses give instruc-tions for divorce papers and divorce procedures?"
>
> Jesus said, "Moses provided for divorce as a concession to your hard heartedness, but it is not part of God's original plan. I'm holding you to the original plan, and holding you liable for adultery if you divorce your faithful wife and then marry someone else. I make an exception in cases where the spouse has committed adultery."
>
> —Matthew 19:4–9, MSG

We know God hates divorce, and yet there is no difference between the divorce ratios inside and outside of the Christian church. Why? Because of-ten we are gripped tightly by hopelessness. We know the mindset of God is "until death do us part," but because of all the misery occuring within

---

21   Silvoso, p. 155.

marriages, people have many manmade excuses: the fighting, the hurt, the shattered hopes, coupled with Satan's barrage of lies, saying "Give it up, what's the use?," "My wife has no love for me," "It will only get worse; get out before you destroy the kids," "Surely God doesn't expect me to stay married to a husband I no longer love,"[22] or "Surely God doesn't expect me to change my lucrative career just because I can't be with my family on weekends."[23]

This is a critical place of decision, a crossroad: at this point, if we make our decision for God, saying He hates divorce and choosing His way, we have all Heaven on our side. But if we believe the evil one's lie that our situation is unchangeable, we have established a pretension that sets itself up against our knowledge of God's Word. We might find ourselves saying, "It's hopeless," while we claim to believe that all things are possible with God. If we fail to choose God in this critical moment, our enemy seizes the opportunity to apply a storm of confusion to our thoughts. Consequently, the pretension and hopelessness prevails.

The apostle Paul, in writing, *"For our struggle is not against flesh and blood, but against the rulers, against the authorities, against the powers of this dark world and against the spiritual forces of evil in the heavenly realms"* (Ephesians 6:12), is telling us to be aware when we find ourselves in hard times relationally, hurting and angry with each other. Remember that there is another component at work here: the *spiritual forces of evil*. Knowledge is our ammunition against the spiritual forces trying to establish a stronghold of hopelessness and despair in our family unit.

Let's use the example of marriage again. Suppose you're at the point of turning your back and walking away from the commitment you made to your wife. That small voice in the back of your mind saying "till death do us part" is almost smothered. You know that small voice is God. But you feel this overwhelming, almost consuming, sense of hopelessness. Such a feeling causes us to see our marriage as unrepairable, and we accept the situation.

Hopelessness is defined as "a state of being desperate, or affording no hope."[24] Hopelessness is a loss of hope, leaving a person in a state of despera-

---

22   Jeremiah, p. 142.

23   Jeremiah, p. 142.

24   http://webstersdictionary1828.com/Dictionary/hopelessness

tion with no expectation of good. Hopelessness, like a cancer, can eat away at our ability to trust God and can undermine our faith. All hope in God to restore can disappear. Now, where on earth does hopelessness come from? No doubt Satan preaches that message to each one of us, in some way, every day.

4.7.2. Stronghold 2 – Deception (The Battle for the Mind)

"…many deceivers, who do not acknowledge Jesus Christ as coming in the flesh, have gone out into the world. Any such person is the deceiver and the antichrist" (2 John 7). This verse shouts out loud and clear instructions for us today! John is warning us to look out for those who do not acknowledge Jesus Christ as coming in the flesh. This mindset is rampant in our world today and comes at us from many different channels of thought, often from deceived Christian organizations. God has given us His Word for this very reason: that we would know His truth, and that this truth would be the platform that exposes deception. But our real concern is not the risky theology of the unorthodox—the real peril is our relentless foe.

> Today Satan continues his strategy of division. He injects the poisons of suspicion, intolerance, hatred, jealousy, and criticism into humanity. These poisons seek an outlet and finds it in the human tongue. James describes the result in his letter: *"…the tongue is a fire, a world of iniquity. The tongue is so set among our members that it defiles the whole body, and sets on fire the course of nature; and it is set on fire by hell… It is an unruly evil, full of deadly poison"* (James 3:6, 8). This poison ejected through the tongue is one of Satan's most divisive tools. It divides husband from wife, brother from brother, friend from friend, family from family, church from church, and even nation from nation. All these divisions are steps toward Satan's ultimate goal: to divide the soul from the body, bringing us down into eternal separation from God. Only our utter dependance on the unifying sacrifice of Christ can prevent this from happening.[25]

Ira Milligan says this about Satan and deception:

---

25   Jeremiah, pp. 44–45.

Jesus said Satan was a thief and that his purpose was to steal, kill, and destroy God's works (see John 10:10). This is also revealed in Satan's four primary natures. The first designated nature of the thief is that he is a tempter. Working through people's senses and using people's own passions, he discretely stimulates their feelings and tempts them with imaginations of sinful pleasure… The second nature of Satan is to deceive. Through reasoning, lies, self-justification, the thief labours to steal the use of people's bodies. By suppressing the human spirit, he tries to use people's flesh and minds to please himself at their expense (see 2 Cor. 10:5; Rev. 12:9). The third nature of Satan is to accuse. By accusing people before God, through the brethren, the murdering thief strives to take their lives, both natural and spiritual… The fourth and final nature of the adversary is to destroy. Satan uses God's Law to his own advantage, working similar to an evil police officer. Using entrapment, he persuades people to sin and then penalizes them for their trespasses.[26]

Whether deception comes through the spiritual or the human realm does not matter to Satan; if we bite the hook by believing his lies, he has liberty to hold us and feed us thoughts which he will use to deepen his scheme and eventually hold us in a stronghold. In giving this foothold to Satan, we lose to some degree our freedom of thought. If we do not uncover the scheme, but rather believe it, it becomes a possible door opener—something the evil one is always looking for. Unchecked, it becomes a stronghold in the mind.

4.7.3. Stronghold 3 – Temptation

Satan is called the "tempter" (Matthew 4:3). James, the brother of Jesus, describes sin thus: "…each one is tempted when they are dragged away by their own evil desire and enticed. Then, after desire has conceived, it gives birth to sin; and sin, when it is full grown, gives birth to death" (James 1:14–15).

If our foe managed to lock us in the stronghold of the particular sin in which we were involved, we would be giving birth to death. This is not physical death, but separation from God—exactly what happened to mankind's

---

26   Milligan, pp. 75–76.

first parents because of Adam's sin. Adam's son, Cain, suffered similar consequences: being sent away from God's presence (see Genesis 4:14). History repeats itself in a generational curse of disobedience to God's spoken Word!

See Chapter 6 on Spiritual Warfare, Section 6.2., for aditional teaching on sin.

4.7.4. Stronghold 4 – Passivity
Jessie Penn-Lewis in her book, *War on the Saints*, states this:

>...the chief condition for the working of evil spirits in a human being, apart from sin, is passivity, in exact opposition to the condition which God requires for His working. Granted the surrender of the will to God, with active choice to do His will as it may be revealed to him, God requires cooperation with His Spirit, and the full use of every faculty of the whole man. In brief, the powers of darkness aim at obtaining a passive slave or captive to their will; whilst God desires a regenerated man, intelligently and actively willing and choosing, and doing His will in liberation of spirit, soul and body from slavery. The powers of darkness would make a man a machine, a tool, an automaton; the God of holiness and love desires to make him a free, intelligent sovereign in his own sphere—a thinking, rational, renewed creation created after His own image (Eph. iv. 24). Therefore God never says to any faculty of man, "Be thou idle." God does not need, nor demand non-activity in a man, for His working in and through him; but evil spirits demand the utmost non-activity and passivity. God asks for intelligent action (Rom. Xii. 1-2, "Your reasonable service") in cooperation with Him. Satan demands passivity as a condition for his compulsory action, and in order compulsorily to subject men to his will and purpose.[27]

Analyzing the word "passive" exposes the deceitful backstabbing ways of our enemy.

---

27 Penn-Lewis, p. 51.

Where sin is active, accusations are passive.

Passive, according to Webster, means "acted upon rather than acting or causing action."[28] Most of us would agree that Satan knows our weaknesses and attacks them. He is always alert for any "garden mentality," hoping that we will make our decisions based solely on what looks or tastes good. As Satan spoke to Adam and Eve in the first person, he speaks to us in the first person with statements like "I failed" or "Poor me" more than we would want to admit. He shoots "thought-arrows" in and mixes them with our own thought processes so well that we have no idea that what just went through our mind—what we just passively accepted—came directly from the "accuser." This process plunges us to our defeat. Another definition of passive is "offering no resistance."

Principle #13: Rebuking Satan's accusations will prevent us from being locked up and give us freedom instead.

In the same situation, we hear internally the words, "You sure are a failure, aren't you?" The moment we agree, we give our foe ground to build on the accusation, an open window for him to move in. Once in that vantage point, he accuses us. This a principle that is consistent with every bit of ground Satan has in our lives: agree with his evil accusation, and he will lock you up. But, if you confess, repent, ask God's forgiveness and rebuke the evil one in the name of Jesus, you will send him running!

4.7.5. Stronghold 5 – Self-Sufficiency

A Biblical Example in Laodicea: Jesus has strong words for the self-sufficient.

---

28   https://www.merriam-webster.com/dictionary/passive

To the angel of the church in Laodicea write: These are the words of the Amen, the faithful and true Witness, the ruler of God's creation. I know your deeds, that you are neither cold nor hot. I wish you were either one or the other! So, because you are lukewarm— neither hot nor cold…

Jesus goes right to the jugular here:

… *I am about to spit you out of my mouth. You say, "I am rich; I have acquired wealth and do not need a thing." But you do not realize that you are wretched, pitiful, poor, blind and naked. I counsel you to buy from me gold refined in the fire, so you can become rich; and white clothes to wear, so you can cover your shameful nakedness; and salve to put on your eyes, so you can see."*

—Revelation 3:14–18

The Laodiceans thought they were rich, wealthy and self sufficient. But Jesus called them wretched, pitiful, poor, blind and naked.

Laodicea was situated in the fertile Lycas Valley. The great Roman Road ran right through town, making it a communication and trade centre. The city was a banking centre, with much wealth. It was also famous for its school and medicine, and its eye ointments were famous for curing eye defects. The city seemed to need nothing—totally self-sufficient. This materialistic spirit of self-sufficiency had crept into the church and had paralysed its spiritual life. Jesus told the Laodiceans that they were not what they thought they were

The stronghold of self-sufficiency blinds us from the truth, causing us to become spiritually numb. We see no need to pursue anything more. We perceive ourselves to be *fine as far as we can see*. In reality, Christ finds us sickening, and He is about to spit us out of his mouth.

Spiritually numb, lukewarm, complacent—things just kind of feel "okay." We don't want to move forward in our spiritual growth; the fire inside has gone out, and the cold has not yet set in. It is the worst place we can be, and Satan loves it. If he can build this stronghold, convincing us that all is well within, then he has us. We stop reaching out for fulfilment in Jesus, because we see no need—we have it all, and this allows Satan to hold us in a place of complacency.

My experience as a counsellor working with Christians indicates that a large part of the born-again Christians who come to church tithe almost every Sunday, then they go home, lay their Bible on the mantle, and never think of God again until next Sunday.

Why? Because everything apears to be well. We do not appear to have any need (defined as external, tangible, materialistic), and thus we feel no deep need for God. At least until the next crisis. History repeats itself—we have been deceived by the Serpent, and complacency becomes the end of many families. Their relationships can be crumbling around their feet, while the parents wear a plastic smile and say that everything is great. Parents might talk about the raise they just received from work and how they thanked God for that blessing. But often, they haven't said much more than hello and goodbye to their spouse, or even to their children, in the past six months.

It's possible that Satan ensured that the raise came through, just to cancel any motivation to call on God, and any need to exersise their faith? This stronghold is deadly—without something catastrophic happening to shake it loose, it is difficult to convince these people of their ongoing deeper need for God.

4.7.6. Stronghold 6 – Double Mindedness

James says, "... *you must believe and not doubt, because the one who doubts is like a wave of the sea, blown and tossed by the wind. That person should not expect to receive anything from the Lord. Such a person is double-minded and unstable in they do*" (James 1:6–8).

Double-mindedness "in strictest literalness means double-souled."[29] It is as though one soul declares, "I believe!" and the other shouts, "I don't!" This leads to difficulty making proper choices, but more than that, it makes it hard to receive help from God. "*Come near to God and he will come near to you. Wash your hands, you sinners, and purify your hearts, you double-minded*" (James 4:8). "*Then we will no longer be infants, tossed back and forth by the waves, and blown here and there by every wind of teaching and by the cunning and craftiness of people in their deceitful scheming*" (Ephesians 4:14).

---

29   Burdick, p. 169.

God "does not give divine insight to such vacillating unstable men."[30] Why? Because they have no faith. Keep that conclusion in mind. I believe there is a key here to understanding some of our struggles in decision making. Do you ever find yourselves pulled between two opposing thoughts? I am referring to what Paul was talking about, *"For the flesh desires what is contrary to the Spirit, and the Spirit what is contrary to the flesh"* (Galatians 5:17).

4.7.7. Stronghold 7 – "Good" Thoughts

We would never suspect that the enemy might bind us up in a stronghold of our own good thoughts. If our good thoughts supersede God's, then the enemy has caused us to miss God's best for us. In Matthew, we see Jesus with His disciples, talking about what will happen to Him *"at the hands of the elders, the chief priests and the teachers of the law"* (Matthew 16:21). He is trying to convey to His disciples that He will die. Peter then takes Him aside and very strongly rebukes Jesus by saying, *"Never, Lord… This shall never happen to you!"* (Matthew 16:22).

Was there any good on earth that Jesus' death could bring? None, as far as Peter could see. In this case, the thoughts of a man became Peter's problem. Jesus countered back, *"… you do not have in mind the concerns of God"* (Matthew 16:23). How many times do we take second best, when we could have had God's best for us?

What are some of the "Good" Thoughts that we Commonly Use or Hear?: Ed Silvoso, in his book *That None Should Perish*, says this,

> I am not so concerned with the ill thoughts our minds produce. Those are more easily spotted and identified. It is the good thoughts that our minds are capable of that often lead to disaster. Let's take the case of church splits. When neutral parties analyze a church split, they never find a group of good people being opposed by a group of evil people. Usually, the arguments on both sides of the split are quite reasonable. In fact, they both sound good. And that is the problem! They are good rather than excellent. Only God

---

30   MacDonald, p. 2219.

can provide the excellent thoughts. Church splits often take place because people, relying on their own understanding, choose not to deny themselves. Both parties provide "good reasons" for their point of view that blocks God's best.

Something similar occurs during the process that eventually leads to divorce. Well-meaning, compassionate advisors counsel divorce on the basis of some very good reasons. They say, "It is better for the children, because they won't continue to be exposed to a bad example" or "It will give you a fresh start, and you certainly need one. You will definitely learn from this mistake, and next time you will do better." These good thoughts cloud the reality that God hates divorce and that He has already provided us with divinely powerful weapons to deal with its cause. This, in turn, keeps us from using those weapons and we thus settle for a good solution rather than God's best. Instead of denying ourselves, standing on God's promises and fighting for our marriage, we choose divorce for "good reasons." As good as they are, they are short of excellent.[31]

4.7.8. Stronghold 8 – Doubt

Is it possible that man has elevated his base of modern-day knowledge above God's written Word? In the schools of higher learning, that certainly has taken place. We are living in the time of "great wisdom"—man's wisdom. But what is man's wisdom compared to God's? *"... the foolishness of God is wiser than human wisdom, and the weakness of God is stronger than human strength"* (1 Corinthians 1:25). It's possible that, in our reasoning and speculating, we have reasoned away the validity and infallibility of the Word of God. Remember, we are looking at this in the context of spiritual warfare. Is it possible for mankind, in our doubt-riddled reasoning, to take anything away from the power and authority of God's Word? A resounding no! The Word is written on the granite rock of Jesus—the Word—Himself.

There are many, many people who ask, "How do you know the Bible is true today?" They say the Bible has been translated over and over, and it is now, therefore, far removed from the original text. I hear this excuse for

---

31   Silvoso, p. 160–161.

not trusting the Bible constantly. However, the Bible itself testifies to its own inerrancy: *"Above all, you must understand that no prophecy of Scripture came about by the prophet's own interpretation of things. For prophecy never had its origin in the human will, but prophets, though human, spoke from God as they were carried along by the Holy Spirit"* (2 Peter 1:20–21).

We cannot build a foundation of faith in God's Word from the shifting sands of doubt. When we look at the bigger picture of doubt and strongholds and then consider the time we spent in doubt, do we have any foundational faith, or do we find ourselves in Satan's stronghold of doubt?

Imagine ministering to a man who has been born again for years, but whose sins on the day of salvation are still his sins today. This man's life depicts little change since his salvation, and he is now in counselling with great expectations. The counsellor has chosen Ephesians for his text: *"You were taught, with regard to your former way of life, to put off your old self, which is being corrupted by its deceitful desires; to be made new in the attitude of your minds; and to put on the new self, created to be like God in true righteousness and holiness"* (Ephesians 4:22–24).

In the process of counselling, the client might say, "I believe in the Father and the Son, and have no doubt that I will one day go to heaven. But it is the validity of the Word of God, in our modern Bibles of the last generation or two, that really worries me." An interesting note here on the word "worry": in German, it means "to strangle the mind," while in Greek, it means "to divide the mind." One of our clients made the choice not to "waste" his time trying to find application in a Bible that he felt was inaccurate because of the many translations over time. This is the work of our enemy.

> One of the first works of the devil mentioned in Scripture was to call into question the fact of a revelation from God. God had said to Adam: "When you eat of it you shall surely die" (Gen. 2:17). The devil appeared on the scene and asked: "did God really say...?" (Gen. 3:1). The same devil who asked that question is at work in the world today, calling into question the fact of a revelation from God. "How can you be sure the Bible is true and is from God?"[32]

---

32   Hughes & Brooks, 2012b.

This sort of reasoning builds a stronghold in our minds—doubt in regard to God's Word. With a stronghold now established, what happens when the enemy challenges us with this question: "What makes you think you have authority over me, when you doubt the validity of your God's Word—has He really said you have authority over me?"

There is no room for doubt. The doubter needs to look at Acts 19: *"One day the evil spirit answered them, 'Jesus I know, and Paul I know about, but who are you?' Then the man who had the evil spirit jumped on them and overpowered them all. He gave them such a beating that they ran out of the house naked and bleeding"* (Acts 19:15-16). If you doubt the accuracy of the Bible instead of standing on the inerrant Word of God, you are wide open to the assault of the enemy. It is by the Word of God only that we stand. *"Put on the full armor of God, so that you can take your stand against the devil's schemes. ... so that when the day of evil comes, you may be able to stand your ground, and after you have done everything, to stand"* (Ephesians 6:11, 13b).

I am often reminded of some words spoken by Billy Graham. When he was a guest on a radio talk show, he said, "There came a time in my early ministry that I had to come to grips with the question if God's Word really is the inerrant, infallible Word." He took his Bible, laid it on the ground and stood on it. He stayed there until he had confirmation that God's Word really is the true living Word of God upon which we can stand. His final words were, "I never looked back from that moment in time!"[33]

Over time, many, many individuls have asked me that same question: "Can you stand on the Word of God?" My answer always is the same, "The God I know and live for is big enough and strong enough to keep His Word in as many translations as it may go through, true to the original words." We need both of our feet planted firmly on the written Word of God, or we are not going to stand until the end!

4.7.9. Stronghold 9 – Pride vs. Humility

In Satan, pride raised its ugly face for the first time, as described in Ezekiel: *"You were the seal of perfection, full of wisdom and perfect in beauty"* (Ezekiel 28:12). One commentary states that "God had positioned Satan to the highest place,

---

33   Paraphrased from Graham, 1997.

next to God Himself. But in a short time (see Ezekiel 28:14) we see jealousy has given birth to pride, and then death (i.e. separation from God, cast out of heaven). All because of what Satan thought or said in his heart."[34] According to Isaiah 14:13–14, Satan told himself, *"I will ascend to the heavens; I will raise my throne above the stars of God… I will make myself like the Most High."*

God still today *"judges the thoughts and attitudes of the heart"* (Hebrews 4:12b). This is His ongoing work in our lives, whether we are asleep or awake. He is constantly identifying the works of the old man, bringing death to pride and the long list of other sins that follows. His desire and purpose is not just to develop our spirit man in preparation for eternity. No, it is to develop it for today also.

We can see why God hates pride—it is worshipping another god. Satan pictured himself rising above the Most High God. This cost him his already-elevated place in Heaven, as he was cast out from the presence and fellowship of the Most High God.

We aren't immune to pride in our battle against Satan. This battle hasn't changed since the beginning of time. Paul says, *"But I am afraid that just as Eve was deceived by the serpent's cunning, your minds may somehow be led astray from your sincere and pure devotion to Christ"* (2 Corinthians 11:3). Still yoked to our old sinful nature, at times we find ourselves mimicking Satan in his rebellion against God. Our old nature resists God and His call on our lives. Most of us are like two-year-old children who want to do things their own way, and that's that! However, doing it our own way is rebellion against God. It is pride.

Proverbs 16:5 tells us, *"The Lord detests all the proud of heart. Be sure of this: They will not go unpunished."* We also know that *"God opposes the proud"* (James 4:6, quoting Proverbs 3:34). If I understand James properly in this passage, when we are proud, God's arms are closed to us. Think about what that means for us—separation from God. Where would this leave us?

The decision is ours; God doesn't make it for us. There are only two ways to go: our way or God's way. When we fall into pride, God turns his back on us in a way, and without Him moment by moment, we will surely fall. The Bible says, *"Pride goes before destruction, a haughty spirit before a fall"* (Proverbs 16:18). God has given us the ability to make choices. If our desire

---

34   Deere, p. 1283.

is to be in God's presence, then we obviously must choose His way over our self-seeking, selfish ways. This requires us to put our own desires to death, picking up our cross daily to follow Jesus (Luke 9:23).

4.7.10. Other Strongholds

There are many other strongholds which we could cover, but the bottom line in each and every one is this: if the enemy has a stronghold in your person or your family unit, there is a sin problem that needs your immediate attention.

> **Principle #14: If the enemy has a stronghold in your person or your family unit, there is a sin problem that needs your immediate attention.**

Since sin is literally the food of Satan, he is not unlike a bird of prey, perched on a treetop, waiting for a mouse to reveal his hiding place. Such are the works of Satan's demons: they are ever ready to drop from their lofty viewpoint and hook their claws into the meat of our sin.

This is the the high cost of sin in our lives!

We see an example of these high costs in the life of Moses, as he finds himself face to face with his sin of a few years past, and now stands looking over the long-anticipated promised land:

> *On that same day the Lord told Moses, "Go up into the Abarim Range to Mount Nebo in Moab, across from Jericho, and view Canaan, the land I am giving the Israelites as their their own possession. There on the mountain that you have climbed you will die and be gathered to your people, just as your brother Aaron died on Mount Hor and was gathered to his people. This is because both of you broke faith with me in the presence of the Israelites at the waters of Meribah Kadesh in the Desert of Zin and because you did not uphold my holiness among the Israelites. Therefore, you will see the land only from a distance; you will not enter the land I am giving to the people of Israel.*
> —Deuteronomy 32:48–52

The sin God referred to took place some years past when the Israelites cried out for water. The cost of Moses' sin was colossal. Moses was not ready to die—he had led his people all these years, and was set on leading them into the promised land. But God said no. It appears that Moses argued with God at this point. According to *The Bible Knowledge Commentary*:

> The text says God would not listen to Moses, that is, He would not grant his request. In fact the Hebrew sentence implies that Moses had kept on asking God for permission, and that God became "furious" (an intensive form of 'ābar) with him (NIV has a milder word, angry; cf. 1:37; 4:21). This conversation reveals something of the intimacy of Moses' relationship with God. It also heightens the feeling of tragedy in the experience of a man who devoted his life to fulfilling God's promise for Israel but knew he would never see its completion. But Moses could at least look at the land from the peak of Mount Pisgah.[35]

Basically, God told Moses, "This is not for you to do. Today you will die and be buried on the mountain top, and Joshua will lead My people into the promised land." Moses paid the ultimate price for his sin, which itself was one or two minutes of anger directed at the thirsty Israelites, during which he misrepresented God by choosing not to speak to the rock but instead striking it twice and telling the Israelites, *"Listen, you rebels, must we bring you water out of this rock?"* (Numbers 20:10).

Envision Moses, the servant of God who spent forty days on the mountaintop with Him, the man who pleaded with God to stay His hand of judgement against His people (Exodus 32:11–14), the man who daily led God's people as God directed him. There was a deep, intimate relationship between God and Moses, but God still wouldn't let Moses cross over into the land. Sin that is not dealt with always costs. Firstly, it costs us the presence of God. Secondly, if sin tarries, we begin to lose the day-by-day life of God that is ours while in a relationship with Him. Thirdly, we come under the law of decay.

---

35   Walvoord, p. 268.

Principle #15: Sin not dealt with always costs: first, we lose the presence of God; second, we lose the day-by-day life of God; third, we come under the law of decay.

When we sin, we sin against God, in the very image of whom we were created (Genesis 1:27), with the exception, of course, of our flesh. Although God cannot sin, we were created with the capacity to sin. We can sin and do sin, as seen first in Adam. We know sin separates us from God. But what, if anything, does our own sin do to our being?

> ...to sin is not only to resist the rule and reign of God but to rebel against ourselves also—to work against ourselves in futility and frustration. God's ways are not simply written in the texts of Scripture but in the texture of our spiritual and physical beings also. God's ways, inscribed on the texture of our constitution, are self-authenticating. One does not need to argue for them; when we live against them, they argue for themselves.... Sin is not the nature of our being; it is against nature—our nature—and against the God who made it.... If the Kingdom of God is within us, written into the constitution of our being—the way we were made to live—then when we sin we not only cut ourselves off from God but we cut ourselves off from our own potential. We disrupt ourselves, our future, our all.[36]

4.8. Oh, the Insanity of Sin

In sharing Moses' example, I hope to provide an analogy by asking a question that begs an answer. Can we, on this side of the cross, lose our promised land as Moses lost his? I ask this question because sin runs rampant in our Christian world today. Let us look first at what sin is for the born-again believer.

---

36   Hughes & Brooks, 2012a.

Simply put, sin is disobeying God—no matter how small or large it may be, no matter how deep or how long we have been in relation with God.

I remember so well an incident that took place in a revival meeting I was leading. I was not far removed from the world at that time, being about five years old in the Lord. I had asked for those that were dealing with sin in their lives and needed forgiveness to come up for prayer. As it turned out, there was a young fellow present who had worked for me for a short time some years earlier. He came up to me, tears runing down his face, with a few coins in his hand, and confessed to eating a chocolate bar he had not paid for. I didn't know what to do—it seemed so trivial, but I knew it was huge for him. The actions of this unchurched, new believer made an impact on my life that I've never forgotten. Sin is sin no matter the size.

4.8.1. The Consequences of Sin

Most of us would see the few minutes of Moses' anger to be about as significant as the fifty-cent chocolate bar. Reiterating the question, can we as Christians lose our promised land, lose our salvation? After giving my life to Jesus, for many years I believed that "once saved, always saved." According to the Bible,

> *And you also were included in Christ when you heard the message of truth, the gospel of your salvation. When you believed, you were marked in him with a seal, the promised Holy Spirit, who is a deposit guaranteeing our inheritance until the redemption of those who are God's possession—to the praise of his glory.*
>
> —Ephesians 1:13–14

As we read on, we are instructed to follow God's example, *"… as dearly loved children and walk in the way of love, just as Christ loved us and gave Himself up for us as a fragrant offering… "* (Ephesians 5:1–2). As we move on in this Scripture, the language becomes much more instructive relative to how we live out our life: *"For of this you can be sure: no immoral, impure or greedy person—such a person is an idolater—has any inheritance in the kingdom of Christ and of God"* (Ephesians 5:5). This verse challenges the concept of "once saved, always saved." It puts the responsibility on us to live such a life that would not hinder our entering the kingdom of God. Another interesting point is made in Ephesians 5:18: *"Do not get drunk on wine, which leads to debauchery."* The word "debauchery" means *"depravity, dissipation,"*[37], which gives a sense of separation. In our application, it would mean the departure of the Spirit of God.

Those who continue to sin will not enter the kingdom of God according to Galatians 5:19–21 and 1 Corinthians 6:10. Also, *"But the cowardly, the unbelieving, the vile, the murderers, the sexually immoral, those who practice magic arts, the idolaters and all liars—they will be consigned to the fiery lake of burning sulfur. This is the second death"* (Revelation 21:8).

It's very obvious that people who practice the kind of sins we just read about will not enter the kingdom of God. But what about lesser sins? *"For whoever keeps the whole law and yet stumbles at just one point is guilty of breaking all of it"* (James 2:10). All sins—from the smallest to the biggest—separate us from God's presence. What we need to remember is that God is a God of incredible grace. *"But where sin increased, grace increased all the more"* (Romans 5:20b). Sin for all of us individually is a battle, a battle that we will fight until God raptures us out from this world. On that day, we will be found sinless forever with God! But in the interim, we must stand.

Sin is obviously the biggest problem in our Christian lives, and you must be able to lead by example, living the life God has called you to, and teaching that life for others. It has to be so real that others are inspired by your example. Time after time, you'll find yourself working hard to help individuals realize that what they're doing is a sin. Small actions come from our desires; *"Then, after desire has conceived, it gives birth to sin; and sin, when it is full-grown, gives birth to death"* (James 1:15).

My final thoughts on sin are sparked by the question asked of Jesus by a teacher of the law: *"'Of all the commandments, which is the most important?' 'The most important one' answered Jesus... 'Love the Lord your God with all your heart and with all your soul and with all your mind and with all your stength'"* (Mark 12:28–30). I can tell you by my own experience—and the experience of many others—that when you come to a place where you are living according to the commandment just read, you will find such a love for God that the

---

37   https://www.merriam-webster.com/thesaurus/debauchery

very thought of sinning against Him will hurt your heart. Hear me—I am not suggesting you will not sin again. Sin may still find its way into your everyday life as you persevere in your love for God, but His stronghold of love for you becomes your strength to stand firm against sin. The strength to persevere in righteousness is birthed by an intense desire to know God at a deeper level.

As Hughes says,

> God has built into us a desire for relationship with Him, which if not satisfied leaves us open and vulnerable to other sources of satisfaction. If God is not satisfying our souls, we will seek something else to satisfy us. It is here that our personal problems begin. This desire for relationship with God is described in the Bible by many words—desire, hunger, longing, but perhaps the most descriptive of these is thirst. The soul of man… has in it a raging and inextinguishable thirst.[38]

It is incumbent upon each of us to uncover that deep thirst for relationship with God. As we are immersed in that thirst, the attraction to sin is virtually drowned by the river of God that flows in our soul. My final admonition is to live by the river of God so that sin will have no room to do its evil work. I know some of you reading this are saying, "This will never happen for me." Trust me in this—seeking God with all of your soul will certainly find you in the position of the psalmist: *"Whoever dwells in the shelter of the Most High will rest in the shadow of the Almighty"* (Psalm 91:1). He literally becomes your *"refuge and fortress"* (verse 2). This is the stronghold of God's love.

4.9. Territorial Strongholds

While Satan can bind us up in a personal stronghold because of our personal sin, it is also possible that there are corporate strongholds built by our enemies of the spiritual realm. The following teaching on this topic is supplied by different authors. I understand that many of you may have no interest in this particular realm. But for others, God may have a call on their lives in this

---

38   Hughes, 2001, p. 107.

very area, or will further on down the road. I have several years of experience in this area, and I believe very strongly that we are coming into a season again where God is raising up a militant church to stand against the host of hell. Satan continues to take all he can to hell with him before the second coming of Jesus Christ. We cannot be successful in the Great Commission without the application of spiritual warfare at this level. Thus, the teaching on territorial strongholds is crucial. Edgardo Silvoso says of church splits:

> A once healthy and thriving Brethren assembly in the periphery of Buenos Aires is undergoing a bitter split. Church leaders who have known and loved each other for decades are at each other's throats. Tempers flare quickly.
>
> Accusations are freely hurled at people who, until recently, have been the embodiment of godliness. After every major outburst, the leaders seem to come to their senses and break down and cry, embracing the ones who, until moments ago, were the object of their attacks. Yet, when it's all over, the head elder has submitted his resignation, and those who remain are ready to fight for the shredded mantle of leadership. Others are quietly making preparations to leave the church. A feeling of precious things slowly beginning to rot pervades the atmosphere. Something awful is happening.
>
> Before he leaves, the head elder makes a last-ditch effort to stem the tide of destruction. He calls for a day of prayer and fasting at a retreat centre two hundred miles away. As the warring factions gather for prayer and Bible study, God begins to teach them about spiritual warfare, about forces of wickedness, about rulers of geographical darkness. Slowly, the Biblical truth begins to emerge that the struggle is not against flesh and blood but against those principalities who hide their presence behind misguided human beings and mask their designs under the guise of irreconcilable differences.
>
> At the end of the day, there is true reconciliation between the elders. They choose to come under the mighty hand of God, and in doing so they bring the church with them. They pledge to use

the spiritual authority delegated to them by the Lord Jesus Himself "against all power of the enemy" (Luke 9:1), and to put a specific section of town under that spiritual authority. They challenge the principalities and powers in charge of the darkness over that region, and pledge to resist the devil until he flees.

Shortly after returning to their hometown, they encounter a new convert in their church. She had been a leader in a spiritist centre in the section of town these elders have placed under Jesus' authority. She confesses that thirteen of these centres had made a pact to break up their church. They had been praying to Satan and his demons for strife among the Christian leaders! What these Brethren elders were unable to understand at first is now something in which they are becoming experts in overnight: spiritual warfare! Immediately they organize a counteroffensive and, in a short time, see a large contingent of people living in the area placed under spiritual authority make a public commitment to Christ. In less than a year, an interdenominational crusade in their town produces tens of thousands of decisions of faith.

All but the Western world considers spiritual warfare a very vital part of end-time evangelism.[39]

Kinnaman, whom I quoted in Section 4.3. on other types of strongholds, has this to say of the territorial version:

These have to do with the hierarchy of dark beings strategically assigned by Satan himself to influence and control nations, communities and even families. A multilevel system of spiritual beings is suggested by Ephesians 6:12: rulers, authorities, the powers of this dark world, the spiritual forces of evil.

C. Peter Wagner, author of numerous books on the principles of church growth, has been researching the subject of spiritual warfare and territorial spirits for several years. He has concluded that identifying and pulling down the strongholds of territorial spirits is

---

39   Kraft & White, pp. 265–266.

one of the most significant factors in church growth or the success of ministry. Wagner's hypothesis, offered at the Academic Symposium on Power Evangelism at Fuller Seminary, is that Satan delegates high-ranking members of the hierarchy of evil spirits to control nations, regions, cities, tribes, people groups, neighborhoods, and other significant social networks of human beings throughout the world. Their major assignment is to prevent God from being glorified in their territory, which they do through directing the activity of lower-ranking demons.

In the Old Testament, the angel Gabriel apparently wrestled with a territorial spirit: "I have come in response to [your prayers, Daniel]. But the prince of the Persian kingdom resisted me twenty-one days. Then Michael, one of the chief princes, came to help me, because I was detained there with the king of Persia" (Daniel 10:12-13).

There is a growing awareness in the Church of the power of territorial spirits. Recently, I met Dr. Paul Cho, pastor in Seoul, South Korea, of the largest church in the history of Christianity. Speaking to a ministers' luncheon on the subject of prayer, he told the story of an American chaplain stationed in Korea who was having an unusually good response to his ministry among U.S. military personnel.

He visited Dr. Cho and asked him, "Why am I so much more effective in Korea than I was in Europe? Same minister, same message, same kind of audience—American servicemen—but significantly different results." Dr. Cho's answer: The spiritual "air" is clearer over Korea, because tens of thousands of Korean Christians are praying fervently.

Have you ever attended a church camp or retreat away from a metropolitan area? Why do you suppose it "feels" better in the mountains or in the forest? Why do you think it is so much easier to seek God? Certainly the social environment of Christian camping has its effects, but I believe the spiritual highs we experience in those settings are due largely to the general absence of principalities and powers in the air.

The missions director on our church staff attended the great Lausanne conference on world evangelism in Manila in the summer of 1989. She reported that "territorial spirits" was a subject of great interest and inquiry. One of the most striking examples of the influence of territorial strongholds, and the power of Christ to break those strongholds, was reported by Edgardo Silvoso in "Spiritual Warfare in Argentina and the 'Plan Resistencia' (the Plan of Resistance)," a workshop at the conference. I have inserted portions of the report:

The Argentine Church never experienced great growth. The average congregation was smaller than 100 members.

Then in 1983 something happened that changed all that. Carlos Annacondia, a lay preacher, was invited to hold a crusade (in a church in La Plata). After four months of boldly preaching the Word and heavily relying on spiritual warfare, over 40,000 had made public commitments to Christ. It was totally unheard of.

As the churches grew in their understanding of spiritual warfare, one aspect that became clear was that of territorial powers.

In the fall of 1984 a group of pastors and leaders gathered [to pray for] 109 towns within 100 miles [that] had no Christian witness.

The pastors and leaders came together in one accord and placed the entire area under spiritual authority. Positioning themselves across the street from the headquarters of Mr. Meregildo's [a warlock famous for his dramatic cures] followers they served an eviction notice on the forces of evil.

Less than three years later 82 of those towns had evangelical churches in them.[40]

These words show us not only the power and unity, but also the need to understand the territorial powers that are at work in our country.

---

40 Kinnaman, pp. 54–56.

Chapter Five

GENERATIONAL SINS AND CURSES

I ONCE COUNSELLED A PASTOR'S WIFE WHO WAS NEVER ABLE TO SPEAK publicly because of a very strong fear, regardless of the number of people present. When we were unable to find the source of the fear, I said, "Let's ask God where the fear has come from."

He spoke immediately into my mind with one word only: "Spartans." I found this to be very exciting, for there could be only one reason that would cause God to speak the word "Spartans" at that time. The woman's fear must be connected to a generational curse of fear that had come down all the way from the time of the Spartans. This should speak volumes to us. It shows that God is concerned about generational sins hidden from men, who are unknowingly bound up by them.

In this situation, we did some research and found that the Spartan civilization started approximately in the tenth century. We also found that at that time, everyone was the property of the state, and wives were assigned to husbands; in all likelihood, women would have lived in daily fear.

The pastor's wife did try to trace her family line back to the Spartans without any success. But she did say that while searching out her ancestry, there was a real possibility that her family line had roots in the area where the Spartans once dwelt.

There is a very small possibility that any one of us could find ourselves in this situation of having roots in Spartan history. I don't want to write that which is obvious, but generational sins are birthed by sin issues that are not dealt with specifically—through acknowledgment, repentance, receiving forgiveness, and then reconciliation. If these generational sins are not dealt with before the carrier dies, then the next generation will inherit the sin issues. This plays out not just with individuals or families, but also with corporations and nations and so on.

5.1. What are Generational Sins?

Generational sins: Sins passed down through family lines.

Let me make clear to the reader, in the context of this chapter, what "generational sins" are. God warns his people in the Old Testament (Exodus chapter 20 and Deuteronomy chapters 5 and 20) that sin can be passed down in the family, from generation to generation. God's desire is to forgive and bless to the thousandth generation; however, if people refuse to recognize, repent and turn away from iniquity, the blessings are forfeited. Generational sin can include most sinful acts, attitudes, devilish deeds, vows or ungodly loyalties that have not been previously identified, specifically confessed to God, and renounced.

If these sins are specifically confessed and broken off, they are certainly forgiven, like any other sin. The problems and solutions discussed in this chapter refer to sins that remain unconfessed, unidentified and even unrecognized. These sins, passed down through families or relatives, by nationality, or by any other inherited connection as well as accompanying problems, may or may not be recognized by those currently troubled, ensnared, afflicted and damaged by the demonic power associated with the inherited sin or sins. The problems—guilt, repeating sin, and affliction—will continue to be inherited by successive generations. The only way to destroy the devil's access to people through sin is through recognition, confession, repentance and receiving God's forgiveness.

This truth has easily recognized examples. Take, for instance, the Freemasons, who appear to have their roots in Britain. Ireland may have given us Druidism, and Holland, where my forefathers' roots are, has earned a worldwide reputation of financial gain via legalizing the pornography and drug industries.

Freemasonry, Druidism and the pornography and drug trades are curses that hold individuals, families and nations in captivity. They are carried like an infection from nation to nation all around the world.

My point here: people are often aware and alert regarding dealing with their daily sin issues, seeking and finding, in Jesus' name, forgiveness and freedom from the guilt and power of these "everyday" sins. This is important! However, unrecognized generational sins, due to their hidden presence, may be even more damaging. There is no thought given to the generational sin issues from the distant past that could be coming at us like a runaway train, destroying everything in their path.

5.2. What is Coming Down my Generational Line?

In this chapter, I will discuss the reality of generational sins and curses, and then examine how these sins might be working against you and your extended family. I will answer the questions, *"Where do they come from?"* and *"How do we deal with them?"* There are many good books written on this subject, and some are referenced in the bibliography. I will present this material from a practitioner's point of view. My prayer is that this information will be helpful to you personally, and subsequently enable you to help others apply it in their lives.

As there are many who still do not believe in the fact that generational curses are pertinent today, *I will first establish a Biblical foundation from which to work.*

Generally speaking, our Western worldview does not make room for a teaching on generational sins or what the Bible generally calls "iniquities." Scripture, however, makes note of different types of sin. For example, *"... he does not treat us as our sins deserve or repay us according to our iniquities"* (Psalm 103:10, emphasis added).

Often a common response to this subject is, "When I gave my life to Jesus, His blood covered all my sin." In one sense, that is true. When Jesus comes into our heart, He does deal with all of our sin: past, present, and future. We are Father God's sons and daughters, taken out of the kingdom of darkness and brought into the Kingdom of Light: *"And God raised us up with Christ and seated us with Him in the heavenly realms in Christ Jesus..."* (Ephesians 2:6).

I completely agree with theologians who teach that at the time of salvation, God saved us from all of our sins. However, this has to do with the relational position only. When we are born again and forgiven, God becomes our Father and we become His children.

But we are not physically home yet; on this earth, we still have to contend with our old nature. Once saved, we begin working out our salvation; we are in the process of transformation. While we are still wearing our earthly suit, it is still possible for us to sin—and sin we will until Jesus comes and raptures us from this earth. God, in His love and wisdom, gave us repentance as a means to daily have our sins forgiven, so that we may have an ongoing relationship with Him on this side of Heaven. We are called now to put off the old self and put on the new, which is created to be like Christ Jesus. An important part of "putting off" is exposing and cutting off all sins—and this, of course, includes all generational sins.

Some people may ask, "What does that mean?" Here is the answer. A generational curse is, "An uncleansed iniquity that increases in strength from generation to the next generation affecting the members of that family and all who come into relationship with that family."[41]

Olga Willms, formerly of Burden Bearers Counselling Centre in Grande Prairie, Alberta, stated, "Generational sins are habit structures or patterns that have developed through the generations and are causing problems in our lives... Sin and its effects may descend through family lines."

As we move along, I will present many illustrations that will bring an understanding of how generational sin continues down family lines. The following is an example of sinful habit structures that make their way into a family unit.

Suppose that a young couple gets married, and in a short period of time, the young wife finds that her husband has an anger problem. Before long, the wife is using the same anger tactics as her husband. Several years later, still together in spite of their ongoing anger, they find themselves with two children, aged two and five years old. The kids are lashing out with the same anger that Mom and Dad display daily. From birth, children learn how to respond to situations by watching how those around them do so. By the age of five, most children will have established a working, perceptual platform of how to respond to most situations, at least in their home environment.

---

41   Hickey, p. 13.

If there is no intervention in their lives to change their faulty thinking, it will carry on for a lifetime. If the sin isn't dealt with properly through repentance and forgiveness, this anger has the potential to become a generational sin and a psychological affliction.

They connect sins of past generations to the current generation.

Thank the Lord that few of us carry on with our five-year-old perceptions (see "Perceptions" in Toolbox). Graciously, God has put many people in our path—parents, siblings, teachers, and bosses—to expose our faulty thinking. We may sense, through our God-given conscience or revelation, that something is amiss in our behaviour or responses.

We aren't looking specifically for psychological traits or thoughts that follow down family lines. What we are looking for is something much more dark and sinister, something that hides in the presence of its own darkness. We must always be aware that our wrong thinking produces wrong and sinful thoughts, which in turn produce hurtful words and actions.

Generational sins are schemes of Satan that don't only hide in the presence of their own darkness, but enable Satan to "ride on the backs" of God's own people, connecting the sins of the past generations to the current generation through the powerful bondage of unconfessed sins.

These schemes, as mentioned before, extend beyond behaviour or responses that are simply psychologically ingrained—they are also spiritual in nature. They are not of the Spirit of God, which is light and life for all whom are His, but a spirit of darkness and death, emanating with force from Satan himself.

Generational sins allow Satan to reap a bountiful crop. Seldom does one use the concept of sowing and reaping when dealing with the satanic, but there is no doubt that Satan mimics the ways of God as much as he can, and in this area, Satan has been very successful. The way sin reaps is laid out for us: *"Do not be deceived: God cannot be mocked. A man reaps what he sows."*

Whoever sows to please their flesh, from the flesh will reap destruction; whoever sows to please the Spirit, from the Spirit will reap eternal life" (Galatians 6:7–8).

This law of sowing and reaping is never more obvious than in generational sins. Reaping from sin is seldom immediate; it is also never without increase. Time is not the only factor, but it remains a major reason why children reap what fathers, grandfathers, and great-grandfathers have sown. Our children reap the root, the seed, and finally the evil fruit of our sins.

I have always believed the law of increase in the area of blessings: *"Honor your father and your mother, so that you may live long in the land the Lord your God is giving you"* (Exodus 20:12). If we plant a little good, we will reap a harvest of good. However, for most of us, we fail to understand that the same law applies when we sow a little evil—it comes back to us, not as life-producing and God-glorifying, but as a curse. The Message Bible puts it this way, *"Don't be misled: No one makes a fool of God. What a person plants, he will harvest. The person who plants selfishness, ignoring the needs of others—ignoring God!—harvests a crop of weeds"* (Galatians 6:7, MSG).

If we apply these verses to the family of four that I spoke of above, these children are already sowing the seeds of anger into their generation, and if there is no intervention, the children will also reap a crop of weeds. These curses, unless dealt with, will never stop; each generation will allow the same weed of anger to take root in their lives. Sin, like a cup that is full and running over, is coming up from all the generations behind you (Dad, Mom, Grandpa, Grandma, aunts, uncles, and all those who have married into the family ancestral line). There is only one way of stopping those curses: searching out and identifying all enslaving sins that come from our ancestors. When each sin is repented of, God's spiritual herbicide (the atoning blood of Jesus) is applied directly to the root of the weed. Then—and only then—does it stop. Later in this chapter, I will share tools to set you and your family free.

The first mention of the concept of generational sins is in Exodus. God says, *"You shall not bow down to them or worship them; for I, the Lord your God, am a jealous God, punishing the children for the sin of the fathers to the third and fourth generation of those who hate me…"* (Exodus 20:5). This is not a one-time statement. The second is,

And he passed in front of Moses, proclaiming, "The Lord, the Lord, the compassionate and gracious God, slow to anger, abounding in love and faithfulness, maintaining love to thousands, and forgiving wickedness, rebellion and sin. Yet he does not leave the guilty unpunished; he punishes the children and their children for the sin of the fathers to the third and fourth generation."

—Exodus 34:6–7

We also learn in Leviticus 26:36–39,

As for those of you who are left, I will make their hearts so fearful in the lands of their enemies that the sound of a windblown leaf will put them to flight. They will run as though fleeing from the sword, and they will fall, even though no one is pursuing them. They will stumble over one another as though fleeing from the sword, even though no one is pursuing them. So you will not be able to stand before your enemies. You will perish among the nations; the land of your enemies will devour you. Those of you who are left will waste away in the lands of their enemies because of their sins; also because of their fathers' sins they will waste away.

When the Israelites refused to enter the Promised Land, Moses prayed before the whole Israelite assembly *"the Lord is slow to anger, abounding in love and forgiving sin and rebellion. Yet he does not leave the guilty unpunished; he punishes children for the sin of their fathers to the third and fourth generation"* (Numbers 14:18). The effects of sin can be felt for decades or even centuries.

We need to be aware of the potential ancestral problems in our families, so we can stand against Satan's attacks, as he schemes to make sins from the past active in our lives today. Because their effects will be felt for generations, it is imperative that we exercise due diligence in exposing ancestral sins and generational curses that have held family lines in a vice-like grip, sometimes for hundreds of years.

In Numbers, Moses pleads with God, *"In accordance with your great love, forgive the sin of these people…"* (Numbers 14:19). The Lord's answer follows, *"I have forgiven them, as you asked"* (verse 20).

104

The penalty for this sin will be carried by this generation. *"Every one of you twenty years old or more who was counted in the census and who has grumbled against me. Not one of you will enter the land I swore with uplifted hand to make your home…"* (Numbers 14:29–30). Now listen to the words of the Lord, *"As for your children that you said would be taken as plunder, I will bring them in to enjoy the land you have rejected"* (Numbers 14:31). The word "enjoy" means that they will be free of all the baggage of their forefathers. The King James Version uses "know" in place of enjoy, meaning they will know and enjoy the greatness of this land of milk and honey. This speaks of freedom with abundance!

But there is something quite different for those whom the Bible calls grumblers. We see the severity of God's judgement on the nation of His people—a people God called grumblers, a people who began complaining even before they left Egypt. They are looking at the Promised Land in rebellion against God, and expecting His response to be accepting.

There is evidence enough in the preceding Scriptures for us to understand that God takes the passing of sins from generation to generation very seriously. So seriously in fact, that we see Him essentially saying, "Enough is enough; I will not allow this sinful generation to enter in and defile this land that I had promised your forefathers to give to you. As for you, you will die in the desert and be buried with your disobedience and contempt towards me, your God. And the next generation, undefiled, to them I will give this land."

Please, pay close attention to what God has said: *"… every one of you twenty years old or more… who has grumbled against me. Not one of you will enter the land…"* (Exodus 14:29). The following urgently requires the attention of those of you who are, or one day will be parents: we are witnessing what I call the *idea of age accountability*. In this Old Testament situation, we see God punishing those twenty years and older for their sins. This means that the parents bore the responsibility for the sins of all their children that were nineteen years and younger.

5.3. The Idea of Age Accountability

In the Old Testament, adult children became accountable to God for their own sins at twenty years of age. Now, I understand we cannot make a case for parenting from the Old Testament model of child accountability today, because we are in an entirely different dispensation, manner and way of life. The point I am attempting to make is that in the Old Testament era, God had established that parents were responsible for their children's decisions and sins up to the age of twenty. Does God follow a similar principle in this day and age, where the parents bear their children's sins? I have no doubt that God does. God Himself declares that He does not change—have no doubt that He continues to this day to hold parents responsible for their children's attitudes and actions. Without this, it will only cause another generation of sins.

An example of age accountability today may be our sons and daughters who are eligible for a driver's license at sixteen years of age. Once they have passed the theory and road tests and received a valid driver's license, they are then accountable for their actions relative to driving. In a sense, this is a measuring stick for maturity in our society. Therefore, let us say that all our children are accountable directly to God for their sins from the age of sixteen onward.

This would have the parents responsible for decision-making and sins up to the age of sixteen. But in our modern day society, what we see is parents allowing their children to make their own decisions at a much younger age. Children are making decisions for their own life, such as what they are going to eat, what they are going to wear, what school they will attend, where they are going to go, what they are going to do, and when they will return. For example, it is very common today for twelve and thirteen-year-old children to already be significantly engaged in sexual activity.

The idea of an age of accountability at around age twenty is possibly Biblically justifiable. There is no Biblical illustration of accountability at age sixteen, though this seems more functional today in the Western world. In reality, if a child is determined to place himself or herself beyond the control of parents, the child can accomplish self-rule long before age sixteen. The laws and practises of our nation can enable a child to effectively escape parental control and authority even before that age. At sixteen, a child can apply to the courts to be "emancipated" from the control of parents and make decisions free from outside control or hindrance. I use this age as a good example of where we are when it comes to parenting, and for what God is going to hold parents accountable.

"Emancipation" is a precise illustration of the fact that in our society to-day, a large portion of children are making life-changing decisions at a very young age, and have no experience that would give them the basis from which to make proper, sound decisions that honour God and their parents. We live in a time where many of the household activities and choices are determined by the children, maybe not so through their spoken words but through the fuss that many children bring into play if they do not receive their way. Un-fortunately, in today's society, many moms and dads cave in to the wants of their children just to end the argument. If this is not dealt with in the first generation, it will become a generational curse of abandonment of the head-ship position of the father, mother, or both, in the next generation, which of course gets handed down to the generation after that, and so on—exactly as it happened in Exodus 20:5.

It is the enemy's intent to demote parents and have children reign. If this dysfunction continues, it becomes a generational sin which empowers the child(ren) to rule both parents and home. This concept of a "child-ruled" or "child-centered" home, if carried on uncorrected, becomes a generational curse.

I believe the biggest curse we face in our generation is children ruling their homes. It has been this way for possibly the past two or more genera-tions—parents kneeling at the altar of their children.

The biggest curse in our generation is children ruling the home.

At times, while walking in our local mall, I have witnessed a small child lying on their back on the floor, screaming and beating the floor with their feet, while Mom is kneeling on the floor beside the child, pleading and beg-ging, "Tell me, please, please, tell me what you want. I'll get it for you." The problem is that many of these children are going (or will soon be going) into the workforce with the mindset that they are to be served. Parents alone are to blame, all due to a lack of biblical parenting.

The Bible says, *"Train up a child in the way he should go: and when he is old, he will not depart from it"* (Proverbs 22:6). The consequences of not training up our children will be the punishment pronounced in Isaiah 3:4: *"I will make mere youths their officials; children will rule over them."* And again, in Isaiah 3:5b, *"The young will rise up against the old, the nobody against the honored."* Today we are witnessing what Isaiah prophesied so long ago. We are seeing our youth governing and officiating in their own homes.

Lack of sound parenting and guidance creates a void, and this void must be filled. The enemy and his cohorts immediately flood in to fill it. Parental position, authority and power are usurped ("Usurp—Seize (a position or power) without authority"[42]). Unrestrained, immature, sinful and selfish children will seize the opportunity to rule the house, running the parents off their feet, and eventually exhausting them mentally, physically, and even financially. We see evidence of this usurping of authority when parental authority, teachers' authority, and other forms of authority are challenged and scoffed at by the children and youth

Some years ago, I was working with a family unit: Dad, Mom, son, and daughter. Mom was a believer, Dad was not, and neither were his extended family members. The mother came into my office one morning, crying and very distraught. She revealed that her twelve-year-old son had beaten her up that morning, just before she came in. This had been happening for some time, but she had never mentioned it. What made it worse was her ten-year-old daughter was becoming just as abusive. As we progressed into the counselling session, I put pressure on the enemy spirit we had already exposed, querying the demon about his access to the family and then the children. The demon responded that since these parents didn't teach their children to be obedient, respectful, and self-controlled, it had "taught" them to be angry, abusive, and arrogant instead.

This is exactly what demons do—they put pressure on areas of anger, frustration or aggression, along with many others. They do anything they can to create animosity, resentment and division within the family. In this case, they caused division between the parents and children. One interesting point is that the enemy had no access to this family for the past three generations—because these generations were Christians, and they lived their lives for the Lord. During the counselling session, I asked the enemy, "What on earth made you think you could get in three generations later?" The demon answered, "We watched and waited."

Principle #16: A disciplined, self-controlled godly life can delay generational sins.

When children and youth literally control their homes, we see the chaos this could bring worldwide. There is a curse of child-headship over the home, which is increasing dramatically! This has given the enemy ample opportunity to gain access to families, usurping God's intended parental authority. The enemy's goal is to gain access to and ultimately rule homes by directing selfish, immature, and rebellious offspring. Alas, in our current day, the powers of hell are successfully teaching children to control the home.

While you are trying to take this all in, remember this: God did not remove any of Satan's God-given and brilliant intelligence when he fell from God's presence. He is described as a subtle, scheming, lying and murderous thief in the Scriptures. Satan knows that a child, well-trained, submitted to Jesus, and under righteous authority, is a massive threat to all his destructive activities. It is no wonder the family is under attack as Satan maneuvers to gain control of each child, parent and family unit.

God holds us accountable for our young children's sins. This truth should make parents stand up and pay attention to this present generation of children and youth. For parents and those of you who will be: let this be your wake up call!

Unwittingly, we as parents may have loosed curses onto our kids and grandkids—but don't be discouraged! As long as we are alive, there is opportunity to redeem the territory that was knowingly or unknowingly gave over to the enemy simply because we were unaware of generational curses. Some sowing occurred in ignorance, and our response could easily be, "I didn't know what I was doing." Don't take that excuse to God. Why? Because we are really without excuse. He gave us His Word to provide direction. If we've been negligent by not discovering His will and ways through reading and heeding His Word or spending time in prayer, we have chosen the alternative to the abundant life God has for us in Jesus Christ: a dry desert. I often use this passage: *"Do not merely listen to the word, and so deceive yourselves. Do what it says"* (James 1:22).

God never changes; therefore, as curses were passed from generation to generation in Old Testament times, so are they passed from generation to generation today (Malachi 3:6–9).

Principle #17: Once sin passes to the next generation, a foothold is established.

I have endeavoured to build a platform that would alert you that generational sins are a problem for Christians. Many Christians believe generational sins aren't relevant today. This theory contradicts Exodus 20:5, which as a part of the Ten Commandments is God's moral law, a law which never changes (Malachi 3:6).

The verdict is in! It is incumbent upon us today to deal diligently with our current generation and search out and address past generations, so we won't send children out to live their adult years cursed by our generational sins.

Generational sins are birthed by multiple means and ways—so many ways that they likely couldn't all be named. Any sin that passes from one generation to the next becomes a generational curse. Once sin has passed into the next generation, it no longer works from the outside but has established a foothold or a stronghold that works, to at least some degree, from the inside.

God has given the father leadership of the family; he is also called the priest of the home. God made the family structure to put the father, as "Father-Priest" and leader over the home, in a place of covering. This would ensure they are blessed and equipped to raise up a generation that would glorify God.

Are you a believing single mother? In a spiritual sense, God has become your husband and the father of your children. You also have authority through Jesus to effectively root out and destroy generational sins and curses.

A generational curse is like the power lines that follow alongside most of our country and city roads. Today, most homes in North America are hooked up to power. (Not so at our home when I was younger! The farms on our right and left were hooked up, but our home wasn't.) Imagine we could drive along the miles of road that carry sins. Generational sin lines work very much in the same way. Sins, prevalent within a family line, represent the main power line, and each family member represents a separate farm. Some family members are "hooked up" to the power, while others aren't. Picture, if you will, your generational line. As you look a great way back down that road, it is indescribable—it seems to go back forever and ever. But now, as you allow your gaze to fall on the road closer to you, you begin to see some images that are hard to make out, but it appears as if it may be your great-great-great grandpa and grandma from your father's side. Now, looking just a little closer, you see your great-great grandpa and grandma, and then Grandpa and Grandma. Finally, you are looking at your father and mother, the family you grew up in, along with your sisters and brothers.

What you may not have seen as you looked at your generational line is a power source of another kind travelling forever alongside your family line. Satan has his wicked powerline following alongside our generational line. He is the provider of the unseen dark power working its way into the family. Satan doesn't ask to come in; day and night he is relentlessly working his schemes to get into the house. But he isn't satisfied just to get inside; he's working to be hooked up to every room and person in the house. What would that look like in the spiritual realm for the family line?

Let's take a look: The wife is a Christian and the husband isn't; he accepts her "as is" and gives her room to live her Christian life. He is a good husband, kindly, with a passive personality. The wife wishes her husband would be more proactive in raising their kids, disciplining their growing anger and abuse. The son, at three, began to show signs of anger and abuse that continued as he grew. The younger daughter, by the time she was in her teens, was displaying the same attributes as her older brother. The husband's generational line has no such behaviours, but looking far back into the mother's generational lines, we see that her great-great-great-grandpa returned home from the war as a very angry man—verbally and physically abusive. His children, a girl and two boys, also grew up very angry and abusive. Upon closer inspection, it appears that anger and abuse are family traits that were in the young mother's preceding generations.

Faith in Jesus greatly reduces the generational curse.

The previous case study is indicative of generational sins for perhaps any family you could select. A question you must ask yourself is: what is in my current generation, and more importantly, what is in my past generations?

Generational curses are not unlike the data lines that now travel alongside our roads. These cables have the capacity to carry hundreds—if not thousands—of tiny transparent fibres on the inside that each feed different homes. Generational sins follow the same pattern, going from person to person and family to family due to unconfessed anger, abuse or any type of sin. Just because the curses have made their way into a lineage does not mean Satan has taken each and every individual captive. The reason for this is that some individuals, even though not born-again Christians, have unknowingly chosen not to sin. Because of that choice, Satan cannot gain ground into those people, who have therefore blocked the evil from themselves. Some unbelievers make better, healthier choices than some Christians.

Principle #18: Even non-Christians can delay generational sins by a disciplined, self-controlled lifestyle.

Righteous living or not, if we do not deal a deliverance death-blow to our generational sins, they will travel to the next generation, providing Satan with a legal right to ensnare each new generation.

5.4. How Can the Enemy Gain Access?

"'In your anger do not sin': Do not let the sun go down while you are still angry, and do not give the devil a foothold" (Ephesians 4:26–27).

"Foothold" means a place in your heart. If we do not deal with our sins, they may carry on successively to future generations, giving the devil a foothold within us to be inherited. He and his cohorts have a legal right to thrust his schemes and manipulations on us, entangling us in anger or abuse (only two of the many types of generational sins).

We know that Satan and his demons cannot just walk into our lives any time they please. According to the Scripture that I just presented, they gain access to us through continued, habitual sins. Where generational sins operate, our enemy has a right to work the family line, which they do in varied ways.

Perhaps, unbeknownst to you, a demon is trying to work a generational curse of anger into your soul. The most common way is through what I will call "thought-darts." These are short phrases dropped into your thoughts relative to what is happening currently in your family—thoughts such as, "Dad is always mean to me. He gave me a licking again today for swearing, which my brother does all the time and he doesn't say a word to him. Dad is always mean and picks on me. Mom never stands up for me. My little sister laughs at me every time Dad gets mad at me." On and on it goes for weeks, months, sometimes years, until finally, without realizing it, you become angry, hateful, in a constant place of unforgiveness. Then comes the train of generational anger. It's not hard now for the enemy to drag in boxcars full of revenge, jealousy, and spite through the door of your soul. Not far behind come hatred and murder.

With this added information in hand, look for the final time at the family of four that we have been following. The husband is quiet-spoken and kind. He certainly didn't give in to anger and abuse, but we see it in his children. Why? Maybe the husband was raised in a home that taught that it was wrong to be angry and hurtful, along with other life principles that simply promoted good and right living. Thus, any time the enemy came promoting anger and abuse, he made the right decision and said "no" to the temptation.

Just a few days back, when working with a client, I was dealing with a rather arrogant demon. As I was sending it away, it said, "Okay, I will go. But as soon as you are gone, I will be right back in." I reminded the demon that this man had repented of his sin, that God had forgiven him, and that he had committed not to enter back into that sin. I reminded the demon that he, and even Satan himself, cannot just march into our lives.

The response from the demon was, "You're right, we cannot just march right in. We are not allowed, but we can always at any time put pressure on the area of possible sin."

In other words, Satan knows our areas of weakness, and very often, he provides the temptation there. Don't be discouraged by that demon's statement! You can be absolutely certain that our God will not allow more than you can bear. As is written in 1 Corinthians 10:13, *"No temptation has overtaken you except what is common to mankind. And God is faithful; he will not let you be tempted beyond what you can bear. But when you are tempted, he will also provide a way out so that you can endure it."*

See also the teaching on deliverance in Chapter 9 (Freedom through Deliverance).

5.4.1. Family Unity

The father in the family unit we have been following made some correct choices that blocked out the curses of anger and abuse from entering his life, but those two curses did make it into the lives of his children. Why?

There is a clue in the mother's desires. She encourages her husband to be more proactive in raising their kids, to discipline them in their growing anger and abuse, and to teach them to become individuals that make a difference for God on this earth. Let us assume this unbelieving father, who is kind and gentle, is also extremely passive, abdicating his position of leadership. He is neither equipped through Jesus, nor willing to meet the challenges of training his children in spiritual matters and necessary respect for authority. The authority structure of the home is now upside down, opening the door for the enemy to come in like a flood (Isaiah 59:19). (See Chapter 9 on the passive spirit of Ahab and the controlling spirit of Jezebel.)

Had the husband been more proactive in disciplining the children, he would have made it much more difficult for the enemy to take the children captive. Although the curse came down from the mother's side, the father, being the head of the home, could have used his authority to effectively battle it.

A Christian home that has God's love and principles to live by gives children an inner sense of peace and purpose, along with the experience of truly belonging and being loved. When this is coupled with strong Bible-based discipline, it gives the child a sense of being cared for and protected. The home becomes a safe place, a place of refuge, a place to have questions answered safely. It is a place where the father is the head, the doorkeeper, and the priest—effectively applying the blood of the Lamb to the windows and doorposts, and declaring that all enemy spirits must pass over their home. We must understand and carry out the roles of father and mother in breaking generational sins and curses.

5.4.2. The Importance of Bible Knowledge and Application

Whenever I am with clients, I remind them that the Word cannot just leap into needy areas in our hearts. We are individually and solely responsible for reading and applying God's Word in our lives. We cannot blame God, our pastor, or our counsellor for the lack of growth in our lives. If we are not applying, we are dying!

Hughes says, "Don't be surprised to discover that many Christians are far more interested in interpretation of the Bible than the application of it."[43] I have often thought of those words when coming across Christians who were indignant that someone disagreed with their particular pet doctrine, but showed no concern whatsoever about massive contradictions with Scripture in their own lives.

Hendricks and Hendricks remark,

> Observation plus interpretation without application equals abortion. In other words, every time you observe and interpret but fail to apply, you perform an abortion on the Scriptures on terms of their purpose. The Bible was not written to satisfy your curiosity; it was written to transform your life. The ultimate goal of Bible study,

---

43   Hughes & Brooks, April 12, 2011.

then, is not to do something to the Bible, but to allow the Bible to do something to you, so truth becomes tangent to life.[44]

You see, once we stop applying the Word, it loses its influence over us. We will never find the Bible to be dynamic if we do not surrender to its truths and obey its commands.

The Word of God is alive within us, judging the thoughts and attitudes of our heart. In other words, God is identifying areas of sin in our lives, thoughts that need His transforming touch. He whispers into our hearts, saying, "You need to put off this habitual sin and put on Christ Jesus." The startling truth is that if we are not reading and directly applying the principles of what we read, God is hindered in what He can do in and through our lives. Let us get back to the principle of the application of God's Word in our individual lives. What would that look like for a father, a priest of the home?

Principle #19: The father is the priest, gatekeeper, and doorkeeper of the family.

Throughout the Bible, the father is understood to be the covering, the priest, gatekeeper, and doorkeeper of his family—the protector. We need to understand that where the Bible refers to the "father's sins," it does not say that the mother's sins have no impact on the family or future generations. But the implication is that fathers are held responsible for dealing with the mother's sins and those of her lineage. The mother, similarly to the children, comes under the father for protection and direction. This requires the father, in his position as priest, to ensure that all generational sins and iniquities from his own lineage are exposed and dealt with, as well as the generational sins from his wife's lineage. Then a spoken declaration is required, declaring that all is cut off and cannot ever come back to connect itself to the family unit and future generations again! (See Ephesians 5:15–6:4.)

---

44 Hendricks & Hendricks, pp. 283–284.

Husbands, we are to love our wives as Jesus loves us; in that, we can present them back to ourselves as a radiant bride. This has always challenged me. Do it, husbands—it's a win-win. By loving your wife as Jesus loves you, you are applying the Word to your wife, so that she, your children and you yourself will become benefactors.

5.5. The Blessing

A picture of God's blessing is painted for us as follows.

> *If you fully obey the Lord your God and carefully follow all his commands I give you today, the Lord your God will set you high above all the nations on earth. All these blessings will come upon you and accompany you if you obey the Lord your God: You will be blessed in the city and blessed in the country. The fruit of your womb will be blessed…*
> —Deuteronomy 28:1–4

This is the blessing available to every one of us. The only requirement is to follow His commands by applying the written Word to our lives, and as husbands and priests of the home, to apply that Word to our families.

> *You were taught, with regard to your former way of life, to put off your old self, which is being corrupted by its deceitful desires; to be made new in the attitude of your minds; and to put on the new self, created to be like God in true righteousness and holiness.*
> —Ephesians 4:22–24

If we choose not to walk in the blessing, the following will be our lot. "You will be cursed in the city and cursed in the country. Your basket and your kneading trough will be cursed. The fruit of your womb will be cursed…" (Deuteronomy 28:16–18). There is a need today, possibly like never before, for husbands and fathers to be the spiritual doorkeepers for their homes. We husbands have been given the responsibilities of the priest in our homes by our heavenly Father. Are we standing in our position of authority over all things that come knocking on our family's door, attempting to move us off the track? Jesus, in His wisdom, has carefully laid out plans for us in this generation, and for the generations that will follow us. Will your steps be a continuing path of God's light for them to follow?

Stop reading right now! With the book in hand, listen for God's voice. I have written the last few paragraphs with tears flooding down my face like a river and my spirit ablaze. I believe that some of you will, even right now, receive from the Lord a blessing of faithfulness as father-priests.

For those of you who have never performed your role of husband-father-priest, God, in His great love, is for you—not against you. Even in the most shameful sin you have ever sinned, He was still for you. Now He is saying, "It's time, my son—you can do it. I've been waiting for this moment for a long time. Now is the time to step into the pivotal role of husband-father-priest."

Maybe you are a mother, son, or daughter, and God is dealing with your negligence in addressing generational sins. Whatever it may be, this is for you right now. First, this is God's portal of love for you. Maybe He is affirming His love for you; maybe He is reaffirming His call on your life. Maybe He is saying, "You have been running too hard, come and receive a river of life from Me—I AM." (See Exodus 3:14.)

I have witnessed God work this way many times over the years. Just spend some time with Him. "*The Lord appeared to us in the past, saying: 'I have loved you with an everlasting love; I have drawn you with unfailing kindness'*" (Jeremiah 31:3).

Stay here until you hear from God.

He is the High and Holy One who lives in that high and holy place, and desires to reign in the tabernacle of your heart. He is the God of the generations. He alone has planted seed in the heart of every one of us that produces a harvest of righteousness in the soil of our hearts. Our children are the recipients of that harvest and, in turn, carry it on for the fulfilment of God's purposes throughout future generations.

A wife with no husband or father filling his role will become, by God's design, the head over her home; she now stands in the position of priest over her home and children. With the help of her Heavenly Father, she can fill the position of headship, ensuring that God's purpose relative to her generations will continue throughout the generations. Let the following quotes be an inspiration.

> If you believe that your ministry can be fulfilled in one generation, then your vision of God is too small. Our God is the God of Abraham, Isaac, and Jacob. The blessing of previous generations must pass down to the next generation, or Kingdom manifestation will be contained in momentary outpourings limited by time and space. For the entire earth to be filled with the glory of God, we must understand that our harvest will never be greater than our seed. A father must understand that his greatest ministry is bequeathed in sons and daughters who bridge the gap of generational inheritance in the Spirit.[45]

God's design and desperate need in our modern times is for men: men who will strike the blow of courage to be what God purposed each one of us to be, them to be and believe an impression of character on a disintegrating society. Observing the overwhelming confusion about what has been brought about by the lack of distinctive masculinity that has plagued our world, the Biblical model of manhood ushers in a breath of fresh air to an age suffocating from the humanistic approach to manhood which has resulted in a society spiralling out of control (2 Tim. 3–13). If we ever hope to recover what God had in mind regarding living as a human race, Biblical manhood must be revisited and its spiritual principles must be lived out in our lives amid a world that is crying out for help. Men who are children of God dare not do otherwise.[46]

5.6. The Three Steps to Freedom

1. Acknowledge the sins of iniquity, generationally and personally.

---

45   Nori, p. 3.
46   Hayford, 1995, p. 693.

2. Confess them as sins. Use Nehemiah 1:6 and 9:2 as a guide:

"... *let your ear be attentive and your eyes open to hear the prayer your servant is praying day and night.... I confess the sins we... including myself and my father's family, have committed against you*" (Nehemiah 1:6).

"*Those of Israelite descent had separated themselves from all foreigners. They stood in their places and confessed their sins and the sins of their ancestors*" (Nehemiah 9:2).

"*But if they will confess their sins and the sins of their ancestors—their unfaithfulness and their hostility toward me...*" (Leviticus 26:40).

"*... and purify us from all unrighteousness*" (1 John 1:9b). That little word "all" takes in this whole area of generational sins. But the key is that we need to confess them as sins.

3. Take back every bit of ground given to Satan and declare freedom.

"In the name of Jesus, I take back every bit of ground given to Satan, declaring that every legal hold and every legal ground of the enemy has been broken and destroyed. Satan, you no longer have a legal right to harass my family.

Father God, I stand in for my whole family and ask that you forgive us for all of these sins mentioned here. Forgive our parents and ancestors generationally. I receive your forgiveness and thank you for it. Now I stand in for my family and cut all of the evil curses and ties that have bound us in the past.

In the Name of Jesus Christ, I now renounce all generational curses that have been put on my family through my ancestors, parents, or myself. I break the power and reject all the sins of my ancestors, by the power and authority of Jesus Christ; I renounce all Satanic assignments that have been put against me and cancel every curse that Satan and his forces have put on me. I cancel all the power of the curses spoken against me, from the moment of my conception in my mother's womb until this moment. I am under the covering of the blood of Jesus Christ.

I command every familiar spirit and enemy of the Lord Jesus to leave my family and me now, and in the name and authority of Jesus Christ, I cut these ties, now and forever. Amen."

Claim this verse for you and your family: *"But from everlasting to everlasting the Lord's love is with those who fear him, and his righteousness with their children's children—with those who keep his covenant and remember to obey his precepts"* (Psalm 103:17–18).

5.7. Explanation of Word "Curses"

The very concept of cursing is very non-Western; we really don't want to accept it. However, the Bible is far from being silent when it comes to this topic. *"With the tongue we praise our Lord and Father, and with it we curse human beings, who have been made in God's likeness. Out of the same mouth come praise and cursing. My brothers and sisters, this should not be"* (James 3:9–10).

Principle #20: Word curses are angry, negative words that allow a foothold or stronghold into our lives.

Many people, when talking about curses, say something such as, "Oh yes, I know. I'm working on it. I'm trying to clean my mouth up; I'm not swearing so much." This is not what James is talking about, although swearing does condemn us and can put us under a curse. *"But now you must also rid yourselves of all such things as these: anger, rage, malice, slander, and filthy language from your lips"* (Colossians 3:8). We have already read that, *"Out of the same mouth come praise and cursing"* (James 3:10). We are usually very much aware of what we are saying when we praise, but not so when it comes to cursing. Curses roll off of our lips often, and we are totally oblivious.

Not long after I gave my life to Jesus, I began seeking freedom in my life from Satan's power. I met with a man who worked in the area of deliverance. We were not far into the session when he asked, "What does 'God damn you' mean to you?"

I replied, "That was one of Dad's favourite phrases." It was one that he spoke over me many, many times, totally unaware of the cursing power of his words. That, coupled with anger on his part and fear and shame from me, gave the lord of the dark realm the opportunity to bring condemning power down upon me. Many people think that cursing is just something witches do—it really has no power. But when somebody curses you, you are damned by the power of words. The only way out is to forgive the perpetrator, and then smash and destroy the curse of damnation, along with the attached foothold or stronghold, sending away any attached demons that work at fulfilling the curses of damnation. Take the curse to the feet of Jesus.

In the Bible, blessing and cursing are often linked. We enjoy and accept the blessing part, but we turn a blind eye to the curses. I have found that curses are very real, even in our churches, although most are not spoken purposely. We curse out of our own ignorance.

A good example of how people curse in their hearts unknowingly is, *"With their mouths they bless, but in their hearts they curse"* (Psalm 62:4b). It could happen this way: suppose you and I are having a rather heated conversation because of a betrayal of some type. You're sitting across the table from me, and I'm looking at you with a big smile on my face, saying, "It's okay; no problem, I forgive you." But in my heart, I am boiling with anger. In this way, I have cursed you in my heart. How? It is rooted in a lie of deception.

Cramer says,

Cursing is in reality, a fact, a biblical fact. The dictionary defines curse as "an appeal to a supernatural power for evil to befall someone or something." Roget's Thesaurus suggests these synonyms for the term curse: "poison, vex, afflict, wound, trouble, plague, torment, and torture." "To curse" means: To damn, denounce, and slander. Cursing is malicious, spiteful, hateful, venomous, malevolent, begrudging, vicious, hostile, and evil. It contains threats, endangers the one being cursed, and is a menace to one's spiritual, mental, and physical safety and well-being. Indeed, to be cursed is a frightening, terrifying, even paralyzing experience. In ancient thought, the belief existed that curses carried an intrinsic power to accomplish their intended goal. The speaking forth of the particular curse somehow released this evil power. Thus, the person or persons who were "cursed" came under those words and under the power released when they were uttered. [47]

We, as Christians, would never intentionally "appeal to a supernatural power for evil to befall someone or something." Yet, we do it all the time, unknowingly. Angry words and actions can greatly damage a person or family unit, without the family or the one who spoke the angry words having any idea that a curse was released. Over the years, I have seen many individuals, and sometimes even whole families, bound up by angry words. When I'm working with a person that has a disease or some type of chronic illness, I ask God to bring to memory whatever the incident may have been at the root of the health issue that this person has been unable to overcome. Often it is because of a spoken curse, unknown or forgotten by the recipient. Almost always, there has been no consideration given to the possibility of there being a curse invoked. This gives our enemy a handle by which he holds individuals and families in captivity to him, even Christian families.

Consider carefully the following words: "Sometimes Satan has a tight hold on Christian families and Christians." *"If anyone, then, knows the good they ought to do and doesn't do it, it is a sin for them"* (James 4:17). This means that Satan could find you or me in sin just about any time. This makes it very easy for the dark realm to slip in a bit of deception to blur your perception— just enough to have you bite into his tempting apple. What does God's word say? *"…for when you eat of it you will certainly die"* (Genesis 2:17).

Now, just to ensure I am understood, the reference to "die" is not instant physical death. It means separation from God. To continue in sin is to widen and deepen the chasm between you and God. This is still one of the greatest illustrations in the Bible for us today. It is our choice. If we choose the apple, we die. Separated from God, we become an unprotected and easy target for Satan to work his ways into our life.

Blow the horn! I believe this is an important issue for the Church of Jesus Christ today. In my experience, a great deal of born-again believers are living

---

47   Cramer, p. 2.

in soft sin—unrepentant, lulled to sleep by Satan's song of complacency, "All is well." Meanwhile, Jesus is saying to us today, *"I know your deeds, that you are neither cold nor hot. I wish you were either one or the other! So, because you are lukewarm—neither hot nor cold—I am about to spit you out of my mouth"* (Revelation 3:15–16). No word of commendation was extended to the Laodicean church. They were pictured as utterly abhorrent to Christ because they were lukewarm. Content with their material wealth, they were unaware of their spiritual poverty.[48]

Almost always when I read, *"I am about to spit you out of my mouth,"* I gasp! I'm not insecure in my position in Christ Jesus. I know in whom I have believed, and know that He is able to keep that which I have committed unto Him against that day. But shame on us, should Christ ever find us lukewarm.

5.7.1. How is it that a Christian Needs to Worry about Curses?

"Like a fluttering sparrow or a darting swallow, an undeserved curse does not come to rest" (Proverbs 26:2).

> **Principle #21: Christians who are undisciplined, disobedient, and out of harmony forfeit their claim on God's protection.**

Wherever there is a curse at work, it has a cause. Consider just one word in Deuteronomy 28:1, "obey." This word has a double meaning. It means the conditions for enjoying the blessings are firstly, to listen to God's voice, and secondly, to do what He says.

"Do not be idolaters, as some of them were; as it is written: 'The people sat down to eat and drink and got up to indulge in revelry.' We should not commit sexual immorality, as some of them did…" (1 Corinthians 10:7–8). This is a reference to Exodus 32:4–6, and a warning for us today. Obviously, it is for believers in the new covenant. The central lesson is simple: Christians who are living in disciplined obedience to God and in harmony with each other can

---

48   Walvoord, p. 940.

look to God for His protection against Satan. But Christians who are undisciplined, disobedient, and out of harmony forfeit their claim on this protection.

5.7.2. Spoken or Thought-Imposed Curses

You have minds like a snake pit! How do you suppose what you say is worth anything when you are so foul-minded? It's your heart, not the dictionary, that gives meaning to your words. A good person produces good deeds and words season after season. An evil person is a blight on the orchard. Let me tell you something: Every one of these careless words is going to come back to haunt you. There will be a time of Reckoning. Words are powerful; take them seriously. Words can be your salvation. Words can also be your damnation.

—Matthew 12:34–37, MSG

Proverbs 6:2 says, "*… you have been trapped by what you said, ensnared by the words of your mouth.*"

I unknowingly had a curse placed on me by a very, very angry man. I had to personally deal with this individual in a rather strong way. I was completely respectful and proper in my approach, but he went ballistic. I did what had to be done, and I was praying that that would be the end of it. A few weeks later, I was in a deliverance session with an individual I had never seen or worked with before. We had finished all that we could find to deal with. But I could not cast the demons out, even though they confessed to have no hold on this person. Finally, after putting on much pressure, I was able to cast out the demons, but not before one said, "Okay, we are going from here. We have you anyways, and I'll see you in hell."

I wasn't sure what that meant, and at that point I didn't care. Demons do a great deal of boasting, and as far as I was concerned, we were finished. About a week or so later, I was meeting with the man who had gone ballistic on me. We knew each other well and had spent a great deal of time together over the years. Because of that, I shared the rather unusual comments from the demons. But before I could get all the demon's words out, "I'll see you in hell," this man gasped, and said rather loudly, "Those are the words I spoke!"

He acknowledged that he had inaudibly spoken those very words in anger towards me. Because we reconciled, the curse was rendered null and void.

This incident had a happy ending, but when you find yourself being cursed by somebody, more often than not, there is no reconciliation. In those cases, the curse is left out in the atmosphere, alive and well, giving the enemy the ability to take liberties because of unforgiveness. That curse will continue to work by whichever means it can to bring about the curse words originally spoken. *"Surely they intend to topple me from my lofty place; they take delight in lies. With their mouths they bless, but in their hearts they curse"* (Psalm 62:4).

5.7.3. Is it Possible to Curse via our Prayers?

Unexpectedly, our prayers can be used to curse!

A women called me with a need for prayer. She had experienced something evil coming against her during a recent morning devotional, and couldn't understand why. She had asked God what she was supposed to do with this darkness that had settled on her. The Lord told her to "command it to go to the tree in the centre of your garden," which she did. Not many days later, the tree fell over, dead. A few weeks later, her husband noticed when he arrived home that the tree that was parallel to the first tree was dying from the top down. Within a few days, it too fell over dead. As we prayed together asking God what was happening, we felt the Lord say, "Those who removed you from the church are now praying for you, but there is still anger towards you. Therefore, their prayers are a curse, not a blessing."

As Christians, we are not exempt from curses.

Most often we just forget angry words, and because we are Christians, we walk away instead of retaliating. We put the incident behind us—or so we say. But the curse is still active, empowered by its own evil intent. When we say, "a curse without cause shall not alight," we Christians tend to believe this means that we cannot be touched by a curse. Why? Because we are Christians.

Consider this: does God protect Christians from committing idolatry or adultery, or any other kind of sin? Certainly there is a measure of protection when we purposely live for God, but if we choose to sin in some way, despite knowing it will harm us, God won't violate our decision. So it is with curses. We aren't exempt from a spoken curse (known or unknown), or unable to pronounce or institute a curse just because we are Christians. The "cause" or opportunity for it landing on you could very well be from an incident twenty years prior, where you unknowingly humiliated a brother in Christ. But every time this person sees you or thinks of you, it gives the demons an opportunity to bring to mind that the curse.

5.7.4. A List of Seven Conditions that may Indicate a Curse

This list of conditions that may indicate a curse can be generational but can also be self-imposed.

1. **Mental and emotional breakdown.**

   "It's driving me crazy."

   "I just can't take it anymore."

   "It makes me mad to think..."

   I know of a strong Christian woman whose parents told her repeatedly that her religion would drive her crazy. After a time of much victory, I noticed she said quite regularly, "I think I'm going crazy."

2. **Repeated or chronic sickness (especially if hereditary).**

   "Whenever there's a bug, I catch it."

   "I'm sick and tired..."

   "It runs in the family, so I guess I'm next."

   Rheumatoid arthritis is often the result of a word curse. In some cases I've seen, once the curse was uncovered and forgiveness was granted, gnarled fingers have straightened out for the first time in years.

3. **Barrenness, a tendency to miscarry or related reproductive problems.**

"I don't think I'll ever get pregnant."

"I've got the 'curse' again." This is said often by women referring to their monthly period.

"I just know I'm going to lose this one—I always do."

4. **Breakdown of marriage and family alienation.**

"The palm reader said my husband would leave me."

"Somehow I always knew my husband would find another woman."

"In our family we've always fought like cats and dogs."

5. **Continual financial insufficiency.**

"I can never make ends meet—my father was the same."

"I can't afford to tithe."

"I hate those 'fat cats' who get all they ever want—it never happens to me."

6. **Being "accident prone."**

"It always happens to me."

"I knew there was trouble ahead…"

"I'm just a clumsy kind of person."

7. **A history of suicides and unnatural or untimely deaths.**

"What's the use of living?"

"Over my dead body."

"I'd rather die than go on the way I am."

Sometimes our own words come back to us as a curse.

We must choose to bless and not to curse ourselves, our families, and others. *"This day I call heaven and earth as witnesses against you that I have set before you life and death, blessings and curses. Now choose life, so that you and your children may live…"* (Deuteronomy 30:19).

5.8. Breaking the Generational Sin or Curse

If you have cursed someone:

1. Repent. We must confess if we have spoken a curse, or for the part we played which allowed a curse to settle on us, and then repent of it.
2. Rebuke. We must cancel whatever we have said.
3. Replace our wrong talk with right talk. Simply put, *speak a blessing.* Usually, if not always, there needs to be forgiveness.

We must deal thoroughly with all sin issues, or our sins become generational sins.

I have worked with different families where the grandmother gave birth out of wedlock at the age of fifteen years, and likewise her daughter and granddaughter.

Spoken curses normally come out of an angry, hateful, jealous, or proud heart—and we can curse ourselves in the same way. The first tiny seed of a curse is able to take root as we submit to its cause. The way a generational curse gains an entrance in the first place is the same as with spoken curses.

The most commonly used method of Satan is to continually speak "thought darts" over and over again until we accept them as a reality. Unless we are aware of his ways, we will never recognize the voice as being any other than our own. Thoughts like "I'm going to divorce my wife" can get stronger and stronger until we find ourselves submitting to them and facing divorce. At this point, we can either accept or reject the thought. If we accept it as a possibility, the curse has gained the upper hand. How do we get free?

5.8.1. Practical Application

We need to recognize and renounce any family patterns or habits (curses) that we are aware of by naming them, asking God's forgiveness for the whole family, and severing all negative ties. There is a list below with some possible results of generational sins. Check any below that you feel may be in your family.

☐ Abuse: physical, sexual, emotional

☐ Adultery

☐ Addictions: alcoholism, drugs, sex, food

☐ Allergies

☐ Alzheimer's

☐ Anger or bad temper

☐ Anti-Christian

☐ Aphasia, i.e. "speech problems"

☐ Barrenness

☐ Bestiality

☐ Betrayal

☐ Blame

☐ Blindness: spiritual or physical

☐ Blood disorders, circulation problems

☐ Cancer

☐ Co-dependency

☐ Conceived out of wedlock

☐ Controlling

☐ Crime

☐ Critical spirit, shrikism (picking someone apart)

☐ Deafness

☐ Deceitfulness

☐ Depression

☐ Destruction, dying out of family

☐ Diabetes

☐ Dishonouring parents

☐ Divorce

☐ Dyslexia

☐ Epilepsy

☐ Fears and paranoia

☐ Gambling

☐ Hate

☐ Heart problems

- ☐ Homosexuality
- ☐ Idolatry
- ☐ Incest
- ☐ Infirmity: physical or emotional
- ☐ Insanity/breakdown
- ☐ Insomnia
- ☐ Kidney problems
- ☐ Laziness/lethargy
- ☐ Legalism
- ☐ Lying, falseness
- ☐ Manipulation
- ☐ Materialism
- ☐ Migraines/headaches
- ☐ Miscarriages, abortions
- ☐ Multiple Sclerosis
- ☐ Obesity, anorexia, bulimia
- ☐ Occult involvement
- ☐ Pornography
- ☐ Poverty, destitution
- ☐ Prejudice
- ☐ Rebellion, disobedience
- ☐ Rejection
- ☐ Schizophrenia
- ☐ Scoliosis
- ☐ Sects, false religious cults
- ☐ Silent treatment
- ☐ Suicide
- ☐ Untimely or violent deaths
- ☐ Violence

See also the occult in Chapter 6.

5.9. The Blessing

I have said much about the curse, but now for the Blessing. *"For our light and momentary troubles are achieving for us an eternal glory that far outweighs them all. So we fix our eyes not on what is seen, but on what is unseen, since what is seen is temporary, but what is unseen is eternal"* (2 Corinthians 4:17–18). These verses reveal the two realms that determine the course of history. These two realms, warring against each other, determine our personal history on a daily basis. Many things that happen around us in the seen world cannot be explained without the unseen. Our success in life depends upon our ability to comprehend and to relate to the invisible and spiritual.

When it comes to blessings and curses, we understand that both are vehicles of supernatural power. But let's take a look at the blessing.

I had no comprehension of blessing when I began to pray for others. I had two or three sessions with an elderly woman who was confined to her home with her alcoholic husband. I helped her through some issues in a session and then prayed for her. As she was getting up to leave, the Lord said, "Pray a blessing over her."

Now, I didn't know what to do. I had never even considered what a blessing was, let alone prayed a blessing prayer. I told the woman what God had said, and then I told her, "If you don't mind, I will hold your hands and pray." As I began to pray, my mouth filled up with a substance—it was as if I had drawn deep on a cigarette until my lungs were full. And as I spoke in prayer, that substance went forth. I knew without a doubt that my words were the wings on which God carried His blessing into this woman's life. And blessed she was—as she sat crying, she received the full measure of God's love and life. I have never forgotten that incident, and still today, I try to close counselling sessions by sending my clients home with a blessing.

The main vehicle of both blessings and curses are words. *"With their mouths the godless destroy their neighbors, but through knowledge the righteous escape"* (Proverbs 11:9). *"The words of the reckless pierce like swords, but the tongue of the wise brings healing"* (Proverbs 12:18). *"The soothing tongue is a tree of life, but a perverse tongue crushes the spirit"* (Proverbs 15:4).

We also see, early on in the Word of God, the concept of blessing with Jacob. *"Then Jacob called for his sons and said: 'Gather around so I can tell you what will happen to you in days to come'"* (Genesis 49:1). These words had generational ramifications in Jacob's time, and they still do in our day.

5.9.1. Blessings for Obedience
Deuteronomy 28:3–14 says:

You will be blessed in the city and blessed in the country.

The fruit of your womb will be blessed, and the crops of your land and the young of your livestock—the calves of your herds and the lambs of your flocks.

Your basket and your kneading trough will be blessed.

You will be blessed when you come in and blessed when you go out.

The Lord will grant that the enemies who rise up against you will be defeated before you. They will come at you from one direction but flee from you in seven.

The Lord will send a blessing on your barns and on everything you put your hand to. The Lord your God will bless you in the land he is giving you.

The Lord will establish you as his holy people, as he promised you on oath, if you keep the commands of the Lord your God and walk in obedience to him. Then all the peoples on earth will see that you are called by the name of the Lord, and they will fear you. The Lord will grant you abundant prosperity—in the fruit of your womb, the young of your livestock and the crops of your ground—in the land he swore to your forefathers to give you.

The Lord will open the heavens, the storehouse of his bounty, to send rain on your land in season and to bless all the work of your hands. You will lend to many nations but will borrow from none. The Lord will make you the head, not the tail. If you pay attention to the commands of the Lord your God that I give you this day and carefully follow them, you will always be at the top, never at the bottom. Do not turn aside from any of the commands I give you today, to the right or to the left, following other gods and serving them.

"*The tongue has the power of life and death, and those who love it will eat its fruit*" (Proverbs 18:21).

"*... for the Mighty One has done great things for me—holy is his name. His mercy extends to those who fear him, from generation to generation. He has performed mighty deeds with his arm; he has scattered those who are proud in their inmost thoughts*" (Luke 1:49–51).

5.9.2. Reverse the Curse

This is a final story on God's generational blessing, drawn from my experiences with Family Foundations Institute (FFI) seminars (see FFI info and seminars at the back of this book).

I was facilitating a small group, which had a participant who was born and raised in Africa. His father was a chief of their community—a very wealthy and well-respected man. During his move from Africa to Canada, his father had been killed. The rules in his country at that time were if the father died, the closest brother to the father inherited all that he had, including the father's wife, children, and finances. As it turned out, the father's brother took all the money and the home, leaving no inheritance for any of the family members. This participant worked through the FFI seminar and through it, he forgave and received forgiveness.

As I was closing the session, the Lord spoke to me and said, "Jan, I want you to pray for this man, specifically that the generational blessings of family, finances and home would be returned to him." So I immediately prayed as the Lord had asked me to. As I was praying, I literally heard in the spiritual realm what sounded like a train roaring down the tracks towards me.

That night I didn't share what I had heard. But the next morning, I was asked to come up and speak. With this man's permission, I told the story about him and the train. When he heard me tell the story, he came running up from the back of the church weeping, crying, and shaking, saying he had also heard that train during the small group. I was able to track his family for a few years, during which there was a significant change in his countenance, in his heart, in his finances, in his relationship with his wife and his children, and in his relationship with his next door neighbour, who had been cursing him every time he saw him. Never doubt the power of the blessings of God.

God is as concerned for the passing on of the generational blessing today as he was in Jacob's time. I remember well the first time I received a blessing prayer.

I had brought into my hometown, under the auspices of Craig Hill, FFI International, a team lead by George and Marion O'Neil, who brought along with them a team of eight or so people from Ontario, coordinators for the Ancient Paths Seminars. As I had brought them in, it was my obligation to coodinate all arrangements for the three days they were there.

We completed four seminars back-to-back. This meant I missed much of the teaching, but worse than that, I missed most of the ministry during the group time. Finally, on the last Saturday, George said, "Jan, you have had very little ministry time. For the most part, you missed all the blessings, and we as a team are not leaving until we see you thoroughly blessed." So I agreed.

As they prayed, I began to cry. All the leaders prayed once or twice or even more for me in different ways. Some of them recognized curses and burdens I was carrying, all of which had to be removed from my soul. God, in all of His wisdom and glory, used His leaders to bring me into a place of blessing—something I never could have imagined.

I literally felt God's love, life, and future flowing into me. My life had changed—even my outlook. That was a time of being loosed from curses, but also from my own incorrect perceptions of myself. Satan no longer had his hand on the throttle of my life; I had been blessed and blessed and blessed, and the blessings wiped out the curses.

We all need to experience and receive the fullness of God's blessings. And I can truthfully say this: when I was blessed by that team, my life inside and out was changed forever.

These FFI seminars are available in many different countries around the world.

Chapter Six

SPIRITUAL WARFARE

A war between the Saint and Satan.

And it is such a bloody one that the cruellest war ever fought by men will be seen as but sport and child's play compared to this. It is a spiritual war that you shall read of; not a history of what was fought many ages past and is now over, but of a war now going on—the tragedy is present with us. And it is not taking place at the farthest end of the world; it concerns you and everyone who reads of it. The stage on which this war is fought is every man's own soul. There are no neutrals in this war. The whole world is engaged in the quarrel either for God, against Satan, or for Satan against God.[49]

THE PURPOSE OF THIS CHAPTER IS TO UNDERSTAND GOD'S SOVEREIGN plan in allowing evil. In all my years of counselling, I have seen firsthand that many born again Christians would agree that we are in a spiritual battle, but they lack the understanding of its severity. They carry no sense of urgency for themselves, let alone for others.

They believe that "Because I am born again and blood washed, Satan and his underlings cannot get to me." Therefore, they refuse to take a stand against the evil ones. This twisted theology leaves all of mankind, particularly believers, wide open to whatever schemes or agenda the evil one would like to impose upon us.

Many of God's people assume, "No worries, I am a believer. God will protect me and provide all my needs." And to some degree, God does do that. But the problem is that Satan does not war against God personally. Should he

---

49   Gurnall, p. 20.

try, he would prematurely find his toes dipping into the burning fires of hell. Satan is too sharp for that—he knows there is no contest.

We have an enemy that works against God's people day and night. Christians are in a war fought in the unseen realm. This "spiritual warfare" has far too many faces to cover in this manual.

As a practitioner with more than twenty-five years of practice in this realm, I aim to provide you with practical tools along with a greater understanding of spiritual warfare.

"You said in your heart: 'I will ascend to the heavens; I will raise my throne above the stars of God; I will sit enthroned on the mount of assembly, on the utmost heights of Mount Zaphon. I will ascend above the tops of the clouds; I will make myself like the Most High'" (Isaiah 14:13–14). Those are Satan's words!

At the moment of Satan's fall from glory, God could have wiped out evil forever had He chose to do so. However, today humans are still led into rebellion against God by the Devil and his cohorts.

This war is a result of the finished work of Jesus Christ, who died on the cross and rose again for the salvation of all mankind. Christ's resurrection is what really turned the heat up on Satan's side. Jesus's resurrection is the thorn of hatred that drives the enemy.

I truly believe that Satan is loosing thousands upon thousands of demons—equipped, knowledgeable, and full of hate—with the thought that they can destroy mankind. It cannot be denied.

The body of Christ needs to be intentional; we can no longer be casual in our walk with God. Jesus Himself identified Satan as the father of murder and untruth, and explained that we do have an enemy. Revelation 12:7–9 tells us that he has a vast army under him.

Ever since the moment of Satan's fall, these two kingdoms have been in conflict. Spiritual warfare is not just two superpowers fighting for control. A fight between good and evil is too simplistic a description for what it really is: major warfare between Satan and God's saints. Today, we not only participate in the conflict, but we become the central focus around which this conflict revolves.

6.1. The Occult

There are many faces of the occult, described by the following quote by Hoover.

"Occult" is used to describe those happenings which either transcend or seem to transcend the world of the five senses (sight, touch, taste, smell and hearing). The word itself comes from the Latin and can be correctly translated with the following words: hidden, secret, dark, mysterious, and concealed. Using the above definition, three distinct characteristics of the occult come to the forefront:

1. The occult deals with things secret or hidden.
2. The occult deals with operations or events which seem to depend on human powers that go beyond the five senses.
3. The occult deals with the supernatural, the presence of angelic or demonic forces.

Using that broad definition of the word occult, all phenomena which properly fall under that definition can be included in one of three categories:

- Fortune-telling—the art of forecasting future events and human character.
- Magick—the ability to bring about results beyond human power by recourse to superhuman spirit agencies (Satan and demons). The magic referred to in this monograph is not the "pull-the-rabbit-out-of-the-hat" type of magic. Technically speaking, the magic we are dealing with in the study of the occult is spelled M-A-G-I-C-K in order not to confuse it with popular entertainment.

- Spiritism—a spiritual activity grounded in the belief that by means of certain persons, certain mediums, people can make contact with the deceased and obtain revelations from the beyond. While almost all occult phenomena can be included in the three categories listed above, in many instances, an occultist can be involved in more than one of the categories. For example, a person involved in black magic may also practice some of the phenomena occurring in spiritism.[50]

6.2. Examples of Spiritual Warfare

The following quotes provide information about different areas of spiritual warfare.

6.2.1. New Age

The New Age Movement appears to be a confusing and contradictory mix—until one understands that there are two distinct expressions of the movement: the occult and the humanistic. The occult expression involves such ideas and practices as reincarnation, crystal power, channeling spirit guides, UFO phenomenon and the worship of self. The humanistic expression focuses on developing unlimited human potential and an ethical system centered in responsibility only to one's self. The occult expression of the New Age attracts those interested in the latest fad. For that reason it is often dismissed as trivial. While the practice of some New Age fads—the use of crystals, sitting under a pyramid—may decrease, the occult New Age is not trivial. It has left behind a trail of spiritual death, and it continues to endure because of the great number of its participants. The humanistic New Age Movement has been around ever since Satan convinced Adam and Eve that they could be the equal of God. Down through the centuries, like a chameleon, it has

---

50   Hoover, p. 8.

changed its colors in order to blend into a new environment. It continues to promote Satan's agenda as it seeks to involve every social, cultural, and religious aspect of life in his deceptive lies. Since New Age humanism is synonymous with the fall of humanity, it will remain until Jesus comes again.[51]

6.2.2. Schools Exposing Children to the New Age

Even the very young are being targeted.

Saturday-morning cartoons are proving to toddlers that "I AM THE POWER!" They are told that there are "good" sorceresses and witches and shamans and wizards who have access to untold power, and that telepathy and telekinesis (and those words are the exact ones used) are normal and useful abilities to cultivate. In growing numbers of schools around the country, the children are being taught how to contact their spirit guides (euphemistically called their "Higher Self" or their "Inner Wisdom") to help them solve problems. They are being sent home with assignments to research their astrological sign or to draw a mandala for art class or to practice the exciting rituals which little Elizabeth and Jennifer and Amanda do in some very popular children's books in order to become initiated into Witchcraft, just as they were. In Gifted-and-Talented programs children are given projects dealing with Ouija boards: how to build them and use them, how to read palms, and how to be like the "amazing Mrs. Hughes," who helps policemen find missing bodies. They are being taught Yoga, meditation and techniques of guided imagery/visualization long used by shamans, mediums, and other occultists in the practice of their religion. Despite overwhelming documentation of suicides and murders associated with it, Dungeons and Dragons now has a special edition of their "game" especially for use in school.[52]

---

51   Lochhaas, pp. 8–9.
52   Michaelsen, pp. 13–14.

Hatha-Yoga. There is a common misconception in the West that hatha-yoga, one of about ten forms of Yoga that supposedly leads to self-realization, is merely a neutral form of exercise, a soothing and effective alternative for those who abhor jogging and calisthenics. After all, the YMCA, the Boy Scouts, and the Girl Scouts (and any number of schools and churches) include it in their programs, so there couldn't possibly be anything dangerous or mystical or religious about it, could there? An article entitled "What is Yoga?" that appeared in Boy's Life, a magazine popular among the Boy Scouts, presents Yoga as "a set of ancient poses and exercises that stretch the muscles, strengthen the body and discipline the mind," a "sport" that "promotes strength and calmness," a "good tool for dealing with whatever challenges—mental or physical—that come along." The author of the article informs her young readers that "Yoga... means discipline," and heartily encourages them to become involved in it. Actually, the Sanskrit root word for Yoga, yug or yuj, means "to yoke, to unite or to bind." It also means "union" or "communion." The whole point of Yoga is "Self-Realization"—that is, to experience your divinity as you yoke yourself to Brahman (the "Infinite," the "Universal Spirit," the impersonal force that the Hindus call "God").[53]

6.2.3. Halloween

We can trace the beginnings of Halloween all the way back to the practices of the ancient druids at their winter festival on October 31.

Although Halloween as commonly practiced today is a seemingly innocent time for most youngsters, it is a very serious observance for many witches, neo-pagans and other occultists.... Reading through various histories of Halloween one is struck by the large number of superstitions and divinatory practices involved.... All things considered, however, we think the most prudent and wise decision for Halloween is abstinence. Why? ...Halloween

---

53   Michaelsen, pp. 93–94.

symbolism and activities today, although technically removed from their ancient practices, nevertheless retain the underlying associations for which they were intended. In other words, the very act of dressing or costuming oneself heralds back to the original purpose for which this was done.[54]

If we are involved in Halloween, we are sinning by association. *"Although they know God's righteous decree that those who do such things deserve death, they not only continue to do these very things but also approve of those who practice them"* (Romans 1:32).

We must remember, the smallest seed of curiosity or engagement gives the enemy legal right to take us deeper in his schemes. *"For you were once darkness, but now you are light in the Lord. Live as children of light (for the fruit of the light consists in all goodness, righteousness and truth) and find out what pleases the Lord. Have nothing to do with the fruitless deeds of darkness, but rather expose them"* (Ephesians 5:8–11).

In addition to Halloween, there are other days where we must be on guard. Think of these days as a call to action to pray against the attacks of Satan and draw closer to God in praise and worship.

There are documented unholy days when certain rituals and sacrifices (animal and human) are performed in formal satanism: February 2, March 20 (spring equinox), April 26–May 1, June 21 (summer solstice), August 3, September 22 (fall equinox), October 29–November 1 (All Hallows' Eve), and December 22–24 (winter solstice). Christians should be aware that hideous abuse of children, defamation of Christ and human sacrifices do occur on these dates. We should follow the Lord's signals in prayer. Some of us can sense or feel the added pressure and power of evil in the atmosphere on certain days or seasons. How should we respond during these times? We should watch for an increase in depression, discouragement, and disturbance of sleep. We should engage in prayer that is proactive and pre-emptive and guard ourselves, our

---

54   Ankerberg & Weldon, pp. 9, 15, 22.

family members and our fellow workers. We must learn to pray with knowledge and discernment, releasing the light of the Holy Spirit to penetrate and weaken the effects of darkness and convict those practicing these things and lead them to truth. These dates and seasons should be opportunities for the Church to enter into strong praise, worship and celebration of the Lordship of Christ.[55]

Spiritual Warfare has Many Faces: In the early 1980s, my wife and I took a road trip down through the central part of the province of British Columbia. We were going to visit some friends, and do some ministry with them. When we entered the home of our friends, something hit me on my forehead, wrapped itself around my head, and left as fast as it had come. As we were moving into some ministry time with our friends, I told them what had happened to me when I entered their home. With their consent I was able to command that demon to identify itself (see Chapter 10 on Deliverance for the method to deal with demonic activity).

The demon claimed to be the overarching demonic authority over that particular area, working through the Women's Liberation Movement (WLM), and there was no doubt that he was. This demon was livid because his scheme to promote WLM was uncovered. He boasted that after many tries over many years, they had finally broken through into the central part of British Columbia and had become deeply rooted in key people who were promoting the movement.

In those years, I took this demon to be just another demon. Today I would say that it was a principality over the city and area, and without a doubt, it was reaching as far and as wide as it could into the surrounding areas. The demon's intent was to saturate those areas with Women's Liberation propaganda.

This husband and wife had both grown up in strong Christian homes, and were living a life that glorified Christ. The wife admitted that she had been involved in the WLM several years ago in a different province. But when she realized the intent of the movement was to remove men from their God-given headship, she removed herself from the organization and become an advocate against it.

---

55   White, p. 204.

So, why the exposure of the demon in their home that night? In hindsight, I believe this demon didn't voluntarily identify itself, but was forced to do so by the hand of God, specifically for His purpose and timing in exposing Satan's current activities in that area. I believe it was also so we would uncover the movement and give the wife some understanding of WLM's purpose and goals (although that would have been unknown to her), so we could stand against the evil schemes of the devil in relation to this movement.

Interestingly, on our way home from this trip, we stopped for lunch. Attached to the restaurant was a New Age store; of course, we had no interest in purchasing from there. We had our meal and on the way out, we decided to walk through the store. We were in there for only two or three minutes when I began to get sick. I was worsening each second. Needless to say, we left. Our car was parked close by, and by the time my wife and I had reached the car I couldn't stand without support. I was on my knees with both hands on the door handle trying to open the door—all my strength had left me.

We left, and about fifteen or twenty kilometers down the road, we could feel the darkness lifting off us. A few hours later we were fine.

A few years later, we were driving through that little town, and as we drove by the New Age store we felt the darkness we had experienced years ago coming upon us again. Our snap decision was not to gas up there!

The New Age Movement may be new to this generation, but it is as old as Satan's deception to Eve. It is just one of many of Satan's schemes.

Here is an interesting tidbit of information relating to the incident I just shared:

Have you ever come away from contact with a place, such as a New Age bookstore or movie theater, and found yourself feeling fearful, confused, even doubting your faith? When this happens, don't be so quick to ignore your feelings or rationalize them away. Ask the Holy Spirit for discernment. Be quick to respond with prayer for protection. As ambassadors of an invisible kingdom, we simply need to understand the reality behind the veil of visible events. We may unknowingly find ourselves caught between the clashing of the kingdoms of light and darkness.[56]

I have shared these stories to give you a picture of our enemy who never sleeps and is always looking for ways to employ his schemes. You may be asking, "How on earth could this ever take place?" Remember, we are dealing with spiritual warfare.

6.2.4. Binding and Loosing

Matthew 18:18 is the biblical platform upon which we base our teaching on binding and loosing: *"Truly I tell you, whatever you bind on earth will be bound in heaven, and whatever you loose on earth will be loosed in heaven"* (Matthew 18:18).

I have included the concept of binding and loosing in this chapter so you will understand it is also a form of spiritual warfare. When this Scripture is applied properly, it has incredible ability to assist in the work of setting the captives free from demonic attachments (see Chapter 10, Deliverance, Section 10.8.1., for the practice and application of binding and loosing).

What I endeavour to do in this chapter is to deal with the current day questioning of the relevance of binding and loosing, by professionals as well as lay people. If you carry out a bit of research on this topic, you will find that binding and loosing was considered the job of the priesthood. Many in our day are not far removed from that way of thinking, claiming that binding and loosing are not for laypeople. Others I have spoken to or ministered with believe that binding and loosing is not relevant for us this side of the Cross of Jesus Christ.

But time after time and in numerous ways, I have found that binding and loosing has only enhanced my success as I work against the powers of darkness in setting the captives free!

Foster & King say, "The work of binding and loosing—binding the strong man and losing his captives—the work that dominated Jesus' ministry

---

and filled his vision, will be the work of his disciples during the period of his absence."[57] (Please refer to Chapter 10 for further information.)

6.2.5. Demonized Children

One of the horrors from hell that always lies on my heart is the demonization of the very young. This might come about through incest by a family member or molestation by somebody like the next door neighbour's son, a friend of the family, and the list goes on.

While counselling, I've often come across children that were demonized while in utero. This is more common than you would think. This occurs as a result of a mother having intercourse with multiple partners while pregnant. These children begin to act out sexually by the time they are three or four years old.

It is impossible for children that young to be sexually active. But what appears sexual to us is actually the demon who gained access to the child via the mother's sexual activity. This allows the enemy to demonize her on the inside—to come in like a flood and live inside her person. From within, the demons manifest through the child.

The first time I became aware of this type of child sexualization was while attending an Ancient Paths seminar, taught by Craig Hill, founder of Family Foundations International, a ministry that works all over the world today (see Toolbox at back of this manual). I said to myself, "I simply cannot believe this." But God must have had me there just to hear that story, for less than a month later I had an almost identical situation in my office.

Now, many years later, I've worked with a few dozen families where this has been an issue. The symptoms are often quite similar. For example, a four-year-old boy sitting on his mom's friend's lap reaches into her dress to touch her breast. The mother, embarrassed by her son's behaviour, scolds him, but her friend says, "Don't be angry with him, he's only four, and he doesn't know what he's doing." This is true; the child doesn't know what he is doing. But the demons know very well.

One family that I worked with had an eighteen-month-old daughter and a son who was not yet four years old. The mother left the little girl naked on

---

57   Foster & King, p. 64.

the bed while grabbing a diaper. By the time she came back, her son had taken off all his clothes and was on top of the little girl, attempting penetration.

This type of activity doesn't happen by chance. No, Satan and his cohorts are on duty twenty-four hours a day to ensure no evil opportunities are missed, and he knows how to move people into place at the right time—to bring about a marriage breakdown as a result of a few minutes of lust, or to line things up so a four-year-old girl is sexually violated by an uncle while her mom was out for morning coffee with a friend.

I've worked with many individuals over the years (fathers, mothers, older siblings, or the boy next door) that have come in for personal ministry because, years back as a child, they were sexually violated. I've also ministered to perpetrators seeking personal freedom and reconciliation. God has created us as sexual beings and has given us what we need to be sexually active, not just for propagation but also for our pleasure—within the confines of marriage. However, mankind has perverted our sexual being by giving lust freedom to do what it desires to do. In our society today, lust runs rampant.

The following is a simple illustration of the flow of lust. In this particular scenario, a fifteen-year-old male babysitter became curious and looked, just a bit, while changing the diaper of the little girl—a seemingly harmless act. But the next time the babysitter came, the outcome was a little different. This time, he'd been thinking about touching what he'd seen last time—and he did. The third time, the babysitter was of course totally unaware that he was now lusting, and what was attached to him was a demon of lust. He intended just to touch the little girl's private parts, but again he found himself doing with his fingers something he didn't want to do—but he wasn't to stop himself: This is spiritual warfare.

Before I was born again, I was like the fellow on the radio, singing the song of that day: "I'm just standing on the corner, watching all the girls go by."

After I became a believer, I worked to bring a stop to this sin. Once when a beautiful girl stepped out in front of me, I immediately turned my head to avert my eyes, but they were involuntarily driven back to look at her. I was a new Christian, and I experienced for the first time—or at least recognized for the first time—demonic working from inside of my person. This, of course, caused me to look for someone with experience in this realm.

I know this might sound unbelievable, but I've seen it personally, and have heard stories from many that have come in for ministry. The fact is, demons cannot just crawl or walk into our person. If a demon makes its way in, it's because of some personal ongoing sin issues. But there are other means by which the enemy enters, as you will see throughout the book.

Generational sins often chisel their way into our soul. They aren't just looking for a home to live in. No! They have their plan—to control you from the inside, with what I call "personality demons" (see more on this type of demon in Chapter 10 on Deliverance). If they aren't found out, little by little their thoughts become yours. They will look through your eyes and talk through your mouth, while using your hands, fingers and feet for whatever evil intent they can conjure up.

Stop! Don't Burn the Book! Remember, this is Spiritual Warfare. It was a demon that literally forced my eyes off to the left to watch the woman in front of me walk away. It was a demon that moved the hand of the four-year-old to touch the breast of his mother's friend. It was a demon using the hand of the male babysitter to do things to the little girl he would have never had done if he'd had control. We all say, "I would never, ever do that." Well you can say that, but if you are living outside the center of the road of righteousness, wanting and lusting after the things of the flesh, then you too may very well find yourself involuntarily doing what you want not to do. (Side note: a demon cannot just come in by their own free will and molest a child. It needs a helper, and that helper can be many things, but often lust permeates a home simply because of the sexual content on television and the adult reading material that is left for all to see. It can be as simple as that.)

I have heard many similar stories, and have prayed for many now in their thirties, forties, and even older who want to deal with sexual issues that began in their very early teens. They are now married and passing this sickening spirit of lust on to their next generation.

That initial seed of sexual lust, from the very early age of ten, has now become generational:

Inherited spirits of lust are frequently to blame for allowing the sexual spirits of Incubus and Succubus to operate while a person is asleep. What happens is that the individual will have a very vivid dream in which he or she is approached by a "person" who either asks to have sex with him or her, or actually engages in sex. The "person" may act in a heterosexual or homosexual manner, and a sexual climax ensues as the individual awakens. The "person," if acting as a male, is not just a mental fantasy, but actually a demon called Incubus; and if it acts as a female, it is a demon named Succubus. I find these to be very foul, uninvited evil spirits that often, but not always, follow family lines. Some very bold ones will even attack a person during the day. When evicting them, I call them by name, and they often leave with a pronounced jolt in the body of their host. It seems as though their cover is shattered when they are called by name.[58]

I have ministered to some individuals who were involved with these Succubus (female) or Incubus (male) demons. People with these demons, even those confessing to be born-again believers, were still fighting to get totally free from demon-driven sex. It is said that breaking free from this kind of sex is akin to quitting street drugs. This too is spiritual warfare.

A Footnote to the Material Just Read: You may be the parent of a child who was molested. No matter how minor or far back in time, the incident may need prayer for inner healing and forgiveness. Then authority needs to be taken and the demon must be removed from the individual (please see the process of deliverance in Chapter 10). It is very common for demons of lust to attach themselves to or hang around those who've been sexually violated, waiting for an opportunity.

In my experience, the majority of the young who are sexually abused come from family lines with generational sins. This is critical information: it may have been the boy next door who sexually violated your daughter. But it was the unknown and *undealt with generational curse* of sexual molestation in *your family* that allowed the enemy to use the boy to molest your daughter!

---

58   D. Wagner, pp. 159–160.

When ministering in this area, refer to the chapters on forgiveness (3), generational sins (5), prayer (7 and 8), and deliverance (10).

One other type of spiritual warfare against young children is the stuff that makes its way into their bedrooms during the dark hours of the night. Many of us parents experienced this weird phenomena when we were children. Despite this, we often have no comfort to offer our young sons or daughters as they come crying into our bedrooms because of something that spoke to them out of the darkness of the night.

Because this activity is a mystery for most parents, they tell their young child to go back to bed. The child then is left to deal with the situation on their own, feeling fearful and abandoned. This is good news for Satan and his crew. He will begin by increasing fear, providing some bumps throughout the night, which only increases the feelings of loneliness and abandonment.

Worse yet, actual spiritual torment in the child's sleeping state is far more common than you realize. A few years may have passed, and some may still be experiencing odd things during the dark hours of the night. For others at the age of ten or twelve, they haven't experienced anything in years, and it seems that whatever it may have been, it was harmless. Maybe a friendly "ghost," like Mom said, that would harm no one. But what Mom and Dad don't realize until it's too late is that their fifteen-year-old daughter has become captivated by the things that come and go at night. No more youth group or church for this girl—just a bedroom full of all she can find on the dark side of the supernatural.

These things that make their way into our bedrooms at night are nothing other than Satan's demons, as are the beings that move about in haunted houses. These demons are commonly portrayed as spirits or ghosts of the dead, looking for a dwelling place. They're all demons. Ankerberg says, "Witchcraft, poltergeists, and other forms of spiritism tend to go hand in hand. Biblically this means witchcraft is involved with the powers of darkness. If these spirits and ghosts are really demons, no other conclusion is possible."[59] Ankerberg continues: "These spirits are not what they claim (spirits of the human dead), but are lying spirits that the Bible identifies as demons."[60]

---

59   Ankerberg & Weldon, p. 55.

60   Ibid., p. 46.

The jury is in. The verdict: all the spooky nighttime phenomena in homes are nothing other than Satan's evil angels. So, assuming they are generated by the powers of darkness, let us now go back to the fifteen-year-old girl who, born and raised as a Christian, was not protected from the darkness that knocked on her bedroom door. No doubt, there were many reasons why this girl ended up where she was. But the biggest reason is because much of the Body of Christ Jesus does not believe that these nighttime encounters that have our children running into our bedrooms in the middle of the night are a very powerful type of spiritual warfare. We have never taken time to determine the sources of this nighttime activity. Why? Because we think it harmless.

This ideology leaves the father, mother, children, and home spiritually naked—a wide-open target for the evil ones. Others never inquire about the bumps in the night because their belief is that Satan was defeated by Jesus on the Cross (which is absolutely correct). But their belief that "once born again, Satan and his demons cannot get to us or harass us in any way," is deeply flawed. This skewed theology leaves God's people unprepared, uncovered, and wide open to whatever schemes the hosts of hell may have to fling our way. And our children often take the brunt of it!

Part of being prepared both day and night is living in obedience to the Word of God, where it says, *"Put on the full armor of God, so that you can take your stand against the devil's schemes"* (Ephesians 6:11). Applying this Scripture in the context of spiritual warfare, the armour of God is God's provided protection and direction for all children, which is to be managed by the father and priest of the home.

If this had been in place in the home of the fifteen-year-old girl, with the father giving biblical direction for their protection and covering of the home and family, they would never have lost her.

To illustrate the help and protection that is within the authority of every Christian, please read the factual story a friend allowed me to include in this book. This incident occurred about a year after he and his wife became Christians.

The young father and his wife had recently been saved and were joyfully serving the Lord. Children's bedtime "Jesus songs" and tuck-in prayer had become a nightly practice. One night, shortly after the father fell asleep, his three-year-old boy appeared at his bedside. The boy was frightened, complaining that his bed was shaking so much he couldn't sleep.

Dad assumed it was just a dream. The solid wood-framed bed on a concrete floor couldn't be shaking. He reassured and quieted the boy and sent him back to bed. Dad had hardly drifted off when the little boy appeared again and almost in tears said, "Daddy, it's still shaking." Dad sighed and again calmed the boy, but pulled him into bed to hold him and settle him. After the child relaxed, he once more sent him back to his own bed. In a matter of two minutes the little boy was back and almost shouting through his tears of frustration and fear, *"Daddy, the bed is really shaking!"*

So, Daddy dragged himself out of bed, resigned to sitting with the child until he fell asleep. He tucked his precious little one under the covers in the darkened room and sat on the floor at his side. As soon as he sat down, his son exclaimed, "See Daddy? The bed really is shaking!" Dad reached and placed his hand on the bed. What a shock! The bed certainly was shaking rapidly from side to side. Still not understanding, he placed one hand on the concrete floor under the bed and the other on his son's shoulder. Neither son nor floor were shaking. The floor was concrete, the bed was solid wood, and the walls were not moving...

Suddenly the hair stood up on Daddy's neck as he realized that the presence of a harassing demon was the only explanation. This young dad, an inexperienced but truly born-again believer, was suddenly filled with righteous anger. He spoke out a loud command, "How dare you! You foul spirit, in Jesus' name leave this place and never return!" Immediately the shaking stopped.

To the young father's knowledge, this experience was never repeated. From that day forward, as soon as each child could understand, they began to be trained in spiritual warfare. Each child asked Jesus to be their Saviour and Lord soon after they could understand what that meant. They each learned to effectively use the name of Jesus against harassing, frightening spirits, creatures, noises and any other questionable happenings.

The family was eventually blessed with five children. As they grew up, most of them reported seeing or experiencing at least one or two "visitations" or harassing noises. However, they had been taught that they had power over the devil and his helpers in the name of Jesus, and they used it to drive out the spiritual attack. Though sometimes frightened by the encounters, the children knew Dad and Mom would believe their story and help them. The parents also regularly prayed God's protection and the covering of Jesus' blood over the children.

Thirty-six years have passed since then, and all five children plus their families are Christians and serving the Lord Jesus today. Now, the grandparents and the parents of the newest generation are training and preparing the little ones for victory in Jesus' name.

Instructional Prayer on Headship: The following is a prayer to use as priest of the home. God put the earthly father in place as priest and gatekeeper for the home. As the Israelites applied the blood of the Passover Lamb to their door frames, so shall you, as the priest of your home, apply oil to your door frames and window frames, declaring as you go along:

> This oil is symbolic of the work of the Holy Spirit and the blood of the Passover Lamb, Jesus, against you, Satan, because we are blood-bought, blood-washed, and forgiven; through the finished work of Jesus Christ, you are defeated. I declare, in the name of Jesus Christ, my Passover Lamb, that you, Satan and your cohorts, must leave our individual persons as well as this property and home. I also declare that you cannot return, and should you ever pass by, you also must pass over.

6.2.6. Harry Potter and Stephen King

When I look back, I think of young people who were indoctrinated by Stephen King's books. These books really took off in the early seventies, and were considered harmless reading. Today, though, I have performed deliverance with many individuals for whom the first door for demonization was their involvement in King's books.

However, the Harry Potter series is, in my mind, much more lethal, because it openly teaches witchcraft. What will our world look like, a generation or two from now, should Jesus tarry? There is no doubt in my mind that Satan is working hard for the minds of our young generations, and he is stealing many through gruesome, much-hyped horror novels.

Parents Be Aware:

> Stephen King wrote in the *New York Times Review of Books* ("Wild About Harry," July 23, 2000) that the Potter series, which he loves, would provide children with a good introduction to his own gruesome and demonic horror novels when they are old enough to read them. Contrary to the media hype, this is not good news for the children, or adults, of today. Some celebrate that children are reading the massive Potter books instead of watching television. They need to rethink their options. To be sure, television is, more often than not, a moral, spiritual and intellectual wasteland; but so are the Potter books. In fact, many self-proclaimed pagan groups sing the praises of Rowling's books, and some young people have reported their desire to become witches after reading of their spell-casting hero, Harry Potter.[61]

Abanes, a well-published expert in cults and the occult, meticulously inspects the Potter books and reveals their connection to nearly every facet of the occult—alchemy, astrology, spells, mediumship, and other pagan practices. He demonstrates that these books desensitize children and others to the forbidden and dangerous world of pagan magic (Deuteronomy 18:9–14; Galatians 5:20; Revelation 22:15).

However beautifully Satan has wrapped the package, it is still evil. Satan knows full well that for most believers, if he were to offer us the apple of Adam and Eve, he would be the loser. So, he now comes to us by saying, "You cannot eat of this apple, for if you do, you will surely be separated from your God. But it is okay to look at it, to hold it, and to smell it."

If you were to even smell it, he would surely have you. You see, you smelled it because you were curious, and now curiosity has your attention. All Satan needs is our curiosity to gain an advantage. It may be only the size of

---

61   Abanes, p. x.

a pinprick to start, but he knows how to lure us in. Satan is a master in temptation. If we are not cognizant of his schemes, little by little he will lead us to take that bite. An example can be found in the New Age movement, where some say, "Oh, I really love New Age music; I find it so relaxing." There you are—you bit into the bait. Well, consider this: the host is Satan and his crew.

What Does God's Word Say?: The above is the way of the world. The following Scripture is the way God has set for His people.

When you enter the land the Lord your God is giving you, do not learn to imitate the detestable ways of the nations there. Let no one be found among you who sacrifices their son or daughter in the fire, who practices divination or sorcery, interprets omens, engages in witchcraft, or casts spells, or who is a medium or spiritist or who consults the dead. Anyone who does these things is detestable to the Lord; because of these same detestable practices the Lord your God will drive out those nations before you. You must be blameless before the Lord your God. The nations you will dispossess listen to those who practice sorcery or divination. But as for you, the Lord your God has not permitted you to do so.
—Deuteronomy 18:9–14

And further:

The acts of the flesh are obvious: sexual immorality, impurity and debauchery; idolatry and witchcraft; hatred, discord, jealousy, fits of rage, selfish ambition, dissensions, factions and envy; drunkenness, orgies, and the like. I warn you, as I did before, that those who live like this will not inherit the kingdom of God.
—Galatians 5:19–21

Let us apply the Scripture just read to the messages promoted by Stephen King and Harry Potter. If you allow your children to read such material, you could very well be sacrificing them to wicked gods. That, too, is a form of spiritual warfare!

6.3. The Bigger Picture

6.3.1. The Conflict of Two Kingdoms

The intention of this book is not to establish the reality of Satan and his co-horts. No! This is a battle that is intensifying as we get closer to the end days and the return of Christ. This is a war in which every born again believer enters into by default. He or she is instructed by the Apostle Paul first to be strong (see Ephesians 6:10–18).

A believer who is engaged in the battle here on earth has the protection of Jesus, and regardless of the end result of this raging battle, he or she is guaranteed heaven for all eternity.

6.3.2. Is There Really a Battle?

Some time ago, a pastor asked me to meet with him and a family from his congregation for prayer ministry. In the course of the evening, I mentioned that we are taught by the Word of God to do battle. The pastor replied saying, "I don't see anywhere in the Bible saying we are in a war." Therein lies the problem—we do not see.

Since the fall of man, brought about by the deception of Eve and the disobedience of Adam, and by the evil one, Satan himself (Genesis 3), God's people have been unknowingly engaged in this battle. Because of the battles, the ditches of the highways and byways are filled with God's people, from ancient times until our present day. Satan's ability to deceive—as he did with Adam and Eve—is still his best weapon. There is the battle. Day by day, Satan taunts us, trying to draw us into his wicked schemes, hoping always to bring us into alignment with his evil agenda and turn from God. Once again, this is the battle, and every born-again believer fights it (most of us unaware of the force of Satan's deceptive power).

We, who are His through the shed blood of Jesus, know we are on the winning side. But until Jesus steps onto the clouds of heaven and brings an end to this conflict, and takes us home, we are Satan's target!

When I was two years old in Christ Jesus, I had the privilege of spending time with a pastor who helped me to recognize God's call on my life in deliverance-type ministry. During our time together, he shared with me that he had been setting people free via deliverance for thirty years—and that the battle had intensified over those thirty years.

Well, I can now add my twenty-five plus years of practicing deliverance to his thirty years and say the same. There is no doubt in my mind that Satan is turning up the heat. He does that in at least two ways: by releasing more demons against a deliverance session, and by sending higher ranking demons.

Today, Satan is building up his forces against God's people with a vengeance. Because of his intense anger against God and his hatred for mankind, he is raging around the globe, twenty-four hours a day, seven days a week.

And we are his target. Each one of us really need to consider our part in this battle, and then report for active duty because "... *our struggle is not against flesh and blood, but against the rulers, against the authorities, against the powers of this dark world and against the spiritual forces of evil in the heavenly realms*" (Ephesians 6:12). We're engaged in spiritual warfare—whether we know it or not, whether we want to be or don't.

If you are a born-again believer, you are in the battle by default, and denial of that fact will get you no mercy from Satan's host from hell. There is no doubt in my mind that Satan has a well-structured war machine. The battle is being fought by Satan and his millions, aggressively campaigning against God's chosen. Satan knows very well where he will be spending his time for all of eternity. This knowledge causes him indescribable hatred towards God—it is like gasoline poured on fire, and it will eventually consign him to the burning fires of hell forever and ever.

While casting out an angry demon that is fighting to hang on, I often remind it that it is the defeated foe and its destiny is the fires of hell. And the response back to me by the demon being cast out is often, "Yes, it's true, but we're taking lots of yours with us!" This statement from the demon should provoke a question: What side of the fence am I on?

Satan is not, first and foremost, against mankind. He is against God, and because he cannot destroy God, he pours out all his wrath on God's creation. We know from the Word that Satan was thrown out of heaven.

Principle #22: Spiritual warfare is Satan's quest to take as many to hell with him as he possibly can.

I must reiterate: spiritual warfare is Satan's continuing quest to take as many to hell with him as he possibly can. And he does it in an infinite number of ways, each one drawing mankind into sin. Once he gets us to sin, he then works to turn us against each other, bringing division into our homes, churches, and ministries. Unknowingly, we will soon have joined our enemy in the work of accusing the Beloved of God.

This scheme often backfires on Satan, because more often than not the pressure Satan puts on us to turn our back on God is the impetus we need to open our hearts to Him. Yes, God does use Satan as the refiner.

> *"See, it is I who created the blacksmith who fans the coals into flame and forges a weapon fit for its work. And it is I who have created the destroyer to work havoc; no weapon forged against you will prevail, and you will refute every tongue that accuses you. This is the heritage of the servants of the Lord, and this is their vindication from me," declares the Lord.*
> —Isaiah 54:16–17

Before we move on, these questions beg answers: Where and when did evil come from? How could evil ever fit into God's Kingdom plan? Genesis 1:4, 10, 18, 21, and 25 tell us that God did not create anything that was evil. *"God saw all that he had made, and it was very good"* (Genesis 1:31). God initially created a kingdom of complete sinlessness, but something changed. In Ezekiel 28:11–19, there is a graphic illustration of Satan's fall as explained in the verses: *"You were blameless in your ways from the day you were created till wickedness was found in you. Through your widespread trade you were filled with violence and you sinned"* (Ezekiel 28:15–16).

First Biblical Illustration of Spiritual Warfare: Let us look at a few Biblical illustrations of the ongoing conflict, starting with the creation of mankind in Genesis 1:26–31, where God said, *"It was very good"* (verse 31). Now, in Genesis chapter 3, we see the first recorded encounter between mankind and Satan. Satan is the master deceiver (Genesis 3:1). Consequently, Eve's confession was, *"The serpent deceived me, and I ate"* (Genesis 3:13), resulting in God's judgement on Adam (Genesis 3:17–19).

What a catastrophic event was the fall of man! Going from the fullness of God's blessing to painful toil, giving birth in pain, and eking out a living. Eve was deceived, but Adam was disobedient, choosing to take the fruit from the hand of Eve and eat it. Adam was not deceived, confused, or disillusioned; he just chose to be disobedient, and in that, he sinned. Innocence was shattered, and everyone born from that moment on was born with a sin nature. Sin had entered all of mankind. But God, through Jesus, provided redemption for all who will receive Him.

But we can still find ourselves being sent away from God's presence as a consequence of continued sin. Fear not: God has provided for His fallen a place of refuge, a place where every question can be answered and every sin forgiven. This is a crossroad, the place from where we find our way back to God. (You may tire of the term "crossroad," for it is used many times in this manual. It may apply while working out a principle, or asking God for direction in whatever your need may be. Your success is incumbent upon your ability to stand and listen.)

Spiritual warfare is driven by raging anger and hatred towards the human race. Satan and his millions are working overtime to take as many people as they can with them into the burning fires of hell. Until the final curtain closes on Satan's reign of terror, deception, killing and destroying, it requires that we, the army of God, have an understanding of the significance of our times, and more importantly, the understanding of the potential of Satan and his hosts from hell to do us harm.

Evil is increasing in our time by leaps and bounds. All around the world, God's army is required to be fully dressed in the armour of God, understanding that its strength and protective ability is effective only to the degree of our righteousness in Christ. A full, strong, and protective armour comes only through relationship with God, in Christ Jesus. There is no doubt that what I have just said will be troubling for some people. But the truth remains: if you have been a Christian for some time and have never built a relationship with Jesus Christ, then your armour has no protective strength.

Maybe your response is "Yes, I do have the protective Blood of Jesus." Maybe not, if you are knowingly living in sin.

The existence of Satan and evil conjures up many questions such as, "Why doesn't God deal with Satan once and forever?" Well, one day He will!

God has a place for the evil ones, and they fit right into His plan of salvation for all mankind. God's plan for Satan is that he is to be the chisel, rasp and hammer in the maturing process of His saints. *"As iron sharpens iron, so one person sharpens another"* (Proverbs 27:17). We each become the rasp, shaping each other more and more into the image of our Lord and Saviour Jesus Christ.

If we cannot accept that Satan is a part of God's purpose, then this can lead to tremendous doubts, anger and even resentment towards God. Some people need to repent of their anger for believing that God does not truly care for mankind. Christians and non-Christians alike blame God for many of the bad things that happen in their lives and the lives of their loved ones.

For instance, "If God is a God of love, why did He let my neighbour's little girl get run over by a car?" I can certainly understand those words being spoken by an unbeliever, but by God's own?

6.3.3. Perceptions, and Where They Take Us

The reason people are angry or bitter is because they generally have wrong perceptions of God—for instance, "God doesn't care for or look after His own because He is absent or distant." Let's measure that somewhat common perception against the written Word of God.

"Be alert and of sober mind. Your enemy the devil prowls around like a roaring lion looking for someone to devour" (1 Peter 5:8). God lovingly warns us that if we continue in sin, Satan will do all he can to devour us. But, as I have mentioned earlier, Satan is the pawn in the hands of God, the blacksmith of

Isaiah 54:16–17. He is also called a usurper, which means he uses or takes something without the right to do so. The problem lies not with God, but with us; our sin makes a way for Satan to move in on us and our families. Many, including born-again believers, believe that everything that happens is God's will. But this is not true. God's will is that none shall perish. To facilitate that, He provided for us the road of life, with left and right turns and a free will.

Accordingly, we must contend with evil because of man's choice. *"Therefore, just as sin entered the world through one man..."* (Romans 5:12). People choose to obey or to disobey—God has given us that freedom. *"But if serving the Lord seems undesirable to you, then choose for yourselves this day whom you will serve, whether the gods your ancestors served beyond the Euphrates, or the gods of the Amorites, in whose land you are living. But as for me and my household, we will serve the Lord"* (Joshua 24:15).

Disobedience always opens the door to evil (John 3:19–21). However, Jesus is at the door. *"Here I am! I stand at the door and knock. If anyone hears my voice and opens the door, I will come in and eat with that person, and they with me"* (Revelation 3:20).

The church of Samaria was told, *"Do not be afraid of what you are about to suffer. I tell you, the devil will put some of you in prison to test you, and you will suffer persecution for ten days. Be faithful, even to the point of death, and I will give you life as your victor's crown"* (Revelation 2:10). That is the test for all of us: will we stand to the end? There are many questions we cannot answer, but out of God's wisdom and His great love for mankind, He has allowed evil to remain on the earth. He has given us the right to choose. We are not bound by God's desire for mankind. We can go the way of Satan, if we choose. Without free will, we would be puppets, managed by God. It is ironic that those who choose the dark road will be managed by Satan for his purposes.

Free will is absolutely necessary for the quality of relationship that God wants us to have with Him. God, in His love for man, has given man the ability to choose right or wrong. God has granted dignity to all of mankind by giving us free will (see John 3:16).

Second Biblical Illustration of Spiritual Warfare: My second illustration involving human sin is the very obvious evil found with Cain and Abel. *"While they were in the field, Cain attacked his brother Abel and killed him"* (Genesis 4:8b).

Some time had passed since Adam and Eve hid from God as He called out, "Adam where are you?" The words, "Where are you?" can be rendered, "What have you done?" We all know that God knows all things at all times. Now Adam and Eve find themselves some years later, no doubt remembering what their disobedience cost them, as they look into the face of their first-born son. God asks Cain, now a full-grown man, "What have you done?" *"Then the Lord said to Cain, 'Why are you angry? Why is your face downcast? If you do what is right, will you not be accepted? But if you do not do what is right, sin is crouching at your door, it desires to have you, but you must rule over it"* (Genesis 4:6–7). Or in other translations, "master it."

With Cain, we see for the first time a man under the spell of his own rage: *"So Cain was very angry and his face was downcast"* (Genesis 4:5). Cain is in a state of deep despondency, stubbornly refusing even to listen to God, let alone follow His counsel. This despondency triggered self-pity, deep anger and jealousy—even though God did not reject Cain, only his offering. God asks Cain to reconsider, saying, "Take another look, Cain; bring the right offering, and you will be accepted. Don't be so angry!" God then gives Cain a warning, saying that sin will take him captive if he does not master it. This is relative to our day: we too can be found in exactly the same place.

It's very interesting that Genesis 4:7 personifies sin and gives it independent life, as if it were an animal, perhaps a serpent, lurking in the doorway to Cain's heart. Sin must be overcome or our heart will face its own demise.

The word "sin" in Genesis 4 is believed to be connected with an Akkadian word meaning "demon" (Hebrew had no word for demon).

> Hamilton says that the Hebrew word for sin here is connected with the Akkadian word "demon, rabisum." In Mesopotamian demonology the rabisum (demon) could be either a benevolent being that lurks at the entrance of a building to protect the occupants, or just the opposite, a malevolent being that lurks at the entrance of a

building to threaten the occupants. Wenham refers to an article by Ramaroson who translates the warning in verse 7, "If you do not do well, the croucher (demon) is at the door."[62]

Spiritual warfare is fuelled by Cain's inability to control his anger and hatred. This, coupled with unforgiveness, had Cain seemingly imprisoned (compare again to the parable of the unmerciful servant in Matthew 18:21–35).

Few things are more destructive to Christians than anger. Anger causes us to lose our self-control and to say and do things we would otherwise never consider. Anger, if allowed to remain, turns into bitterness that eats away at our hearts. Scripture consistently commands believers to put away anger, which is one of the sins of the flesh: *"Get rid of all bitterness, rage and anger, brawling and slander, along with every form of malice"* (Ephesians 4:31).

At times, we try to defend our anger by quoting, *"'In your anger do not sin': Do not let the sun go down while you are still angry... "* (Ephesians 4:26). Ephesians refers to anger that does not necessarily lead to sin. As additional proof, we might argue that Jesus cleansed the temple in "righteous indignation," showing that Jesus was capable of being angry without sinning. However, when Jesus cleared the temple, Scripture does not indicate that He was angry (see Matthew 12:12–14, Mark 11:15–18, and Luke 19:45–46).

We must be careful not to justify our anger with Scripture, but to put away all anger (Ephesians 4:31). That doesn't mean that we cease to have strong convictions or lose our desire for justice, but it does mean that we refuse to allow the sins of others to cause us to sin. Anger does not bring about God's redemptive work; far more often it hinders what God is working to accomplish. If you feel that your anger is righteous, see if you are holding anger in your heart. Is your anger turning into bitterness? Is your anger causing you to speak in an un-Christian manner to someone or to gossip about them? Is your anger causing you to make excuses for your own ungodly behaviour? Is your anger preventing you from acting in a loving, redemptive, and Christlike manner toward someone? You must examine any anger within you and allow God to remove any sinful attitudes that it may have produced (see also "Anger" in the Toolbox).

---

62   Murphy, p. 217, emphasis in original.

Principle #23: Anger causes us to lose self-control and to hold onto unforgiveness.

After years of working with many individuals and couples that were locked up in Satan's jailhouse because of unforgiveness, I came to an understanding of what a hellish place it is. I listened to couples tell their stories of anger and even hatred towards each other, accusing each other of every sin they'd committed. When the accusations seemingly have no end, divorce is crouching on the doorstep. Some couples live like this for months or years, testifying of living in fear, anger, anxiety, hopelessness, or pain. They become separated from each other and from God, submerged in their own anger and unforgiveness. They have no idea that they're in the jailhouse, where Satan is the jailer and his demons the torturers.

I have worked with hundreds that have been born again and seem faithful to the Word of God, but fail in this area of forgiveness. Forgiveness is the most critical principle when it comes to relationships between God and people, and men and women at all levels. Through unforgiveness, they enter Satan's realm and find themselves in the spiritual jailhouse. Anger and unforgiveness are "hot buttons" for Satan, and he knows when to push them. Remember, anger is often the fruit of unforgiveness, as is the silent treatment, and the list goes on. As we continue in unforgiveness, the enemy increases the torture. People feel like they're going crazy, and many of these individuals ending up spending much of their lives in hospitals, when all they needed to do was forgive and be forgiven.

Sin separates us from God. For Adam, *"the Lord God banished him from the Garden of Eden…"* (Genesis 3:23). In other words, Adam went out from the presence of God. For Cain, he *"went out from the Lord's presence and lived in the land of Nod…"* (Genesis 4:16). They both lost the intimate presence of God. As it was then, so it is today.

Most often people are unaware of their ongoing sin. When they are aware, they often prefer to deal with it themselves, not really wanting to come for help. The biggest reason individuals seek help is because of the habitual sin in their lives. The thing is, we all sin and need help from time to time, but habitual sin is more dangerous. The truth is, many people live in habitual sin. They have left the intimate presence of God, living in the place of Nod just as Cain did.

As long as we are habitually sinning, we limit God's blessings and help, sometimes even eliminating His ability to change our lives. Now, it's true that we will not be sinless this side of heaven, but God's purpose is that we grow day by day, putting off the old ways and putting on new ones. *"You were taught, with regard to your former way of life, to put off your old self, which is being corrupted by its deceitful desires…"* (Ephesians 4:22).

Many today are banished from God's presence and miss His best for them because of continued sin. Some may weep and scream at God and think He is deaf, or say, "Well, if He's not deaf, then He simply isn't interested in us individually or our hidden pain." These people may have lost the truth of God due to sin. If we choose to do it our way, we immediately put ourselves in a place of rebellion. If we continue on in some little sin, we are very clearly saying, "I don't need the manifested presence of God in my life!" It is no different today than it was in the Old Testament with Adam and Cain.

Third Biblical Illustration of Spiritual Warfare: A third illustration of spiritual warfare is where the Apostle Paul finds himself defending his ministry and lifestyle, saying,

> *For though we live in the world, we do not wage war as the world does. The weapons we fight with are not the weapons of the world. On the contrary, they have divine power to demolish strongholds. We demolish arguments and every pretension that sets itself up against the knowledge of God, and we take captive every thought to make it obedient to Christ.*
> —2 Corinthians 10:3–5

Paul's fear is that *"…just as Eve was deceived by the serpent's cunning, your minds may somehow be led astray from your sincere and pure devotion to Christ"* (2 Corinthians 11:3).

The New Testament leaves open the possibility for God's people to be led into disobedience by Satan, just as Eve was. In Ephesians 6:10–18, Paul makes it very clear that we are to be prepared for war by putting on the full armour of God.

6.3.4. The What and Why of the Full Armour of God

Practically and experientially, does the overarching Western worldview leave open the possibility of spiritual warfare today? Absolutely not! In Africa, India and similar cultures, the demonic realm is close at hand; many people are living their lives to appease the powers of darkness. The Western world has gone to the extreme opposite, believing either that there are no powers of darkness or that the powers of darkness have no ability to work against us.

Let me make this quite clear: this is *not* true! I say this strongly, with a conviction that has been birthed out of more than twenty-five years of deliverance and counselling, consisting of the eviction of thousands of demons from hundreds of individuals. I have put in my time in the trenches, and I know quite well what it is like to be hit by Satan's grenades. We are, in fact, at war!

Listen to what Ed Murphy says about the practice of spiritual warfare. "Can a theology of Satan and demons that is both true and useful for ministry really be developed by theologians studying their Hebrew and Greek Bibles while sitting in their air-conditioned offices apart from at least some personal experience?"[63] I answer with a very loud, resounding *"No!"*

Are we are questioning the Bible? No, God forbid. But what about questioning our theology?

Maybe the first question needs to be, "What is theology?" Basically, theology is man's interpretation of God's word:

1.   the study of religious faith, practice, and experience; especially: the study of God and of God's relation to the world.
2.   a.   a *theological theory* or system i.e., Thomist theology is a theology of atonement.
     b.   a distinctive body of theological opinion ... [64]

---

63   Murphy, p. xiii.

64   http://www.merriam-webster.com/dictionary/theology

Every day, people are having experiences that don't line up with man's interpretation of what the Bible says about spiritual warfare. The bare truth is our current theology of spiritual warfare, at least in our Western world, is in a real and urgent need of a rewrite. As Murphy says, "Theology which is contradicted by experience, or at the least brought into question, is theology that needs to be re-examined."[65] And further, "Our theology of the spirit world must fit the reality of contemporary human anguish."[66]

Remember our Biblical mandate to put on the armour of God (Ephesians 6:10–24).

6.3.5. Breaches in the Blood Covering

Those of us who are practitioners need the naysayers to come on board with us. Current-day theology says Jesus, by the work of the cross, defeated Satan. We are now covered by His blood, so Satan cannot harm us. It is true; by Christ's shed blood we are covered by the finished work of Christ Jesus.

But there is potential for us to be deceived by this comforting concept. We cannot forget that sin in our lives brings about a breach in the blood covering. All the while, Satan is working behind our false hedge of security, tricking us into saying, "Satan cannot touch me." This deception is working well for Satan.

Satan is indoctrinating us and our children in the teaching of the occult with the likes of Harry Potter, Stephen King and many others. Curiosity is, in my opinion, the most used and successful scheme of Satan. He baits us with his propaganda in books, movies, music, and other places.

What we seem to misunderstand is that when we bite onto the hook of curiosity that is attached to something that belongs to Satan, he has a legal right to reel us in in that area of temptation. It is imperative for us, God's Beloved, to know that everything that belongs to Satan has demons attached to it. That means if we have Mormon or Freemason reading material or artifacts of whatever type, or anything else that is not of God, we must get rid of it and then ask God's forgiveness for coveting something unholy. As an adult, you may be strong enough that the Mormon message does not infiltrate your

---

65   Murphy, p. xiii.

66   Murphy, p. xiv.

mind and spirit (do not count on it). But what if you have children? What kind of pictures are the demons speaking into their minds, night after night?

Principle #24: Everything that belongs to Satan has demons attached to it.

That is exactly what goes on every day and night all around the world. It is the devil's schemes, unseen, underground spiritual warfare—a war against the saints of God. We are the children of God, the church of Jesus Christ, the army of the Most High God. We are the ones to whom Jesus gave the authority to trample on snakes and scorpions and overcome all their power so that nothing will harm us (Luke 10:19). We need to give our heads a shake and take a hard look at where we are as a body of believers. Are we advancing? Are we pushing the gates of hell back? Or are Satan and his cohorts doing the pushing?

My answer to that question is that there are many churches advancing, growing, and gaining as they build the kingdom of God. But over the last twenty years or more, I have seen time after time how our enemy is targeting the very young, drawing them away by the thousands if not by the millions.

It is common today for church-going fourteen-year-olds to be sexually involved with many partners. For church attendees, it is becoming "normal" to live together before marriage. The divorce rate is the same in the Church as it is in the world. The world is saying, "What would it gain me to go to your church? I see no difference between lifestyles in the Church and out of it."

This is a little harsh, but I've heard such comments many times. We've been led into spiritual apathy by the soothing soft tone of the evil one, saying, "Don't worry, God is a good God—He won't turn you away. He'll forgive your sins. After all, He's a God of love, isn't He?" And on it goes, with our current reality identical to that of Adam and Eve. We, too, have been sent away from God's presence by His hand. Why? Because as you and I walked through the garden of life, we ate from the forbidden fruit of lust and pride. We listened to the serpent as he encouraged us to fulfill our lustful desires:

"You will not certainly die" (Genesis 3:4). But now as we become banished from God's presence, we have regrets.

This is the essence of spiritual warfare. It is unseen by the natural eye but as real as life itself, with Satan and his cohorts working their schemes to get us in sin. Once we're in that sin, they can shout their words right into our minds—darts accusing us of sin. Next comes discouragement and self-loathing; we hate ourselves for caving into sin once again. In this place we may cry out for God's mercy. But He doesn't listen to us, because in our shame we speak the words, "I'll never forgive myself for this one." That decision has us in the jailhouse, with Satan's jailers throwing accusing darts in the first person and deceiving us: "God will not forgive me this time. I am unworthy of His love and forgiveness."

We must understand that a large part of what comes into our minds daily isn't generated by our own minds or even from God. We need to accept that just as God speaks into our minds, so does Satan; this occurs our whole life. Every hour, every minute, of every day, it is the enemy's intent to slow us down in our efforts to be more like Jesus. The enemy's desire is to manipulate us in such a way that we eventually come to a place of agony, filled with anger towards God for not protecting us from the onslaught of evil.

For others, their anger towards God is not due to the evil one. They may believe that there is a devil, but consider him powerless. These people are angry at God because they say, "If God is in control of all things, why did He let my husband have an affair with my best friend?" "Why did God let my brother's little four year-old daughter be raped by the neighbour's son?" There are no words to explain these terrible atrocities. Many will never need God more than they do when experiencing such horrible things, yet this is exactly when they turn their backs to Him. Why? Partly because they never understood that words like "God doesn't care what happens to me," are really the voice of the enemy, infecting our concept of God with the lies of Satan.

This is typical spiritual warfare! Now we are taken captive and held by a stronghold, believing "God doesn't care." Such is the intent of the evil one against mankind as he works to trap us in his evil schemes!

But God, through Jesus Christ, has provided a bullet-proof means of protection from Satan via the finished work of Jesus Christ on the Cross of

Calvary. For those of us that believe in our heart and confess with our mouth that Jesus Christ is Lord, we have received salvation—a salvation that calls us to walk as Jesus walked. In working out our salvation, we put off the old man and put on of the new man, which teaches us to be like Christ Jesus (Colossians 3:9–10). Within a millisecond of accepting His Salvation, our spirit man, which was dead to God, is exchanged for the righteousness of God (2 Corinthians 5:21). This is the first step towards putting on the full armour of God, which we are instructed to do in Ephesians 6:10-18.

The apostle Paul rallies the saints of God in a call that has reverberated down through the corridors of time, challenging our generation to *"be strong in the Lord and in His mighty power"* (Ephesians 6:10) as we face our unrelenting opponent. He pronounces not so much an order as a declaration, stating that the type of enemy we are facing cannot be fought by human strength and resources, but only by His *mighty* power. From here, we are instructed to take a stand against the devil's schemes—not in our own power, but in the power of God. This requires each Christian to know who they are in Jesus, and who Jesus is in us.

I remember very well working with an early client. I had commanded a demon that was inside this very angry man to identify itself. It shot back with a furious voice, saying, "Who are you to command me to respond to you?" I was very surprised and immediately aware that fear was taking hold of me. However, even then I knew without reservation who I was in Christ Jesus. I was able to throw that in the face of the enemy, which took the wind out of its sails. If you are uncertain who you are in Christ Jesus, then you need to build yourself up in Him before tackling any demons. If not, you may end up like the sons of Sceva, naked and running down the road, chased by demons (Acts 19:13–16).

To allay your fear, I would like to share a story. It is positive proof that if we give ourselves totally to the Lord Jesus Christ and if we are fully dressed in the armour of God, then we have the instantaneous and complete protection of our reigning King Jesus.

Four or five years after I dealt with that angry demon, a pastor brought in one of his members for deliverance. He was about six-foot-six—a well-built oil rig worker. The pastor and counsellee were sitting on a chesterfield facing me; we were about three steps apart. Upon completion of the intake information I said, "Let's pray before we move on." I prayed, and as I said amen, I looked up straight into the hateful eyes of a demon that was peering at me through the eyes of this man, who had gotten up off the chesterfield and was now one step away from me.

Nothing registered with me: no fear, no sense of danger; it all happened in a split second. In the same second as I saw him coming towards me, his head lifted up and went sideways, exactly like when two men are in a fist fight and one executes an uppercut from the side, lifting the other up and throwing him backwards.

This happened just like that. He came right up off the floor and was thrown back the three steps he had come, hitting the wall and then falling behind the chesterfield while crying out, "Help me, help me." Within a few minutes, he gave his life to Jesus.

This very memorable incident is another example of God's unfailing means of protecting His people. I have no doubt whatsoever that God sent me an angel. Our part in securing God's moment-by-moment protection? *"Whoever dwells in the shelter of the Most High will rest in the shadow of the Almighty"* (Psalm 91:1). This is akin to the stronghold of God's love seen in chapter 4.

The Lord does not guarantee that no evil will befall those who trust him ("make the Most High your dwelling"). All who find "refuge" (cf. v.2) in him will rest with the confidence that whatever happens on earth is with his knowledge. Nothing happens outside his will, whether "harm" (lit., "evil," v. 10) or "disaster" (lit., "disease" or "wound"; cf. 38:11; Lev 13:14; Isa 53:8).[67]

While on the topic of standing, the KJV uses the word "wrestle" while the NIV uses the word "struggle." I prefer wrestle, for it is a struggle *as* we wrestle one-on-one against our foe. I stand or fall according to my choices. My wife and I will, at times, come together to do battle against the invading enemies, as does a church or a city or a territory. The armour that we are to

---

67   VanGemeren, p. 601.

put on is singular; each one of us responsible for putting on our own armour as well as the ongoing maintenance of it.

6.3.6. What is the Armour?

When getting ready for a deliverance session, I, along with most of the Christian world, put on the full armour piece by piece. But when the battle ends, we never think to remove this heavy, bulky full armour. The truth be known, not taking off the armour after the battle is about the only part we have right. For the armour is not something we put on and take off.

Actually, we are already dressed in the full armour when we live our life—moment by moment, day by day—in a way that emulates Christ Jesus. C. Peter Wagner lays out our obligation as sons and daughters to live moment by moment in a way that glorifies the Most High God. If we live that way, we'll be able to stand when the day of evil comes—and we'll still be standing when it ends. As Gary Kinnaman expounds,

> Don't ignore it. Don't downplay it. There has been a declaration of war on the saints. But God's Church will never be defeated if we fight against the schemes of the enemy wearing the full armour with which He has equipped us. Overcoming the Dominion of Darkness explores little-understood concepts like binding and loosing, and explains in detail the significance of each piece of your vital armour:
>
> - The Belt of Truth—honesty with God, others and yourself.
> - The Breastplate of Righteousness—obedience in your daily walk with Him.
> - The Shield of Faith—clinging to the truth of God's enduring Word.
> - The Helmet of Salvation—guarding your mind, where the real battle rages.[68]

---

68 Kinnaman, inside cover page.

Take time to understand what is being said here. The armour isn't something we put on—it's something we are. The strength and effectiveness of our armour is determined by the measure of our righteousness. We don't put it on and take it off; we live it. Understanding this concept should spur each one of us to higher levels of righteous living.

Sadly, the Western world has bought into the teaching that, on the cross, Jesus defeated Satan and rendered him powerless; therefore, Satan cannot harm those of us who are Christians. So there is no need to concern yourself with whether your armour is on or off.

Principle #25: God is not in full control, and Satan is not fully harmless.

Generally what follows is, "Don't you worry about Satan, or even think about him. God is in control, and everything will be okay." Is God really in control? Think about this: if God is really in control of all things, would He have allowed the utterly meaningless slaughter of millions of His beloved in the Second World War? Never. We may be able to imagine something like that happening in the Old Testament, but God doesn't treat His people that way on this side of the cross.

Our mandate to be engaged in this spiritual war is made clear by Jesus:

I saw Satan fall like lightning from heaven. I have given you authority to trample on snakes and scorpions and to overcome all the power of the enemy; nothing will harm you. However, do not rejoice that the spirits submit to you, but rejoice that your names are written in heaven.
—Luke 10:18–20

6.3.7. First Recording of Satan's Name in the Bible

Satan is first mentioned by name in 1 Chronicles 1:1: *"Satan rose up against Israel and incited David to take a census of Israel."* The word "incite" is enough to tell the story. It means "to move to action: stir up: spur on: urge on."[69] David had no idea whatsoever that Satan was the prompter of his thoughts. Satan stimulated David's mind to do evil. We see a principle here that is recorded first in Genesis 3 and found throughout the whole Bible: human sin almost always has a double source.

- It has a human dimension because of wrong choices and sin in our lives.
- It has a supernatural dimension because of Satan's temptation.

Refer to the story of Ananias and Sapphira. *"Then Peter said, 'Ananias, how is it that Satan has so filled your heart that you have lied to the Holy Spirit…?'"* (Acts 5:3).

According to Paul, things haven't changed since the days of Adam and Eve: *"But I am afraid that just as Eve was deceived by the serpent's cunning, your minds may somehow be led astray from your sincere and pure devotion to Christ"* (2 Corinthians 11:3). Just as Eve was deceived, so are we today. Deception is still one of Satan's most successful tools against us. Once he gets us into a place of deception—however small it may be—it is a toehold, a place for him or his cohorts to stand.

6.3.8. The Battle has Intensified

From our study thus far, we have come to understand that the battle is against the mind. This is the only way Satan and his demons can get us. Once Satan enters through the mind and gains a foothold that can serve as a landing strip for his demons, we can totally lose control of whole areas of our lives. We have given that control away!

I have already mentioned a growing intensity as Satan sees his time getting shorter. As 1 Peter 5: 8 warns us, things have not changed; we must still *"Be alert and of sober mind. Your enemy the devil prowls around like a roaring lion looking for someone to devour."* The principle remains from Old Testament to New Testament to today.

---

69   http://www.merriam-webster.com/dictionary/incite

Make no mistake here—do not be deceived. The recipients of this epistle are very clear. *"To God's elect, exiles scattered throughout the provinces of Pontus, Galatia, Cappadocia, Asia and Bithynia, who have been chosen according to the foreknowledge of God the Father, through the sanctifying work of the Spirit, to be obedient to Jesus Christ and sprinkled by his blood"* (1 Peter 1:1–2). These words are directed at the New Testament church.

Let's glance back, once again, at Cain as he initiates murder (Genesis 4:8)! God's warning is a word of grace towards Cain. God knew where he was heading and stepped in to warn him. He was saying, "Stop, Cain! Turn back. You're heading for disaster." God continued His attempt to stop Cain by saying *"you must rule over it"* (Genesis 4:7), referring to the personal demon of sin that was crouching at his door. There is a strong emphasis on "you," implying the part of the battle that is our own personal responsibility.

Ed Murphy builds on this thought by quoting a commentator called Herder:

> God talks to Cain as a willful child and draws out of him what is sleeping in his heart, and lurking like a wild beast before his door. And what He did to Cain He does to everyone who will but observe his own heart, and listen to the voice of God.
>
> What was Cain's immediate response? Stony silence. Leupold observes, there is something ominous about Cain's silence. He is not reported to have thanked God for the warning or to have repented of his jealousy, or to have mended his ways. A stubborn silence seems to have been all he had to offer. Anticipating verse 8, he says,
>
> Cain's sin in reference to his brother was primarily jealousy culminating in hatred, a sin that seems comparatively weak and insignificant but which carries possibilities of great development with itself. Anger, bitterness and lack of forgiveness are some of the most dangerous sin handles in a human life.[70]

Here we see the serpent bruising the heel of the seed of woman. Each of us have hidden in our own soul possibilities for evil that we would never

---

70   Murphy, pp. 217–218.

suspect, often due to previous sin. Because this sin is not dealt with, Satan has released his arrow into the already boiling pot of sin, and all of a sudden it bursts and fully inflicts its terrible curse on man.

The New Testament says that Cain belonged to the evil one.

> ... this is the message you heard from the beginning: We should love one another. Do not be like Cain, who belonged to the evil one and murdered his brother. And why did he murder him? Because his own actions were evil and his brother's were righteous. Do not be surprised, my brothers and sisters, if the world hates you.
>
> —1 John 3:11–13

Note how the godly life of God's people provokes jealousy, anger, and resistance from evil people. This resistance can even become open hatred. Why? Because a godly life exposes evil, and evil hates to be exposed. The natural progression is to destroy that which has exposed the evil. Evil is satanic. *"The thief comes only to steal and kill and destroy..."* (John 10:10).

We see Paul warning us away from a similar disaster: *"See to it that no one falls short of the grace of God and that no bitter root grows up to cause trouble and defile many"* (Hebrews 12:15). This verse refers to church discipline, but it is really about God's discipline. Paul also states, *"'In your anger do not sin': Do not let the sun go down while you are still angry, and do not give the devil a foothold"* (Ephesians 4:26–27).

Remember, this epistle is written *"To God's holy people in Ephesus, the faithful in Christ Jesus..."* (Ephesians 1:1). In both Hebrews and Ephesians, Paul addresses the problem of Satan having a foothold in the born-again believer.

The proof is in Paul's choice of words. *"... you must no longer live as the Gentiles do"* (Ephesians 4:17), and *"That, however, is not the way of life you learned..."* (Ephesians 4:20).

The "way of life" here means to know and love Christ. *"... you heard about Christ and were taught in him in accordance with the truth that is in Jesus"* (Ephesians 4:21). "Heard" implies the hearing of faith, accepting Him as Lord and Saviour. And even to the born again, Paul is saying "Watch your step, you people of God. Be alert or Satan will get a foothold." This is exactly what toppled

Cain. In the story of Cain, the ongoing spiritual warfare between the two seeds, the two kingdoms, begins. Spiritual warfare breaks out in full force.

If Satan's methods are the same today as they were at the time of man's fall, the question is, can Satan really do anything to us today after Christ's triumph over him? Much of the church today is telling us to get our eyes off of Satan and onto Christ, and He will protect us. But the Word tells us to watch *"in order that Satan might not outwit us. For we are not unaware of his schemes"* (2 Corinthians 2:11).

In the Western world, we believe that God lives in heaven and man lives on earth. We have downplayed the middle realm, the spirit realm. The truth of the matter is that the spiritual realm is both good and evil.

The church in the Western world needs a paradigm shift (a radical change in thinking) when it comes to what Satan is able to do today. Listen carefully: the very same schemes and tools that Satan used to bring about the fall of man, he has continued to use throughout the ages, and he is still using them now in our time. The only difference is that over time, these tools have been sharpened and improved, like a missile that never misses its mark. As we get closer and closer to the return of Jesus Christ, this unseen warfare will grow to an intensity of hatred and madness that will surpass mankind's understanding.

Many churches today are being deceived and don't see the need to get themselves deeply rooted in the Word—Jesus Christ! And because of that, they will be swept away.

6.4. Early Spiritual Warfare

As I bring this chapter to a close, I want to leave you with a picture of the spiritual warfare that broke out with a vengeance at the fall of mankind, a warfare that still rages today and will grow increasingly heated due to the tenacity of the fallen angel, Satan himself. He knows full well his destiny is a burning fire of hell. Fully aware that his time is running out, his singular intention is to take as many of us, the beloved of God, as he can to hell with him. Could you or I end up there? The Bible does say—more than once—that those who continue to sin will not enter heaven. These are hard words, words which need our immediate and deep attention.

For the most part, we see the battle on an individual basis. We say, "I can stop the odd arrow that comes my way." But Satan has a bigger plan that needs our consideration. Paul's words of deep concern still echo from the past: *"… I am afraid that just as Eve was deceived by the serpent's cunning, your minds may somehow be led astray from your sincere and pure devotion to Christ"* (2 Corinthians 11:3).

Any born-again believers who question these concerns are like the pastor I mentioned earlier—the one who believes there is no battle. If we deny the reality of this spiritual war, we are like a soldier ambling across the battlefield, unarmed and defenseless, denying the reality of the flying bullets and hidden mines. Sooner or later, we will be attacked and wounded.

In our current spiritual temperature, some of us *"dress the wound of my people as though it were not serious"* (Jeremiah 6:14). Charles Dyer explains,

> Jeremiah responded in amazement to Judah's unbelief. But no one would listen to him as he tried to warn them of the coming calamity. This is the first of more than three dozen times in Jeremiah where the people did not listen…. Judah was in danger of destruction because she had strayed from the ancient paths of God's righteousness.[71]

I'm not saying that we're in danger of destruction, but many are living according to their own homegrown and convenient version of righteousness.

It appears to me that divorce among pastors and leaders is increasing. Young children are involved sexually, often with parental knowledge. I once overheard a mother say, "I am so excited for my daughter"—who by the way, was only in her early teens—"I can get her on the pill, and she can go out and have all the fun she wants without the worry of getting pregnant." Those words made me sick to my stomach. What does it do to the holy and righteous heart of God? Even among young married Christians, it is now very common for the wife to be the one in an adulterous relationship. I find this very disheartening, as should you. Throughout history, it has been the wife and mother that has often been the symbol of righteousness in the family.

---

71   Dyer, p. 1138.

One thing that causes my spirit much pain is profanity and crude language, whether by men or women. Even some pastors swear. I've seen individuals placed in positions within the church not because of a proven track record or personal righteousness for the glory of Christ, but instead because of convenience, influence or wealth.

These situations are a pinprick in comparison to the total size of our sins. However, they are enough to show us how we may still be living out of our old sin nature rather than being obedient to the written word of God. Many of us live as in the days of Jeremiah, when the people thought they could get away with their sins as long as they came to the temple for cleansing. In other words, we do not see our sinful ways as very serious.

6.5. Are You Serious about Dealing with Sin?

In Jeremiah 7:5–15 we find "their true safety lay in thoroughly turning from sin and living righteously."[72] My concern for our current time is not unlike Jeremiah's concern for his: "Jeremiah responded in amazement to Judah's unbelief. But no one would listen to him as he tried to warn them of the coming calamity."[73]

Today, it seems many Christians are not concerned about small habitual sins. A common response I've had when addressing the sin in someone's life in a counselling session is, "Hey, I'm okay, I'm born again. God has forgiven all my past, present, and future sins. I'm not worried." The implications of that premise are dangerous, if not fatal—especially if Jesus should return to find us living in a stylish, habitual sin.

If you are concerned at all, take these following words, and write them on your heart, soul and mind. Let them shape your daily walk through Satan's minefield of lust, greed, and hate. Let us never forget that the smallest of continual sins separates us from God. Each sin opens the door bit by bit, until Satan or his cohorts come in like a flood.

---

72   MacDonald, p. 1003.

73   Dyer, p. 1138.

Sin has two components: our flesh and our enemy. The ebb and flow of spiritual warfare is created by Satan, with a raging force to kill and destroy. And there we are, fighting against our old nature even after we are born again.

Let's go back to the time of Isaiah. Here, similarly to Jeremiah, is a picture of God dealing with His people because of the same ongoing sin issues (Isaiah 3:9–11), reminding them of the heritage He has provided (Isaiah 54:14–16). These powerful, ancient Scriptures are as applicable for us today as they were in the days of Jeremiah and Isaiah. If we choose to live a life of righteousness that glorifies God day by day, then *"no weapon forged against you will prevail, and you will refute every tongue that accuses you"* (Isaiah 54:17). If we choose to live habitually in the sinful nature of man, the consequences will be radically different. We will bring disaster upon ourselves—disaster that may come directly from God to meet His refining purposes. As He says, *"See, it is I who created the blacksmith who fans the coals into flame and forges a weapon fit for its work. And it is I who have created the destroyer to wreak havoc…"* (Isaiah 54:16).

6.6. Five Purposes of the Blacksmith

The tool used to "wreak havoc" can be compared to the blacksmith. We all know what a blacksmith is: a skilled metalworker who can bend, shape and mold metal into any number of configurations. His success is measured by his ability to administer fire in the necessary sections of the metal. If he bends without enough heat, he can render the metal useless; too much heat and the metal flows and runs away like water.

The process in the spiritual realm works according to the same principle. God uses the blacksmith to shape our character and to make us grow. Satan is God's blacksmith—a tool that can be used to test us by God's permission, as Job was. God is always at work in multiple ways, working and shaping us into the very image of Jesus Christ Himself.

1. Sometimes Father God chooses to bring in the blacksmith not because of ongoing or active sin, but simply because we think we have reached the pinnacle of our Christian growth. We may believe we have earned a cozy armchair for a time of rest. In His infinite wisdom, God will use the

blacksmith to turn up the heat in our lives. He is telling us, "You have done well, but as of yet, you have not completed all that I prepared for you to do."

2. When we slip off the road of righteousness into sin, Satan turns up the heat with the intent of destroying us. Satan is looking for victims to devour. This scenario is more common than we would like to admit! I know this to be true, because it's been my experience as well as that of hundreds of other individuals who have stepped into my office for deliverance. Truth be told, most of us have been there. For those of you who have yet to experience a situation like this, there are two things you must do even though you are face-to-face with the blacksmith as he is turning up the heat. Firstly, acknowledge and take ownership of your many sins. Right now, get down on your knees and confess your sins. Secondly, ask Jesus to cleanse you from all your sins. Those two actions will instantly re-position you (Isaiah 54:14–17).

3. The blacksmith can be used to build our Christian character. Christian character is not built from the comfy chair on your deck, nor is it built by going to church every Sunday. You may learn something about it at church, but unless you put it into practice—taking it out onto the highways and byways, applying it by being the burden bearer or the disciple maker—it is useless. Be prepared to be ridiculed, laughed at, put down, and betrayed by your family, your church, and your closest friends. This building up of our character often comes through Satan's temptation, but under the close and continuous watch of Father God. He is always ensuring that the refiner's fire is at the precise temperature that will produce the intended measure of godly character in our life.

Jesus went through all of this and so much more. All of the betrayal, the unbelief, the beatings, people spitting on Him—Jesus undoubtedly suffered as He made His way to the cross. God was purposely strengthening, equipping and preparing His Son through trial and tribulation for the time when He would bear the full weight of the cross and be poured out in death. God strengthened Jesus to carry the cross, bearing the full weight of mankind's sin. The hatred put on Him by His own race was so much heavier than that of unbelieving people (Gentiles).

God-applied tribulations, along with the blacksmith's tribulations, are God's way to make and shape us. We, too, can accomplish all that He has in store for us. As a reward, we will one day meet Him, along with Jesus, in heaven. Some of you may be thinking that you have been a Christian for forty years and never yet had a trial. My suggestion for you is to check with Jesus—you very well may have missed the door of salvation. Don't mess with this; don't wait; do something about it now.

Over the years, I have led many people to the Lord Jesus Christ, some in mid-life and others in their late sixties, who had been sure they were going to heaven. Many of these people had positions within the church. But upon some investigation, they realized that they had never prayed the prayer of salvation.

4. "Hard places teach us to love. When God wants to soften and refine our spirits and answer our prayers for patience and love, He has to let the discipline of ill treatment, injustice and often the severest wrongs compel us to go to him for the love (charity, KJV) that "beareth all things, that endureth all things" (1 Corinthians 13:7 KJV)."[74]

We often find out that we do not have enough love for the test. As the Holy Spirit convicts us of our sins, He leads us to the source of strength. Then, as we gradually learn the humbling lesson, He leads us on from day to day in deeper testing and sweeter refining. Eventually, we will be able to thank Him for the fire that brought us more of His Spirit's grace and overcoming love.

5. Job comments about God's work in our lives for the purpose of growth (Job 23:1–10). Today, with God at work in and through our lives, spiritual warfare plays out in all our affairs. In spite of the trials and tribulations, we must stand on the fact that God, in the person of Jesus Christ, is the rock of our salvation. We must equally understand that Satan is also a rock, but a rock made by the hands of God. Satan is the rock that God uses to bruise us as He makes us more like Jesus day by day. It is imperative to understand this, or we can end up fighting against God. At different times over the years, I have discovered partway through a deliverance session that the mountain being faced was put there by God. This is a mountain each individual must climb in order to come to a place of proven and sustaining Christian character.

---

74   Simpson, p.18.

> ## Principle #26: Some mountains are placed by God to prove and sustain our character.

6.7. My Final Word of Wisdom

If you find yourself in a place where it seems that all hell has broken loose, and you cannot make sense of it or make your way through it, don't immediately start accusing Satan for your situation. First ask God, "Are these trials and temptations, or is this the hard place from where I just cannot move on? Are these things from You? Are these actions of Your love for me as You work to bring me more and more into the image of Your son Jesus?"

Remember always that when He has tested you, you will come forth as gold. You can stake your life on that, with the outcome of abiding in peace and joy here on earth, even in the worst of times. How?

> *That is why I am suffering as I am. Yet this is no cause for shame, because I know whom I have believed, and am convinced that he is able to guard what I have entrusted to him for that day.*
>
> —2 Timothy 1:12

PRAYER

Part III

Chapter Seven

LEVEL I: PERSONAL PRAYER SHIELD

Pray hard and long. Pray for your brothers and sisters. Keep your eyes open. Keep each other's spirits up so that no one falls behind or drops out.

—Ephesians 6:18, MSG

PRAYER THAT FLOWS FROM A HEART THAT LIVES IN OBEDIENCE TO THE first and second commandments will provide your every need in ministry (Matthew 22:36–40).

Without a doubt, prayer is one of most important and critical practices in our Christian lives. That being said, this chapter is intended to warn you of the dangers of doing ministry without being in constant communion with the Godhead (Father, Son, and Holy Spirit). It will also facilitate the development of the basic elements of prayer life for those who minister to others.

I will endeavour to provide a platform from which even a beginner can feel confident in taking a stand against Satan's schemes!

When you step up and begin making a difference in other peoples' lives by ministering to their hearts, you can be certain that your enemy will also step up. He will increase the pressure, hoping to stop, block, or at least hinder whatever it is that God would have you doing for His glory.

When you step up, the enemy steps up.

7.1. Satan's Schemes

When we make a decision to do whatever it is that God would have us do for His Kingdom, you can be sure that the devil is going to do whatever he can to discourage us by sending out a low-ranking demon to pester us. If he gains a little toehold here, he will be looking for a foothold there, and if he gets that, the next step is discouragement that depletes our faith level—for without faith we can do very little. Faith comes by seeing and doing, and God will not test you beyond what you can manage!

7.1.1. Discouragement

If you are going to minister to others, you must be aware of the day-to-day schemes of the enemy. Discouragement is a scheme of the evil ones, and if you ponder the situation, wondering if God abandoned you, the devil knows exactly when to drop into your mind the words, "I don't know if I can trust God!"

> *But how can people call for help if they don't know who to trust? And how can they know who to trust if they haven't heard of the One who can be trusted? And how can they hear if nobody tells them? And how is anyone going to tell them, unless someone is sent to do it? That's why Scripture exclaims,*
> > *A sight to take your breath away!*
> > *Grand processions of people telling all the good things of God!*
> > *But not everybody is ready for this, ready to see and hear and act.*
> *Isaiah asked what we all ask at one time or another: "Does anyone care, God? Is anyone listening and believing a word of it?" The point is: Before you trust, you have to listen. But unless Christ's Word is preached, there's nothing to listen to.*
> > —Romans 10:14–17, MSG

7.1.2. Busyness

If it's not discouragement, then maybe it's one of Satan's even more successful tools. Here's an example: while we are totally unaware, our enemy comes alongside us, pushing us onward to do more and more of what we love to do—to minister to others and experience the great joy of seeing the captives set free. This drive to do more and more is often a silent scheme of the enemy at work. Then one day you arrive home from a few weeks of ministry on the road, only to find your family has packed up and left, leaving you with an empty house and in the spiral of family breakdown!

In my experience, the dark realm doesn't mind losing a few battles to us. This is particularly true if the enemy sees that by doing so he may be able to instigate the complete destruction of a family, and in doing that, completely cut a family from a few years or maybe even hundreds of years of generational blessings coming down to those that are not yet born!

In the situation I just shared, you can clearly see the enemy's scheme was to keep the counsellor busy by sending people in his direction—people that not only paid him well, but also demanded his time, even after hours. I summarize with this: [[*Never* go out to do ministry, which is akin to going out to meet the enemy, without first getting your direction from God and the Word.]]

7.1.3. Apathy

On a global scale, God's kingdom daily experiences the loss of many souls to Satan. Why? Because we fail to gird ourselves in the Word of God and prayer. It's that simple! Therefore, if you are going to minister to others in the way laid out in this manual, you will need to live a life of faith and intimacy with the Father. Over time, a level of prayer will grow in you that will shake the spiritual ground on which our enemy stands!

The reality is if you are born again but happy to be an armchair Christian, then you really are no threat to the powers of darkness. In that case, you may be able to get by with very little prayer coverage, because you are not in any way a threat.

But the moment you begin to expose the hidden works of darkness in your mind and soul, or the mind and soul of others, then, naturally, there will be resistance from the devil. If you want to move onward and upward in the Lord for yourself, your loved ones, and for those that daily cross your path, then you will be walking into territory that Satan considers his!

When you begin doing ministry of whatever type, it goes without saying that Satan and his cohorts are going to do whatever they can to shut you down or hinder you. Jesus Christ modelled the prayer life for us by spending time with the Father every morning: *"Very early in the morning, while it was still dark, Jesus got up, left the house and went out to a solitary place, where he prayed"* (Mark 1:35). If we follow his example, there will be times when we become our enemy's target. But fear not, for Jesus has said, *"I have given you all authority to trample on snakes and scorpions and overcome all the power of the enemy; nothing will harm you"* (Luke 10:19). We figuratively trample on snakes and scorpions when we are praying against the schemes of the evil one.

Our success in spiritual warfare is tightly bound up in our understanding and application of the Word!

Remember the words of Luke 10:19, and know that your refuge is found always in them.

7.2. Personal Prayer

Personal prayer may be the most neglected discipline in our Christian practice. Almost all of us claim to have a prayer life, and usually we do. But for many people, it doesn't go much deeper than this: "Thank you Jesus for this meal, and please keep us safe."

I know this to be true, because that's the extent of the prayer life of many believers who come into my office for help. We've all been there, and if we aren't disciplined in our prayer life, we can very easily end up there again. Due to its shallow roots, this level of prayer bears little fruit. It flows only from that which evaporates from God's river of provision and protection, which is ours only through our personal prayer life. Our prayer life is to be developed and matured as we live out the command, *"Love the Lord your God with all your heart and with all your soul and with all your mind"* (Matthew 22:37).

What air is for our lungs, prayer is for our personal and spiritual lives. *No prayer, no spiritual life!*

We will never get to know and grow in God with a haphazard, distant prayer life. Wagner says, "Our personal prayer life is the principal barometer used to measure the quality of our relationship to God."[75]

---

75   C.P. Wagner, p. 103.

The importance of prayer is unequivocal. "Few things have contributed to spiritual barrenness in the church Christ founded as has the idea that prayer is mere quiet, meditational passivism."[76]

7.2.1. Repentance

Note the keys to a successful prayer life, whether for you or for the protection of your family.

> Many Christians, even some Christian leaders, complain that prayer does not work. They say that God seems far away, that they have little or no sense of His presence, that He does not seem to answer their prayers. This problem may be related to something Jesus said in the Sermon on the Mount. "Blessed are the pure in heart, for they will see God" (Matt. 5:8). If we are to "see God," that is, communicate effectively with Him in prayer, we must approach Him with clean hearts and hands. Jesus taught His disciples to pray, "forgive us our sins, for we also forgive everyone who sins against us" (Luke 11:4). Praying this prayer should not become a meaningless ritual. It needs to flow from the heart with sincerity and fervency. "Lord Jesus, forgive my sins, as I forgive others."[77]

We must also understand that in our everyday prayer life we need to be taking a stand against the powers of darkness.

> Prayer is not a piece of antique religious furniture to be displayed on special occasions like an ornament. Nor is it that matter of spiritual guesswork by which a holy role of the heavenly dice is made to see if you might strike it rich; a kind of godly gamble, hoping against the apparently inevitable. That kind of thinking has a name. Snake eyes. Satan, the serpent, has hypnotized most of mankind with an astonishingly complex set of ideas hindering prayer.[78]

---

76   Hayford, 2002, p. 41.
77   Cedar, p. 63.
78   Hayford, 2002, p. 61.

7.2.2. Prayer Shield

Level I Prayer is the level in which we personally begin building a protective hedge around ourselves—not just for material possessions and physical bodies, but also for our soul and spirit man! *"Have you not put a hedge around him and his household and everything he has?"* (Job 1:10).

It is foolish to try and deal with the demonic if we have not first been to the Father, ensuring that we are dressed in the fullness of the armour of righteousness (see Chapter 6, Spiritual Warfare).

> *Therefore put on the full armour of God, so that when the day of evil comes, you may be able to stand your ground, and after you have done everything, to stand. Stand firm then, with the belt of truth buckled around your waist, with the breastplate of righteousness in place, and with your feet fitted with the readiness that comes from the gospel of peace. In addition to all this, take up the shield of faith, with which you can extinguish all the flaming arrows of the evil one. Take the helmet of salvation and the sword of the Spirit, which is the word of God.*
> —Ephesians 6:13–17

For every one of us, this should be a principle that we apply daily before engaging the enemy, no matter what prayer level we are at. If you are the husband, then it is your responsibility to ensure that your headship covers the whole of your family.

Chapter Eight

LEVELS II AND III: MINISTRY AND TERRITORIAL PRAYER

A WORD OF CAUTION: IF YOU HAVEN'T MET THE REQUIREMENTS OF Level I, then you shouldn't take the risk by involving yourself in Level II and III. It is at these levels that the battle begins to intensify, because levels of demonic activity increase as you go deeper in ministry. This is ground level, right where we live and work and raise our families. It's also where countless numbers of God's people find themselves bound up by an endless number of strongholds from Satan's huge arsenal of demonic schemes.

8.1. Level II: Ministry and Prayer

Level II, ministry and prayer, is the level at which we will begin to expose the schemes of the enemy; from there, deliverance type ministry begins to take place (see Chapter 10 for the tools and the practice of deliverance).

We can, at times, also find ourselves here dealing with Level III demonic activity—that of principalities—along with all the levels beneath them (see Chapter 10). Over the years, I've found myself dealing with principalities during everyday deliverance sessions.

8.2. The Why and How

Principalities are territorial—not necessarily looking to expand their own territories, but certainly hanging onto that which they already possess. Therefore, if you are working with a family and find their generational sin roots go back a hundred years or so, sunk deep into practices of Druidism, Mormonism, the Ku Klux Klan, or others that are similar (the worst of all being child sacrifices), then the chance of encountering Level III demonic activity during an everyday deliverance session is very real.

When these high-ranking demons see that they are losing ground because of your ministry, they are going to do whatever they can to hold their territory. Whether a principality, a power, or maybe one of the many high-ranking demons that hold sway over family units, you want to be sure that you have been to Father God via the Word and prayer. It's important not just for today but for every day to be in communion with our triune God. Let me tell you: you don't want to ever get caught by surprise in a dark alley with a principality, only to hear yourself calling out to God, "Oh no! I haven't prayed for days and days!"

Gird yourself in the Word of God, prayer, and worship.

At the very least, you are going to confront some fear and darkness moving into your session at some point in time. But if you start your day girding yourself in the Word of God, prayer, and worship, you will have already fortified yourself.

In such a situation, if you do encounter the higher ranks of demons (whether a principality or Satan himself bursting into your deliverance session), all that will need to be said to the intruder is, "In the Name of Jesus I cast you out, and you cannot return!" Next, if you are an experienced practitioner, you will bind up the intruder and gather information from it that is pertinent to the person or family that you are working with to set free.

8.3. Can We Recognize this Higher Rank?

Usually not. This is due to the fact that demons make their way into a counselling session in varied ways. One possible tip: the higher the rank, the more strategic, the more thought-out, calculated, and stealthy the plan of attack. The lower the rank of the demon, the more pompous, stupid, and disarrayed the barrage will be.

For instance, a head-demon of a lower rank might come barging in, almost announcing their arrival, and scattering helpers all over the place, whereas a principality will most likely tiptoe into your session and switch out the demon(s) you are working against, replacing them with more aggressive demons to take away any ground you had gained.

You won't know this until you command the demon you are working against to give up the information you need from it. If you get a response, you will recognize it is not the voice of the demon you were initially talking to; it is angrier and more aggressive.

Be alert and don't let them get away with this switch! In your God-given authority, and in the mighty name of Jesus, command the demon you were originally working with to come back immediately and cast the replacement one out! Don't let demons play their tricks, because if you do, they will have you in a place of perpetual confusion. However, it is not always the principality that makes the biggest mess when breaking into your ministry session; it may very well be a demon from a lower rank.

8.4. This is War

This isn't a game! This is war, and we need to treat it that way. It is incumbent upon us to know what kind of battle we are fighting!

We must be on guard and day by day—be in the Word of God, which becomes our sword. As we grow and mature in the Word and in prayer, our sword—the Word of God on our tongues and in our hearts—becomes sharper and sharper, discerning more and more. It will become more accurate and concise, both in ministry and in our personal lives.

Being "prayed up" and walking in the Spirit of Righteousness guarantees the protective armour of God. Become familiar with wielding the Word, and you will find the enemy running from you. We are called to literally emanate Jesus—we are to deliver the demon possessed (as in Mark 5:6–13), we are to heal the sick (as in Mark 8:31–35; 9:17–27, 10:51–52), and so much more. Day after day, Jesus willingly and joyfully sets people free.

Jesus' daily practice of rising up in the morning to be alone with the Father in prayer enabled Him to meet the needs of those that He crossed paths with later. *"Very early in the morning, while it was still dark, Jesus got up, left the house and went off to a solitary place, where he prayed"* (Mark 1:35).

We should go forth in the same manner, committing to live daily in the Word and prayer, which provides for us clean hands and a pure heart. *"Who may ascend the mountain of the Lord? Who may stand in his holy place? The one who has clean hands and a pure heart, who does not trust in an idol or swear by a false god"* (Psalm 24:3–4).

These are prerogatives that enable us to work hand-in-hand with the Father, Son, and Holy Spirit! If you receive, believe and then put into practice what you have just read, you will find your faith rising up to a level you never dreamed possible.

How Can This Happen When we Seemingly have More Doubt Than Faith?: Let your doubt turn into hope. The one sitting on the other side of your desk has come to you seeking healing for his body, which is riddled with rheumatoid arthritis and in need of a touch from Jesus the Healer. You will become the conduit through which Jesus heals! Faith, seeing through the doubt, explodes with mountain-moving faith.

> *Then the disciples came in private and asked, "Why couldn't we drive it out?" He replied, "Because you have so little faith. Truly I tell you, if you have faith as small as a mustard seed, you can say to this mountain, 'Move from here to there,' and it will move. Nothing will be impossible for you."*
> —Matthew 17:19–21

I have, at different times, both cried and laughed out loud while watching Father God taking the little bit I held in my hands relative to my knowledge and ability, and then, before my eyes, setting the captives free. Little is much when God is in it. *"Whoever can be trusted with very little can also be trusted with much, and whoever is dishonest with very little will also be dishonest with much"* (Luke 16:10).

There is a real need for those administering healing to have an understanding of the "practice of inner healing." "Inner healing" is often perceived differently by practitioners and those seeking ministry. When most people hear the words, their first thought is counselling. But there are others who would say that "prayer" trumps the practice of inner healing. If it were one or the other, I would pick prayer. But really, it is a combination of the two. John L. Sandford says,

> Like deliverance, inner healing is a rediscovery of an ancient ministry. Inner healing is actually a misnomer. It was first called the "healing of memories," which was even more incorrect. What it truly is and should be called is "prayer and counsel for sanctification and transformation." It is not merely a way to restore hurting people, though it does that. It is a ministry within the Body of Christ to enable believers to come to more effective and continual death on the cross, and resurrection into the fullness of life in Christ. Inner healing is a tool the Lord uses to mature His people. "Speaking the truth in love, we are to grow up in all aspects into Him, who is the head, even Christ" (Ephesians 4:15).[79]

Once again, we see the importance of preparing ourselves in prayer on behalf of those to whom we will be ministering.

Once you are settled in, open each session with prayer, listening always for the Spirit of God within, who is the real counsellor (Isaiah 9:6). Listen for His direction throughout the session. It is imperative that the one you are counselling also be involved at some point in prayer.

Obviously, you cannot repent on behalf of them, nor can you make forgiveness on their behalf; those things are their responsibility. But the majority of people I have dealt with don't understand the concept and responsibility of maintaining a day-by-day life of prayer. This becomes a moment-by-moment practice while we are ministering in whatever form that may be.

Explain to your clients the process. If they lack the knowledge to pray on their own, lead them through word by word, making sure they understood what they just did. At this point you can pray for them, often anointing them first, and then laying your hands on them and praying in many and various ways. You might pray for health, if that be the issue, or pray directly into the

---

79   Sandford & Sandford, 1992, p. 18.

broken part of their marital union and for oneness within the marriage. Be purposeful; don't be haphazard in your prayers for your clients.

In my closing prayer, I always say, "I declare to any demon that has lost ground because of what went on in the session today, I am casting you out right now and you cannot return." *"When Jesus saw that a crowd was running to the scene, he rebuked the impure spirit. "You deaf and mute spirit," he said. "I command you, come out of him and never enter him again!"* (Mark 9:25). Caveat: this is the only time in the Word where Jesus told the enemy he cannot return. We can say that only Jesus has the authority to command a demon never to come back. Our guarantee that a demon cannot return comes from having a life that doesn't allow them room to move back in; this is living the life laid out in Psalm 15.

We don't always have to go into a deliverance session to set people free from demonic activity. If you're working with somebody who has been carrying jealousy towards another for a long time, have him repent of his sinful actions, deal with it properly, and then declare to the enemy that they have lost the ground that they have had for years. Say to them, "I take you, you evil spirit(s), in my spiritual hands, and cast you at the feet of Jesus Christ. He will deal with you." Some people may ask, "What if there is no demon there?" Well, if there is no demon, then no harm has been done. But if the sin hasn't been dealt with and has carried over to the next morning, the enemy will have a legal foothold—guaranteed.

I have already said many times throughout this book that Jesus wants us to walk hand-in-hand with Him always, in all we say and do—but never more than in this area of prayer. Yes, it is awkward for all of us at times, especially in the early stages of working with others. I still ask Jesus to lead the way in every session, and I will do my best to follow. I may be speaking out loud to the individual I am hoping to help, but on the inside I am saying, "Okay Jesus, what do we do with this? What do you want me to say about that?" Pray always in the name of Jesus.

Very truly I tell you, whoever believes in me will do the works I have been doing, and they will do even greater things than these, because I am going to the Father. And I will do whatever you ask in my name, so that the Father may be glorified in the Son. You may ask me for anything in my name, and I will do it.

—John 14:12–14

There is absolutely no better way to say it. That's how I do ministry! It's not that I'm hearing directly from Jesus, but I have a spiritual connection that purposely involves Him, and my part in leading the session is to be listening—discerning the Spirit or Jesus Himself as He leads the way. At the same time, in prayer ministry we must be intentionally involved with both the spirit realm and the individual we are praying for. We listen for the Spirit of God while watching and listening to the client.

The following is a platform from which you can establish your prayer life.

"Then you will call, and the Lord will answer; you will cry for help, and he will say: Here am I.

"If you do away with the yoke of oppression, with the pointing finger and malicious talk, and if you spend yourselves in behalf of the hungry and satisfy the needs of the oppressed, then your light will rise in the darkness, and your night will become like the noonday. The Lord will guide you always; he will satisfy your needs in a sun-scorched land and will strengthen your frame. You will be like a well-watered garden, like a spring whose waters never fail.

"… then you will find your joy in the Lord, and I will cause you to ride in triumph on the heights of the land and to feast on the inheritance of your father Jacob." The mouth of the Lord has spoken.

—Isaiah 58:9–11, 14

8.5. Level III: Prayer for City, Province, State, and Nation

8.5.1. Stewarding your Territory: A Challenge to Be Engaged

The purpose of Level III ministry and prayer is to expose and eliminate the demonic entities that reign over and pervade the atmosphere above a church, community, city, province, state, or even a nation.

... if my people, who are called by my name, will humble themselves and pray and seek my face and turn from their wicked ways, then I will hear from heaven, and I will forgive their sin and will heal their land. Now my eyes will be open and my ears attentive to the prayers offered in this place.

—2 Chronicles 7:14–15

I believe these words you just read are meant for all of us, individually and corporately.

2013 was a hard and trying year—a statement I heard echoed by many pastors and leaders, as well as many others within the corporate body of Christ Jesus. It seemed that any forward movement spiritually required a hammer and chisel. I personally believe it was because the evil ones were shaking in fear as they smelled the upcoming, latter-day rains that will circle the world.

The following experiences come from in the mid-nineties revival that swept through Alberta, British Columbia, and even down into the States. The upcoming revival, of which many are already feeling the heartbeat, will be similar. In the nineties, this was my vision:

I saw snow as far as I could see—snow, extending as far north as it could go, reaching out into British Columbia and downward into the lower mainland. I had a vision of a huge building full of people alongside the revival flow... I asked the Lord who they were, and He said these were those who didn't believe in the coming revival.

The picture of revival I saw in the early years had the same flow as the later vision. Within the last year, God has given me a new vision of the flow of the revival. It appears as a bulging river, pushing north, west, and east, reaching into Quebec and onward. When God showed me this picture (the bulging river), it was already reaching out into Saskatchewan. I believe that if God had not stopped the revival, plainly seen by prophets of that day, because of the disunity among the children of God and, more specifically, the pastors and leaders, it would have developed roots in the communities. Many people, prophets and pastors, believe that this revival very well could have been an end-times revival. It was a signal of the second coming of Jesus Christ.

In this type of prayer, we join together with dozens, hundreds or maybe even thousands of others in an effort to remove demonic control from the territory for which we are praying. We are not praying alone, but corporately—not to set a captive free, but an entire territory!

In this type of prayer ministry, the purpose is to determine what strongholds are holding the territory captive. With that sort of information, you can direct your prayer against the principalities and powers that are holding the church or territory in captivity. There can be many different sin issues, often with a principality assigned to each stronghold over the area. This is a relatively safe environment for those that are praying, because they have joined together with one accord. Their purpose is solely to expose the schemes of darkness over a territory. That oneness of heart, soul, mind and spirit births a shield of protection; it also creates an atmosphere of unity, which becomes a hedge for those joined together. When this effort continues, it evolves into clarity on what the schemes are for the specific territory.

At the time of the early revival, I was leading weekly prayer meetings for men's ministry, along with heading Promise Keepers, a local March for Jesus, and bringing speakers in for conferences. At the same time, I was also sending out a monthly mail-out to over three hundred churches from the Grande Prairie area into the neighbouring province of British Columbia, and all the way into the northern territories.

During this busy time, there were four or five different pastors that were meeting together, praying for their churches and the city. I joined them on a few occasions, but as yet we had been unable to join forces for city and country-wide transformation. What drove this hectic schedule was a fire in my belly to see God move mightily in bringing about not just Grande Prairie-wide transformation, but a Divine transformation across our nation.

I had been to the Lord many times, saying, "Lord, I cannot do all of this; get somebody else." And each time I asked, He responded with the same words, "Jan, it is only for a season; there will come a time when you will hand all this over to the pastors."

That eventually took place, exactly as the Lord had said. I reduced my workload to only doing ministry in my Break Free Ministries office and leading occasional seminars. I was quite settled, and enjoying what I was doing. But because of all that I had been doing, I was exhausted mentally and physically.

I had concluded that, as the Lord said, this "moment of time" wasn't so much about revival but about raising up people of prayer for the times yet to come. The Spirit affirmed this strongly as I wrote this portion of the book.

Are we now living in this time? I believe we're moving into a time of significant prayer for our nations. One reason we need to be involved in prayer for our nations is because of the visible anger against the Christian body worldwide. It is a time for the Church to stand up against Satan and his schemes.

Watching the TV news one evening, I observed how ISIS was able to broadcast information across our nation by literally saying, "Canada, you will pay!" That is a threat from Satan. But what is the message for each one of us? Satan's threats are not idle; they need to be understood. His words are spoken to put fear in the heart of man, but the spiritual battle has been fought throughout the history of Christianity, and it will continue. I believe we cannot consider this in a casual way.

My message to the leaders of churches and spiritual entities throughout the whole Christian community is that we need to step up our praying, establishing a prayer time that penetrates the evil that is pressing in on us. I'm very serious about this—I feel the power of God coming on me to say, *"Church, stand up now. This is the hour!"*

There is a definite sense of revival moving around us. Consider these closing words: God does not just *send* revival upon us, but He works on us to *promote* the movement of revival. In other words, God uses us, through our prayers, to bring about worldwide revival.

APPLICATION

Part IV

Chapter Nine

DISCIPLESHIP AND COUNSELLING

HE IS THE WORD OF LIFE, THE FAITHFUL AND TRUE ONE, THE ROCK ON
which we stand, our Good Shepherd, the great I AM, the First and the Last!
Jesus will be the beginning and the end for you in every counselling session
if you let Him.

Our role in ministry is to be a vessel through which the heart of Father
God flows. Just as Jesus came from heaven to show us God here on earth, we
are here now to show Jesus to the world: first for the salvation of all mankind;
second, that the born again would grow into the very image of our Saviour—
becoming His eyes, His heart, His hands, His feet, and His voice. His purpose now becomes our purpose. We are to reach out to those who are in need
of a touch from God through Jesus in us. This is the first step as we aim to be
more and more Christ-like; it requires no training, only obedience.

As I searched for an appropriate title for this chapter, my thoughts went
to Jesus and the mandate for all of Christendom—the Great Commission.

Jesus, undeterred, went right ahead and gave his charge: "God autho-
rized and commanded me to commission you: Go out and train every-
one you meet, far and near, in this way of life, marking them by baptism
in the threefold name: Father, Son, and Holy Spirit. Then instruct them
in the practice of all I have commanded you. I'll be with you as you do
this, day after day after day, right up to the end of the age."
—Matthew 28:18–20, MSG

The Message version does an incredible job of clarifying the concept of
discipleship, particularly Jesus' promise to be with us *"right up to the end of the*
age." When Jesus charged His eleven disciples to *"Go out and train everyone*
you meet, far and near," He was also speaking to us. Since He has not returned

yet, we need to take these words as seriously as His disciples, the Apostle Paul, and others did. We have the same mandate—and maybe even more so, if we have a particular gifting in people-helping.

It is imperative that we, the Church of Jesus Christ, get serious about what Jesus is saying here in the commissioning of His eleven disciples, a commissioning that comes down through the ages to us. This is not a suggestion. It is a command that requires every Christian to say, "Yes Lord. I will be a disciple, and a disciple-maker!"

When we commit to being disciple-makers, Jesus promises *"... I'll be with you as you do this, day after day after day."* In other words, we aren't doing this on our own. For those of us who are or will be practitioners, what a promise! Write this promise on your forehead and your gateposts, and it will become a reality in your life and practice.

Even while you are in the darkest deliverance session, know that He is there. I understand how difficult it may feel, but if you hang onto Jesus' promise, *"I will be with you... right up to the end...,"* then you will have a peace of mind that surpasses all understanding. Jesus promised it—end of discussion! He will be there! We would do well to carve upon our hearts the words of Christ Jesus, *"God authorized me to commission you,"* as a constant reminder that we need Him every step of the way. Without Him, we can do nothing.

Our mandate today as counsellors, people-helpers, and disciple-makers is seen in the following verse, *"...Then instruct them in the practice of all I have commanded you."* This shows that we are to teach others, just as the first disciples did. Teaching is an important component of our ministry to others.

Jesus follows with the words, *"I'll be with you... day after day after day... ."* He will be with you as you do this!. The words you have just read are God's command to every Christian to make disciples and to engage in the lives of those who cross our paths. There are many different levels of engagement in the lives of those whom we seek to make disciples.

The point I want to make is that you don't have to go to school for six or eight years of training before you can begin to make a difference in people's lives. Most of us won't be full- time workers in professional ministry, but we all need to be prepared to minister to and instruct others at any time. We need to be ready for all who need a drink from Jesus' cup of cold water, a meal, a tidbit of Scripture, a prayer to encourage, or whatever it might be to warm the soul.

9.1. Instruments in His Hands

We are His, hand-picked and chosen for His purpose. At the moment of conception, God placed into us our personal gifting according to His purpose. Over time, this will shape our lives and possibly our occupations. As the NIV puts it, "... go and make disciples... teaching them to obey everything I have commanded you. And surely I am with you always, to the very end... " (Matthew 28:19–20).

This is not a personalized call; it is a call that rests on the soul and spirit of every child of God and will play out for each one in various ways. Some will be involved in disciple-making as their full-time occupation. Others may be making disciples as they work with new believers in their church. For those who use this manual, you will be making disciples as you counsel and bring deliverance.

We must always remember that we Christians are in Christ. He lives *in* us so that He can live *through* us. Our willingness to give Him full reign in our lives will determine how much He can use us.

The same principle applies as we counsel others. I suggest that our call into ministry is not unlike God's call on David to become king (refer to chapter 2). God had sent Samuel to Jesse, asking him to have all his sons at the sacrifice. David was on the far side of the desert, tending the sheep, and wasn't even considered. But God knew him and had him brought in.

We see from the word that God spoke to Samuel: *"Rise and anoint him; he is the one.' So Samuel took the horn of oil and anointed him in the presence of his brothers, and from that day on the Spirit of the Lord came powerfully upon David"* (1 Samuel 16:12–13).

As David pursued God, God in turn anointed and exalted David to be King over Israel. David initially proved by killing Goliath that he had a heart that ran after God. Afterward, a time of impartation and equipping ensued, which enabled him to rise up to the obligation of kingship. It was his heart that brought him into the position of kingship, ruling over God's people.

Our call to be disciple-makers or counsellors is not unlike David's call to be king. As God imparted to David the anointing and equipping required for kingship, He does the same for us when we pursue Him and have a heart after Him, anointing and equipping us for our own particular call into ministry. Today, God calls each and every one of us individually, and at the moment we accept the call, He begins to release His anointing for empowering and equipping our call—His perfect purpose on our lives. Don't question it—only believe, and follow God with all your heart.

9.2. Common Instructional Issues

There are fairly common issues in Christians that must be dealt with before individual freedom and growth can take place. I'm not talking about ongoing sin issues, such as pride or non-forgiveness, which separate us from God. No, I refer to our inner thought-life, those perceptions of God that are never heard and never seen. They can become like an out-of-control fire because of lies that are believed about God.

If your perception is that God doesn't care, or isn't strong enough to protect you, then how can you receive from God? Without faith, you cannot. If you are ever going to receive from God, you must change that perception (see also "perception" in the Toolbox). For the Word says that you can never please God without faith, without depending on Him (Hebrews 11:6).

Another common question that arises from our faulty perception is: why do Christians suffer? Over the years, I have worked with many who are very angry at God for allowing someone close to them to suffer, perhaps with a terrible disease.

"... Do not think of yourself more highly than you ought, but rather think of yourself with sober judgment... " (Romans 12:3).

It is important, and beneficial, to be willing to face up to any struggles and difficulties that may be within us. If we are not willing to face reality, we will never become real people. Self-examination is difficult for some people because they have a tendency to over-inflate any flaws or weaknesses they find in themselves and blow them out of proportion. Whenever people addicted to this form of behaviour discover something they do not like about themselves, they say, "It's awful that I'm like this… I must be the most terrible person in the whole world… It's a catastrophe to discover that I, of all people, could harbour these things inside me." These thoughts are irrational and unrealistic. A healthy perception of ourselves keeps such thoughts in proportion.

The correct way to handle the discovery of anything within us that runs against biblical principles is to say: "I'm sad about this, I'm disappointed about it, but by God's grace I can change. Some things in me may be bad, but I'm not *all* bad. I can still respect myself and love myself in God, even though I have discovered things about myself that I don't like. With His help, I will begin doing something about them right away."

If you keep matters in perspective, then what I have to say to you from now on can be transformative. If you can't, or are not willing to try, then I would encourage you to ponder what we have said before going any further. Perspective is all-important. Of that let there be no doubt.

The following is a bird's eye view of a few Biblical characters that are known for shaping their world for the Glory of Christ. These critical examples can be used for living out your life as well as instructing others.

He first found his own brother Simon, and said to him, "We have found the Messiah" (which is translated, the Christ) (John 1:41). People become known for many things. Noah is known as a righteous man in an evil age. David is known as the man after God's own heart. Peter is known as the outspoken disciple. John is known as the disciple whom Jesus loved. Judas is known as the betrayer. Paul is known as a fearless proclaimer of the gospel. Andrew is known for bringing others to Jesus. The first person Andrew brought to Jesus was his brother Peter. As soon as Peter joined the disciples, he became the spokesperson for the Twelve, while Andrew remained in the background. It was Peter, not Andrew, who rose to prominence as one of Jesus' inner circle of three. We do not read of Andrew resenting Peter; it seems he was satisfied to bring others to Jesus and leave the results to Him. It is not surprising that Andrew found the boy with the loaves and fishes and brought him to Jesus (John 6:8–9). Andrew brought Greeks to Jesus, even though they were despised by pious Jews (John 12:20–22). There is no record of Andrew ever preaching a sermon, performing a miracle, or writing a book of Scripture. He is remembered for those whom he brought to Jesus. Andrew is a good role model for us. Our job is not to transform people into Christians nor to convict them of their sin. It is not our responsibility to make people do what they ought to do. Our task is to bring them to Jesus, and He will perform His divine work in their lives.[80]

The question to you is, "How are you going to shape your world for the Glory of God in your time?" Crabb & Allender say,

> Encouragement is the kind of expression that helps someone want to be a better Christian, even when life is rough. By the grace of God, I can have the effect on your life and you can have it on mine. We must apply our mental energies to the job of understanding precisely how we can perform this important work for each other.[81]

Paul also provides helpful instruction on how we are to live and relate to each other:

> *Let the peace of Christ keep you in tune with each other, in step with each other. None of this going off and doing your own thing. And cultivate thankfulness. Let the Word of Christ—the Message—have the run of the house. Give it plenty of room in your lives. Instruct and direct one another using good common sense. And sing, sing your hearts out to God! Let every detail in your lives—words, actions, whatever—be done in the name of the Master, Jesus, thanking God the Father every step of the way.*
>
> —Colossians 3:15–17

---

80 Quickverse, October 21, 2011.
81 Crabb & Allender, pp. 9–10.

9.3. The Practice of Discipleship Counselling

In discipleship counselling, it is most important to start with a prayer that targets the immediate needs of the individual, along with the application of the Word of God. *"For the word of God is alive and active. Sharper than any double-edged sword, it penetrates even to dividing soul and spirit, joints and marrow; it judges the thoughts and attitudes of the heart"* (Hebrews 4:12).

There is a concept here that needs our full attention: while reading the Word of God, believers often get excited about all that Jesus had accomplished in the New Testament. However, when we lay our Bibles down, we also lay down the excitement of what we just read by believing in our hearts, "Well that was what Jesus did; it certainly is not something I could do." That is blatant unbelief, for John 14:12–14 says,

> *Very truly I tell you, whoever believes in me will do the works I have been doing, and they will do even greater things than these, because I am going to the Father. And I will do whatever you ask in my name, so that the Father may be glorified in the Son. You may ask me for anything in my name, and I will do it.*

Most of us have no problem with the concept that the *written* Word of God speaks to our soul and spirit man. The problem is that we lack understanding in the power of the *spoken* Word of God.

The belief that "Jesus could do that, but I certainly couldn't" is a lie. This lie holds us at a level of unbelief and hopelessness; we certainly don't believe we could bring change to the hearts of others. But when we speak principles and concepts that are righteous and true, those words go forth as if they had been spoken by Jesus Christ Himself, penetrating the heart and soul of the person you are speaking to. See the following Scripture: *"He now spoke directly to the paraplegic: 'Get up. Take your bedroll and go home.' Without a moment's hesitation, he did it…"* (Luke 5:24, MSG).

Through God's power, whether the Word is spoken from the mouth of Jesus or from our own, the results are to be the same. If we would take hold of that powerful concept, it would deal a death-blow to our disbelief and fear.

It would make way for faith to bear fruit, expanding the kingdom of God and setting the captives free!

What a *glorious* truth! We *can do* what Jesus did. In His words, *"Don't be afraid; just believe"* (Mark 5:36).

The spoken Word literally moves into the soul and spirit to expose any harmful thoughts and attitudes. Jesus, the Word, also uncovers that which is God-honouring in our soul and spirit for the purpose of our own encouragement and spiritual growth in those areas.

As you work through this chapter, you will see how you can learn to counsel, without the need of years of training, by making disciples one at a time. It is amazing how quickly your knowledge base will grow, with the Holy Spirit at your side and you in the Word and continually in prayer.

That's exactly how I was trained, as I indicated in the introduction. My wife and I did go to Bible school for one semester to study the basics of Christianity, but we took no formal training whatsoever on counselling or prayer ministry. We had both planned to return to Bible school in the fall season. But when I prayed, asking God for direction, he responded, "No, Jan; so many of My people are hurting, and I want you to begin working with them now."

I told Him that I had no credentials whatsoever, and if I did go to school long enough to be ordained, I could at least hang that on my office door. I was eventually ordained about fifteen years later after my pastor said, "Jan, you've been pastoring in this church and city for fifteen years. Why aren't you ordained?" I was then ordained by Victory Church, where I was attending.

Once I was in full-time ministry, I did take several correspondence courses in my area of need, and they proved to be very helpful. Many correspondence courses are available, on every subject. It's certainly something any one of us can do, even if we are not in full-time ministry. I would encourage you to get the training you need, as training is a part of the work of equipping your toolbox.

But training must always be secondary to the Spirit of God, who is the ultimate Counsellor. As written in John 14:16 & 26, *"And I will ask the Father, and he will give you another advocate to help you and be with you forever... But the Advocate, the Holy Spirit, whom the Father will send in my name, will teach you all things and will remind you of everything I have said to you."*

If you allow your training to supersede Jesus or the Spirit when you are ministering to others, then you will lose much of your effectiveness. You can still do some ministry, but you will never reach into the deep realm of the soul and spirit without Jesus. Only His love can birth life into a sin-sickened, hardened heart that seeks only death. He can restore life!

The following is an example of restoration by the Love of God. I counselled a man who was brought in by his wife. They were on the verge of divorce. The husband was so intent on suicide that I couldn't leave the room—he could easily overpower his wife and leave. As the session moved along, it seemed like all fingers were pointing at the husband as the source for their problems. He was certain suicide was the only answer. There were no other alternatives—he had chosen death.

I could see in his eyes and posture that he had completely given up. We were in a borrowed room which had no access to a telephone; therefore, I was unable to access outside help for the terrible situation. We were truly at a stalemate. Words, Scripture, and prayer were of no effect. I had used all my resources, and there was no doubt we were in a hard place. He was set on driving his car at a high speed into the concrete of an overpass, and I knew he would do exactly that. His wife was quietly weeping.

For what seemed like hours, no one spoke, except for my occasional attempt to engage him and to intercede for him against the seemingly tangible darkness.

Finally, he began to straighten himself up in his chair. I could see a softening in his face. His demeanour began to display a change of heart. Little by little, he climbed out of the hole he had buried himself in. The darkness was dissipating, ushering in a measurable change, which began to give us some hope.

Eventually, he looked at his wife, and repentance followed! When we had finished what we needed to do, I asked him, "What brought you out of the pit? Why such a dramatic change?"

He answered by simply saying these words, "The love in your eyes." It is so profound that man can see the love of God in the eyes of another man. I was the vessel in which the love of Jesus flowed through to reconcile this man back to himself, then God, and then to his wife and children.

What a privilege it is to be a part of what Jesus is doing on earth. Jesus, as a man empowered by the Spirit of God, went about meeting the psychological, "soulical," physical, and spiritual needs of others.

I have found that there is no greater joy than seeing the captives set free, and I will share some more of my own experiences to encourage you to step out. Often, the joy occurs with an almost instant restoration of individual lives, and marriages being noticeably and radically changed.

9.3.1. Christian Counselling vs. Psychology

I want to destroy the myth that we cannot help others because we do not have a Master's degree or Ph.D. in counselling. In the following quotes, I compare results between psychology and Christian counselling. You can see for yourself that Christian counselling is often equal to, or even better than, psychology (in fairness, Dr. Collins' quote was written in 1980, and no doubt the procedure of psychology has improved since then):

> …are not encouraging… therapy does not work very well. Researchers on both sides of the Atlantic, studying adults as well as children, discovered that experienced therapists are not much better than the inexperienced; that untreated people recover at about the same rate as those in treatment…. Such a statement is hardly a rousing cheer in favour of therapy's effectiveness…. More important than any of these are the counselor's warmth, genuine concern for people, and sensitivity to the counselee's feelings and needs.[82]

Keep this thought in mind: our success as a disciple-maker is based not so much on our level of training as on our ability to love others.

> In any approach to counseling of another person, an attitude of caring, warmth, sympathy, and concern is essential. This is sometimes called involvement. In reality therapy it has been suggested that the way in which we become involved in the life of the other person is by being concerned about his personal life and his present concerns

---

82   Collins, pp. 44, 46.

with his present behaviour. This can be done by sharing of our self with him and him with us as we endeavor to get acquainted. We can ask, "What is going on in your life right now and how can I help?" We can show an interest in all areas of his life and we can also expand the counselee's range of interest. One of our objectives in helping the person is to make him aware of life and possibilities beyond his difficulties. Often the person is so bound by his difficulties that he fails to see any hope or accept any help. Through gentle questioning or comments he can begin to see new possibilities. Statements or comments such as, "isn't it just as possible—" or "Perhaps there are other possibilities we haven't explored yet—" may help him become aware of the alternatives. After we have become involved we need to bring the person to the point where he will evaluate his present behavior. He will not do so unless he feels that you care and are involved. He needs to make a value judgment about what he is doing with his life right now. "Are you happy about your life or would you like to change? Is this a negative thing for you or positive? Do you feel good or bad about this? Would you like this to continue or would you like this to see a change?"[83]

Psychology: When I began to walk out my call, I quickly learned that the word "psychology" was akin to a curse word, whether for a client, pastor, or just an ordinary Christian. I want you to clearly see how a working knowledge of psychology benefits us greatly in Christian counselling.

Most introductory psychology texts define psychology as the scientific study of the brain and behavior. The American Heritage Dictionary defines psychology as "the science that deals with mental processes and behavior" and "the branch of philosophy that studies the soul, the mind, and the relationship of the mind to the functions of the body." For our purposes, psychology is the scientific study of the ABCs—affect (emotions), behavior, and cognition (mental processes). As such, psychology and the Bible bring

---

83   Wright, p. 46.

different perspectives and levels of understanding to some of the same subject matter. Of all the sciences, psychology comes closest to the issues the Bible addresses. Psychology and the Bible both deal with human nature, the human condition, and even human salvation. And of all the sciences, psychology has had the greatest influence in the culture, academia, and the church.[84]

The world has a tendency to value the professionally educated unbeliever above the Christian counsellor. But the following quote certainly indicates we need to reconsider Christian counselling and its uniqueness.

Christian Counselling: "…Christian counseling is unique because it seeks to deal with the whole person. The Christian counselor is aware that the physical, psychological, and spiritual aspects of human beings are intricately related."[85] Therefore, when one part is affected, the other parts can be affected also.

Once I received a call from a Christian man who was seeking counselling. I knew the man quite well, and for various reasons I was not interested in counselling him. He was a very outspoken person, and I had been the target of many of his sarcastic words, sometimes even in public with others listening. I certainly didn't want him in my office. While on the phone, I was trying to tell him that I had no room. Meanwhile, the Spirit was telling me to bring him in. I very unhappily booked him in for the next morning. To make a very long story short, God conducted a miracle in this man's life.

The next morning, I had a four-hour drive to make. Once I was on the road, I began to pray, thanking Jesus for what He had done in that man's life. Jesus spoke directly over my prayer, saying, "Jan, you did so well." I knew exactly what Jesus was speaking into.

When I first received the phone call from this man, I had immediately felt anxious. I didn't want to meet with him. It was the anxiety that Jesus was pointing at. It had to be dealt with and removed. There hadn't even been a speck of uneasiness in the session with the man.

---

84   Rice, p. 6.
85   Meier et al, p. 314.

Then Jesus said something that really twisted my brain. He said, "Jan, I just love working with you." Jesus working with me? I could understand it the other way around, me working with Jesus—but Jesus working with me?! It really is a wonder!

Jesus truly sticks closer than a brother. This experience could be yours too if you allow the Spirit to lead!

After all these years of ministering, I can say with all conviction that this type of ministry is only achieved in partnership with the Father, Son, and Spirit—me following in step.

This was illustrated for me one day as I was counselling a dissociated person who had a little girl inside her (see Chapter 11 for more information on Dissociation). Frequently when one uncovers an inner child, they are in a dark place and remain there until you earn their trust.

At a particular point in the session, I felt it was time for her to ask Jesus to open the window for some light.

She responded by saying, "He has already asked if He could, and I said yes."

I laughed and said, "I guess I'm a step behind Jesus."

She answered, "Yes, you are!"

Only the love of Jesus could reach into the broken, shattered heart and soul of a thirty-year-old woman seeking healing from the memories that were breaking through into her conscious mind for the first time—memories of being raped daily by her father, starting at the age of three and up to fourteen. We can do much for these dissociated ones, but only Jesus can bring healing, wholeness and oneness to the soul that has been so horrifically shattered.

As He has done through me, He will also do through you. He isn't waiting for you to complete training. He is waiting for you to begin reaching out to others, speaking into their lives, and encouraging them to do the same.

Remember this: stepping out is level one of your Jesus training, and if you continue in it, it won't be long before Jesus has you plunged into the practice of Christian counselling. He will lead you, teach you, and equip you.

Caution: There is a lot of ministry accomplished in the name of Jesus by individuals who are highly trained, with many diplomas hanging on office walls. But all their training might lead to few, if any, life-changing or lasting results. Why would that be?

Often, it's as simple as this: once trained, we completely depend on our years of training and experience. In doing so, we place Jesus in the far corner of our desk—unseen, unreachable and more often than not, forgotten. How foolish! He has in His hand the Owner's Manual for each and every one of us. This manual has within it the answer to every question and every cry of our hearts, whether for counsellor or counsellee.

As you work through these pages, you will see that the Bible has much to say about counselling and about our individual calling to instruct and build up our brothers and sisters in the Lord. In particular, we must understand the importance of being a disciple before we become a disciple-maker. There is a lot of effective, life-changing ministry achieved by people whose only credentials are a passionate heart for God, along with a passionate heart for those in need. God works miracles in that kind of spiritual atmosphere.

Non-Christian practitioners unknowingly find themselves disadvantaged. It isn't that they have any less ability in working with others. On the contrary, I personally have been the recipient of their counsel. Their knowledge of psychology, along with the depth of their care and concern, made me cognizant of my own inadequacies as a Christian counsellor. But the truth of the matter is, we have the advantage in Jesus. I have no doubt whatsoever that Jesus works in the lives of unbelieving practitioners, and even through them. Absolutely every person is created by God; we are all His. The downfall for the unbeliever, though, is that he lacks the power of the Holy Spirit and the use of prayer for healing.

The difference between Christ-centered counselling and strictly "soulical" counselling is significant! As believers, the love and healing power of God lives in us, via the indwelling Spirit of God, imparting and confirming truth as His healing power flows through us.

What joy it is to work with Jesus. Yet many Christians are standing back, saying, "I cannot do ministry." If Jesus wasn't going before us, I would concur with that statement. But why would we ever do ministry without Him? Simply stated, we cannot, and if we try to, we will surely lose the incredible, cutting-edge advantage that we have as believers. We are empowered by the Spirit to do exactly as Jesus did—and even more, simply because we have been given many years to minister to others, whereas Jesus only had only three years.

9.3.2. Spirit Soul Body

It is imperative that we feed our spirit man with the Word of God. It is literally our life—the source of healing for our flesh and bones and every cell and fibre in between. A person with a wounded spirit does not heal well. Our spirit man is one with our soul—after all, the only outward expression our spirit has is through our soul, the psychological aspect of man.

Our soul is the part of us that contains our life journey, good or bad. This is where the evil one dwells, if he has something on us. This is seen in Ephesians 4:26–27, *"Do not let the sun go down while you are still angry, and do not give the devil a foothold."* The word "foothold" in the original means a place in the soul. If given opportunity, Satan will move in and make our soul his dwelling place, so he doesn't have to work against us from the outside.

In order for us to live in the unchanging peace that is ours through the sanctifying work of God, we need to have a working knowledge of the spirit, soul, and body. Not just for ourselves, but so we can pass it on as we disciple others.

If we are born again, our spirit man becomes the dwelling place, the Tabernacle, of God within our person. How can that be? Just typing those words causes my spirit man to rejoice. Oh, the brilliance of God. This shows His deep love for His creation. It's an illustration of how mankind receives his Son Jesus, so that God himself can come and make His dwelling place within our person. Wonder of wonders!

Sumrall has this to say on the subject:

You have a conflict within you. Your soulical parts want to dominate your spiritual parts… You will know God by saying, "Bring that spiritual, born-again nature into me and revive the spirit part of me!" Immediately new things begin to come into your mind; new feelings begin to come into your emotions, and you become a new person in the Lord Jesus Christ.[86] (See also Chapter 3, Forgiveness, for information on Salvation.)

And further,

As soon as you believe you are a son of God, you move into another realm, and your total abilities, spirit, soul, and body, relate to God and spiritual things ... Through Adam we become living souls, but in Christ we become quickening spirits. We are twice sons; we are sons of Adam naturally, and we are sons of the Spirit supernaturally.[87]

God created man, a three-dimensional personality. Neither psychology nor psychiatry realize this, and humanism will never understand it at all. Everything in this universe that was initially perfect is indelibly stamped with a three. God is Father, Son, and Holy Spirit—the three function as one. Man is a spirit, soul, and body—functioning as one. The will is one-third of the human soulical personality. The soul is one-third of the total personality of the person. Your soulical parts consist of your mind, emotions, and will. This is how you relate to other humans.[88]

9.3.3. In Your Strength or in God's Strength

We are very excited when we first recognize God's call on our life for ministry. Along with the excitement, there is a measure of anxiety, and we may feel, "I can't do this!" But confidence begins to abound when we recall that He is with us and that by His Spirit, He will teach us all things.

I have much more to say to you, more than you can now bear. But when he, the Spirit of truth, comes, he will guide you into all truth. He will not

---

86   Sumrall, p. 76.
87   Ibid, p. 126.
88   Ibid, p. 125.

speak on his own; he will speak only what he hears, and he will tell you
what is yet to come.

—John 16:12–13

We quickly realize that we cannot do this on our own. But over time, maybe in a few years or only a few months of seeing many set free and growing in the Lord, we find ourselves feeling pretty smug. We have been totally unaware that somewhere along the road of life and ministry, we have lost four little words: "In Christ I can!"

It is incumbent upon us to be alert always: *"Be sober; be vigilant; because your adversary the devil walks about like a roaring lion, seeking whom he may devour"* (1 Peter 5:8, NKJV).

For our protection, God has provided us with a "straight and narrow" road, one that you and I travel daily. We cross paths with those in need of fellowship, counsel, or ministry. Or perhaps we are the ones in need. See Isaiah 35:8, *"And a highway will be there; it will be called the Way of Holiness; it will be for those who walk on that Way. The unclean will not journey on it; wicked fools will not go about on it."* If we always choose righteousness, that in itself will keep us in the center of the straight and narrow road, which becomes for us the stronghold of God's love (see Chapter 4).

9.3.4. My Story

About three years into practicing my call, I made a subconscious choice to step back from the deliverance and dissociation arena of counselling due to much opposition against my ministry. The church we attended wouldn't support my ministry, which precipitated a decision from my ministry's board of directors that I leave that church in order to continue in my practice.

At the same time, others in the community wrote an article in our local paper, stating that I had no Biblical platform for the type of counselling I was doing. They claimed that I was demonizing the very people I was attempting to minister to, because—in their words—I was not working from the Word but from my own limited experience, and was driven by emotions only. I carried on counselling, still Christian-based and digging deep into people's issues. However, I avoided controversial issues due to all the opposition from those who believed that deliverance was unnecessary once a person had been saved. Because of that, my ministry was becoming more psychological and topical.

This went on for over a year. I still kept relatively busy, but there was very little fruit. Those that came in were going out in very much the same state, instead of happy and excited people leaving my office looking forward to the next appointment. This went on until I had no steady clientele.

One morning during prayer, as I was preparing for a client, the Lord spoke to me. He said, "Jan, I have let you go this way because you needed to know. You need to now go back to where you began." The Lord wanted me to recognize the huge deficit between ministering through the soul and ministering through the Spirit.

I'm sure you get the picture. I gave ground to our enemy by caving in to the fear of man, which let my flesh take leadership. And where flesh reigns, the Spirit is pushed aside.

Sometime after Jesus had reinstated me, one of our local churches brought in a speaker from out of province. His message was awesome, and I went up for prayer. He saw me coming and walked toward me until we were about two or three feet apart. He said very strongly, *"Started very strong in the Spirit but caved in to the fear of man!"* and he turned around and walked away. This five-second encounter was once again God's way again getting my attention. He used a messenger from a foreign land, so to speak, who did not know me, nor I him, to authenticate His message to me: "Jan, deal thoroughly with your fear of man."

9.3.5. Ministering in the Spirit or Ministering in the Flesh

God has no limitations on His ability to speak directly into our lives, or to send a messenger with words that move us back onto the center of the road, thus enabling Jesus to once again be actively involved. For the Holy Spirit to be actively involved in all our ministry, we must invite Him to lead us and go before us. I very often ask Him to arrange things in the spiritual realm so that the enemy cannot surprise us with some sort of evil intervention.

To minister in the spirit, first remember that the person sitting before you is made in the very image of God. Second, know this person is here because Jesus has a plan and purpose for him or her. Third, acknowledge that

His plan involves you. Fourth, remember that Jesus is there with you, and He is unquestionably excited to be a part of what will take place.

Remember also what God has promised us: *"Be strong and courageous. Do not be afraid or terrified because of them, for the Lord your God goes with you; he will never leave you nor forsake you"* (Deuteronomy 31:6).

I have absolutely no doubt that Jesus goes before us, making a way for us to connect with the individual He has chosen to send our way. It is incumbent upon the counsellor to be focused on the client and engaged in both the natural and the spiritual realm. It is the Spirit of God which brings the potential for supernatural work into the counselling setting.

In this type of supernatural ministry we are never alone—indeed, we simply never could do this on our own. The Spirit leads these sessions, but on an individual level. He works with our unique abilities in various ways, fitting them into the purpose of God for the person to whom we are ministering. This grants us the ability to see, hear, understand, and respond to the counsellee, so they in turn may receive and hear from God in the spiritual realm.

God speaks to mankind most often via 1) the Bible, 2) His Word spoken directly into our mind, and 3) from His indwelling Spirit.

We must be cognizant of what is coming into our minds. The very route God uses to speak to our minds is also used by Satan to accuse, confuse, and condemn. First, if you are not diligent in monitoring what is coming into your thoughts, you can get caught up in agreeing with Satan's schemes. Second, you may think, "God has never spoken to me, so why would He speak to me now?" People do not believe that God speaks to them, and the biggest reason is unbelief. Unbelief blocks, whereas faith unlocks the door for God's voice.

Principle #27: Unbelief blocks but faith unlocks.

Throughout my years of practice, God has been speaking into the minds and spirits of many, many people. You may have heard of "the sixth sense" or "gut feeling" or "intuition." I believe these "senses" *can be* God's voice, often giving direction or bringing instruction to avoid calamity or harm. My point is that you need to learn to discern the difference between the voice of God, the voice of Satan, and your own voice. To reiterate, this is Spirit-lead ministry! By choosing to rely on our own experiences, we transform the ministry into *our* ministry. In doing so, we commission ourselves as the leader and effectively close the door to the voice of Jesus.

We started well as God led us into our call. But here we are now, with a few years of experience under our belt, and a few of our own ideas. After all, there isn't a lot of personal glory in just being a "vessel." It isn't wrong to desire your own personal ministry, but the question is always, "Who is going to lead? The Spirit or the flesh?"

God requires our ongoing and passionate availability. If we continually put off our old person and put on the new, the results will be a spiritual maturing, becoming more competent and more like God in true righteousness and holiness. There it is! We can choose to *put on* that which looks like Christ and reproduce the same in our lives, with the Spirit flowing through us like a river.

To live in the place of daily putting on the new self (Ephesians 4:24) is to be at the very pinnacle of Christian ministry. It's like being on the mountaintop of God with Him. This place is available for everyone that will pay the price. I've been there, but I haven't always lived there. At different times, I've found myself beaten and bruised, looking up from the bottom of the mountain with the painful acknowledgment of how far I've fallen. Sometimes I was actually pushed over the edge. Satan hates deliverance and discipleship ministry with a passion, and he will do everything in his power to bring about our fall. Sadly, our problems are often our own doing.

I know there is a multitude out there living a life for God's glory. But what I am trying to say, somewhat loudly, is, *"Never, ever, do ministry without Jesus being at the very center of it."* If you do, [[You are dishonouring those you are trying to disciple

You are leaving yourself wide open to the schemes of Satan

You are effectively eliminating Jesus from your ministry]]

9.3.6. The Crossroad

God foresaw the pride and frailty of mankind, and out of His great love and mercy, He provided a checkpoint for us, a place to re-establish our footing.

This is what the Lord says: "Stand at the crossroads and look; ask for the ancient paths, ask where the good way is, and walk in it, and you will find rest for your souls. But you said, 'We will not walk in it.'"
—Jeremiah 6:16

A crossroad brings us a choice. This is the place to ask, "Am I in step with the Spirit that dwells in me?" When you find yourself in utter confusion, without direction, and with a hundred questions all aimed at God, step back. This could very well be a crossroad.

I've been there more than once. In 2003, I was burned out and had to close my office for about a year. For most of that time, I couldn't even read my Bible because it caused such intense headaches. The worst thing was that I never heard one word from God, although I prayed and prayed.

Finally, one night while I was praying, God spoke my name. I was beginning to pray, "God, forgive me for destroying the tabernacle of my heart, Your dwelling place in my person." I had only begun my first word when God spoke over my words, saying, "Jan, in the darkest hour of your soul, you never lost sight of your God. And in that, you worshipped Me."

This was a type of crossroad, and it was with God Himself. His intention is that every crossroad would reposition us through a life-changing encounter with Him. A crossroad can be a place where there is only one set of footprints in the sand, where Jesus carries one across a dry and dusty desert. A crossroad can be at the bottom of a ditch where Jesus comes and says, "Although I'm in this ditch with you, it's not where I want you to stay."

While with a client, I often pray aloud so they can hear me ask the question, "God, what is 'the way' for this person you have sent to me today?" God often responds immediately to that question by speaking into their heart to identify an issue that needs some action. I purposely pray aloud with my clients so they can hear and understand my prayer requests on their behalf. This causes them to posture their heart so they can receive God's response.

Because of Judah's sin, God put obstacles in her way. Still today, God disciplines and directs His people in a similar way.

> The elaborate burnt offerings and sacrifices, divorced from a genuine love for God, did not please Him. Instead of accepting this hypocritical worship, God vowed to put obstacles in the way of the people so they would stumble. The nature of the obstacles is not given, but it is likely that God was again referring to the Babylonians (cf. Jer. 6:22).[89]

Today, if we choose to continue in our sinful ways, we will eventually find ourselves facing God's obstacles, which Jeremiah would call a crossroad—a place to stop, to think, to choose His way or ours. This topic has been covered different times in this book, primarily because it is God's means of getting our attention in our times of separation from Him. It is a critical point and one to consider whenever you find yourself between a rock and a hard place. A crossroad is God's grace at work on our behalf. God is still saying, *"Stand at the crossroads and look; ask for the ancient paths, ask where the good way is, and walk in it, and you will find rest for your souls."*

Make Jeremiah 6:16 the place of refuge and direction for you as you work with others, bringing them with you to the crossroad for their encounter with God. As I typed this last sentence or two, the Spirit of God utterly overwhelmed me by His presence—I believe for your benefit. Although I received His presence washing over me, it was to say to you, the reader, "As you walk through the following Scripture, you are making a way for a crossroad, an encounter with God!"

The Word tells us to ask God where the good way is. Craig Hill says the following with regard to verse 16:

> The Hebrew word for "GOOD" used in this passage is the word "TOV." Some of the meanings of this word are: pleasant, agreeable, happy, well-off, prosperous, great, excellent, cheerful, merry, and distinguished. Such characteristics are the result of walking in the

---

89   Dyer, pp. 1138–1139.

ancient paths of God. This scripture passage further says that when you walk in these paths, you will find rest for your soul. So many people today have very little rest or peace on the inside. Life is a constant struggle, and there is a continual torment on the inside of many. God never intended for us to have to live this way.[90]

Ask Him where the rest for your soul is. Ask Him how to walk in it. He very much wants to renovate, making us new on the inside. But without our permission, He cannot. Open up for Him those tear-stained, painful rooms, and ask Him to replace all that with His good way.

I encourage you to lay the book aside for a bit. Right now, you can have a crossroad experience, your own encounter with the Most High God. Receive His answers and the blessings that follow. Remember that this is a place of decision and change. Ask God to identify those areas where change is needed for your life and then commit to bring about the change for which you are responsible. God will certainly be faithful to provide you with what you need from Him. *I urge you to stay where you are until you record what you have heard from God!*

9.3.7. The Good Way

The "good way" is an illustration of everyday Christian life and interaction with our Heavenly Father. Every question you have is a crossroad in real life, and it leads to a choice. Every problem, every heartache, every trial and tribulation produces a crossroad, a place where we can go to God asking, "Which is the 'good way' for me?"

God is a God who answers, but if you aren't hearing back from Him, ask yourself this question: "Is there any known sin in my life that I need to deal with before God can respond to me?" Or, "Is there something God has asked me to do that I haven't done yet?" That could also block the Word of God.

So often in our pride of life, we turn from the instruction of God and do it our own way. This once again places us in the flesh, producing only death instead of spiritual life.

---

90   Hill, pp. 1–2.

9.3.8. The Crossroad: Potential Dangers

Now that we have a better understanding of the crossroad as a safeguard, here are some potential dangers for which we must be watchful.

Most of us started out in ministry desperate for His direction every step of the way. But now we have regularly seen miracles due to "our" prayers and the laying on of "our" hands, and we start to boast "I have done these great things." All the while, the red light at this crossroad is flashing, and the words "*In Christ I can*" are fading away into a distant memory. If this is not nipped in the bud, Satan, who has been busy greasing the slippery slope, will have you in the ditch—a place from which many never escape.

If we, because of our many successful campaigns against the evil one, begin to personalize our successes while thinking or saying, "Look what I can do," we are actually sowing a seed of pride alongside our Christian life's road. Satan will be more than happy to water this seed until it expands to a size that leaves no room in our lives for Christ Jesus, pushing us to the edge of the ditch.

I suppose this may sound a bit judgmental, negative or harsh. But stay with me as I make my point. Remember, this is about the dangers we encounter along the Christian road, and our ability to stay in the centre with Jesus, for the Glory of the Father.

Option number one is staying in the centre of life's road with Jesus, for the glory of the Father. Option number two: living on the slippery slope side of the ditch with sinners by night and living for Jesus in the light of day, so to speak. In option number three, we forsake the road entirely and just live in the ditch. This is a natural consequence of continuing too long in option number two.

The problem is that when we reach the heights of perceived success, we are unknowingly at a place of great danger, which is at the least twofold. First, success for mankind is often fatal spiritually. It is the exact point we talked about before where we drop the "In Christ" and continue on with only two words, "I can." The second danger at this height is Satan's knowledge of the pride of mankind. He knows the buttons he needs to push in each one of us in order to increase our self-pride so much that God can no longer use us.

Your argument right now may be, "I would never choose my way over God's way." But truth be told, the potential for this in any of our Christian lives, including those of counsellors and pastors, is very real. If we aren't careful, after years and years of preaching, counselling and other types of ministering, it can all become rote for us. If we are no longer intentionally walking with Jesus Christ, little by little we begin to drift from centre. Jesus will no longer be our first thought as we prepare to sit down with a client.

Satan won't be satisfied to steal from you somewhere along the side of the road every once in a while. No, he will bring his traps right into your home or office to destroy you.

The following traps or setups were sent by Satan:

- Individuals and couples have come into my office just to judge and harass me. My only option was to open the exit door and point at it, saying "Go!" And they ran out.
- At times, women have come in for counselling and within a few moments, the room was filled with such lust that I canceled the session, saying that I could not meet their need. I believe these women had no idea of the setup.
- One afternoon I was sitting in the back office. My secretary had already left, and I was just getting ready to leave for the day when a very beautiful woman, about twenty, walked in. I turned my chair as she came in so I could see who it was. She just walked right over to me and dropped onto my lap. I scrambled quickly to my feet, and took her out to the outer office, thinking it best to sit in my secretary's chair, which would position me behind the office desk facing outward towards her. I placed a chair for her on the other side of the desk, thinking that from there I could determine her reason for coming in. I sat in my chair, and then turned to reach for my Bible. When I turned back, she had picked up her chair, come around behind the desk, and plunked it alongside mine. By this time, I knew what her intention was, and I said, "I'm going to begin by praying," which I did aloud. It wasn't very many seconds until she stood up, ran as fast as

she could out of my office, and down a long hallway to an exit. I've never seen anybody run in a building like that, but it wasn't really her running. It was the demons scalded by the prayer that rushed her out!

As I write of these experiences, the Holy Spirit reminds me that the people in these instances were not leaving in an upright position, but hunched over like an animal, which is a common posture for demonization.

9.3.9. Dangers of Going Off-Centre

The roads we travel with natural vehicles, be it by train, car or truck, have a ditch on each side, and so it is in the spiritual realm. If we abide in Christ, we are secure in the center of the road, but if we get restless or careless in our Christian walk, we don't have to travel very far before we find the beginning of a slippery slope into darkness. If our curiosity about what the world can offer us hasn't been satisfied yet, the next step has the potential to take us into cold and murky waters, all stirred up by the snake that lives there.

The many ways and means by which our enemy works to get us off the centre line, the centre of the Road of Righteousness, will never be fully counted this side of heaven. One example we do know of is lust. Of course, lust has many faces, but sexual lust has our whole world wired. Thirteen-year-old girls are offering sex to their male peers, and, unknowingly, Christian moms and dads perpetuate this problem by sending their very young girls out all pret-tied up, dressed like twenty-year-old women. God forbid!

This off-the-centre-of-the-road lifestyle can push the whole family into the ditch. Soon the children are adolescents, sixteen-, eighteen-, or twenty-year-olds who never had the opportunity to choose the centre of the road for themselves.

Am I too harsh? Certainly for some, but not for most! Sexual lust today is like a crisp, dry forest fire, out of control and unstoppable.

Here are some examples of how God deals with sexual sin issues.

Do you not know that he who unites himself with a prostitute is one with her in body? For it is said, "The two will become one flesh." But whoever is united with the Lord is one with him in spirit. Flee from sexual immorality. All other sins a person commits are outside the body, but whoever sins sexually, sins against their own body. Do you not know that your bodies are temples of the Holy Spirit, who is in you, whom you have received from God? You are not your own; you were bought at a price. Therefore honor God with your body.

—1 Corinthians 6:16–20

Say to the people of Israel, "This is what the Sovereign Lord says: I am about to desecrate my sanctuary—the stronghold in which you take pride, the delight of your eyes, the object of your affection. The sons and daughters you left behind will fall by the sword.

—Ezekiel 24:21

This is how the Amplified version (AMPC) says it:

Speak to the house of Israel, Thus says the Lord God: Behold, I will profane My sanctuary—[in which you take] pride as your strength, the desire of your eyes, and the pity and sympathy of your soul [that you would spare with your life]; and your sons and your daughters whom you have left behind shall fall by the sword.

Fortunately, we can rely on God: *"But he gives us more grace. That is why Scripture says: 'God opposes the proud but shows favor to the humble.'"* (James 4:6). This refers to Proverbs 3:34: *"He mocks proud mockers but shows favor to the humble and oppressed."*

9.3.10. Other Dangers

We see the examples of the dangers in the Apostle Paul's writings.

Three times I was beaten with rods, once I was pelted with stones, three times I was shipwrecked, I spent a night and a day in the open sea, I have been constantly on the move. I have been in danger from rivers, in danger from bandits, in danger from my fellow Jews, in danger from

Gentiles; … and in danger from false believers. I have labored and toiled and have often gone without sleep; I have known hunger and thirst and have often gone without food; I have been cold and naked.

—2 Corinthians 11:25–27

People are still being persecuted and martyred for the sake of the Gospel in our day, with the same dangers as Paul. We face our own persecution today in many ways. We may be ridiculed by our own families for our decision to accept Christ. The workplace can be a harsh place for a born-again practicing Christian. One of the dangers that many of us fall into is to hide our Christianity, therefore hiding Christ. To deny Him is a sin—once again, it entails separation from the Godhead. Certainly, these things are small when compared to Paul's experiences, but persecution is persecution.

Another potential danger occurs after we have experienced a few good years in ministry to others. At this point, we begin to draw from our own knowledge base and experience. This in and of itself is not wrong, for it is through experience that we increase in knowledge relative to our call or gifting. Building our knowledge base is the process of sharpening our tools; sharp tools give us a sense of being equipped, and what follows is more confidence. This is a very good place to be, but it also has can lead to temptations, for our old nature takes pride in our accomplishments.

At this point, if we haven't dealt completely with our old nature, this is the situation that Satan has been waiting for. He sees us perched on this pinnacle of success, and he knows exactly how to light a little fire of pride in our abilities. If we don't recognize the path we are on, the next step, once again, is the ditch. I know that ditch; I have been there a few times myself.

If you are a disciple that has made Jesus King, and you are committed to advancing God's Kingdom, then look out—you are a target for the enemy. If you say, "Satan has never interfered in my life," that would indicate you are no threat to him. Maybe you need to have a good look at your Christian life. As believers, we *should* be a threat to Satan. When we get up in the morning to go and face life, we should literally cause Satan and his crew to tremble. When we walk by somebody that is demonized, the demon inside should be trembling.

9.3.11. The Price

There is, without fail, a heavy price to pay for sin in our lives. And there are many of God's best that never get up after a fall. It's a terrible personal loss, but it's also a loss to the Kingdom of God when we lose someone to the ditch. We lose a measure of the power we had when we pushed together against the gates of hell.

The following is an interesting teaching by Hudson Taylor on the consequences of sin.

"The world is a hard master;" he wrote, "and sin, even if forgiven, is never undone; its consequences remain. The sin of David was forgiven, but the prophet who announced the pardon was commissioned to tell him that the sword would never depart from his house. Every sin committed is a seed sown, and abides in its consequences; and, however secret it may have been, it shall, as the Savior teaches, be brought to light. This truth needs emphasis in the present day, even among the children of God... Because God graciously promises that forgiven sin shall be no more remembered against the believer, many forget that God's word equally assures us that "God will bring every deed into judgment, including every hidden thing, whether it is good or evil" (Ecclesiastes 12:14), a passage the force of which has not passed away under the new dispensation; for the Lord himself endorses it, saying: "There is nothing concealed that will not be disclosed, or hidden that will not be made known" (Luke 12:2). And Paul says: "We must all appear before the judgment seat of Christ" (2 Corinthians 5:10). "And not only so; for even in this life there is a reaping, in measure, of that which is sown, which may come from the hands of men, who are often God's sword to chasten his children."[91]

---

91   Steer, pp. 87–88.

Charles Spurgeon says, "As salt flavors every drop in the Atlantic, so does sin affect every atom of our nature. It is so sadly there, so abundantly there, that if you cannot detect it, you are deceived."[92]

9.3.12. Am I Called to be a Counsellor, and if so, How Would I Counsel?

If you follow God's command to be a disciples and disciple-maker, what will that look like?

There are many, many types of counselling: grief counselling, anger counselling, family counselling, and so on. Christian counsellors end up wearing many hats, but for our own well-being and the well-being of those we work with, we need to first have an idea of our knowledge base relative to the needs we may encounter, along with our interpersonal skills.

Do you have a deep desire to help people through their struggles, or have you ever pictured yourself counselling and loving others? Just start by being a friend. For your own growth, it would be helpful if you could sit in on sessions with a counsellor or maybe a pastor. It won't be long before you know whether this is your calling or not.

Some of you will say, "I only want to be a counsellor, doing no deliverance," or the other way around, "I only want to do deliverance." Well, you can do it either way if you wish, but you will see as you read on that counselling and deliverance are meant to become one in practice. We need to minister to the whole person. As Meier says, "…Christian counseling is unique because it seeks to deal with the whole person. The Christian counselor is aware that the physical, psychological, and spiritual aspects of human beings are intricately related."[93] Therefore, when one part is affected the other parts probably will be too.

Over the years, I've seen lots of committed Christians who have received solid Christian counselling. They know the Word and daily apply it to their lives, but they haven't received freedom in certain areas of their lives. Often this is simply because they were never delivered from Satan's schemes. So go where God is calling you, but be aware there will be times where counselling and deliverance overlap. This might mean that you will have to leave your

---

92   Carter, p. 53.

93   Meier et al, p. 314.

comfort zone and trust God to equip you as needed, or it might mean working with another practitioner gifted in areas you are not.

9.3.13. Models of Counselling

How will you choose to counsel?

There are many options, but I will only discuss three:

1. Non-Directive Method. The counsellor mainly listens, being a sounding board. The counsellee finds the answers.
2. Alongside Method. The counsellor guides the counsellee. They work as a team.
3. Instructive and Directive Method. The counsellor teaches and directs. The counsellee hears the truth and is taught how to apply it to his actions.

My choice has been number three. People are looking for help, and if they had the answers to their problems they wouldn't be looking to engage a counsellor. Many people come to understand that by themselves, they are unable to bring change to some area of their lives. Therefore, I believe a counsellor should offer good solid Biblical instruction, with the counsellee very much involved in the application of the teaching.

Homework is very effective: you can instruct your counsellee with material to take home. You can also gauge application and change in the counsellee by looking at the results of the homework.

As I have already said, the Bible—the Manual written by God, through man, for man—is a treasure trove of solid, reliable instructions for meeting our spiritual, psychological, and "soulical" needs. The Bible is thoroughly and absolutely adequate in equipping both men and women to do what the Bible calls us to do. *"All Scripture is God-breathed and is useful for teaching, rebuking, correcting and training in righteousness, so that the servant of God may be thoroughly equipped for every good work"* (2 Timothy 3:16–17). The concept that *"All scripture is God-breathed"* is profoundly powerful—it literally sends shivers down my spine.

When we speak the Word of God into individuals' lives, it goes forth, dividing soul and spirit, and it does not return void (Isaiah 55:11; Hebrews 4:12). The Word within us literally exposes our carnality, bringing it out of the darkness of our soul, and exposing it to the brilliant light of *"all scripture."*

When we examine 2 Timothy 3:16–17, we see that God's Word ministers to us in four ways: to teach, to rebuke, to correct, and to train. Firstly, it teaches us how to apply God's Word and builds a platform of Biblical principles that we can stand on. Secondly, it rebukes us we stray away from that which is right and exposes the ways in which our lives are not following the Biblical principles we have learned. Once exposed, God's Word is there to correct us, to bring about changes in our thinking and actions that reflect the biblical principles we have been taught. Lastly, it instructs or trains us how to live righteously. God's word is there to guide us and equip us with the discipline we need to do His work.[94]

We can see that as we move up these steps, each becomes stronger in application. In the process of becoming a counsellor and then practicing, we must always remember that our strength is the Lord. As Isaiah 12:2b says, *"... the Lord God is my strength and my song, and he has become my salvation"* (ESV). We need to be thankful for that, for counselling is hard work and can only be done by the helping hand of God.

9.3.14. Diagnosis

Norman Wright says this of diagnosis:

> My emphasis in diagnosis is interpersonal rather than intrapsychic. Intrapsychic has to do with behavior that is produced by the internal condition of the body and mind. Interpersonal has to do with behavior that is produced by our interaction with people. My diagnosis and therapy has to do largely with helping people understand their problem in terms of their relations with and reactions to other people. Now I don't eliminate the intrapsychic entirely. Any client

---

94   Strong, 1984.

who tends to be depressive I refer to a doctor for a complete check-up before he begins counseling.[95]

I found it to be very interesting that upon researching diagnosis, my process turns out to be very much the same as Norman Wright's, without his terminology. By ourselves we simply cannot meet everyone's needs. We are wise when we refer our clients to a doctor, psychologist or psychiatrist.

When we choose not to refer our clients to others who are more trained, and therefore more able to meet the need, we are hindering their growth and freedom. As counsellors, we may jealously hold onto our clients, often hindering the purpose of God and the client's spiritual growth. Every counsellor will eventually have a client they just cannot work with for some reason. That client needs to be introduced to a different counsellor.

Generally, the first counselling session is a time for the counsellor and the counsellee to begin to get to know each other. I attempt to lead the first session in a way that I can send the counsellee home with a sense of hope because of the options available and the presence of Jesus. That almost always provides a positive expectation of change for the next session.

9.3.15. Homework

Failure in counselling is sometimes due to the counsellor's inability to properly diagnose the client's situation, and a resulting inability to give good and helpful instructions that would help the counsellee overcome his problem. However, my experience is that most failures are simply because the client fails to apply what they learn.

In my opinion, the instructive method of counselling is much more successful with homework than the other two models are. This is an advantage. I believe homework is critical in most types of counselling needs. It helps the client understand their problems. This then aids in bringing change to negative and sinful habit patterns.

The counsellor has a profound responsibility to choose appropriate homework for the specific need of the counsellee. The onus is now on the counsellee to complete the homework and apply it to the areas of need. This

---

95   Wright, p. 191.

is hard work for both, and there are times when a client refuses to do the homework and the application.

Again, the lack of application is the number one reason for failure in counselling. Most counsellees come in with the mindset that the counsellor is totally responsible for the improvement of their situation. They leave the office after the session, excited because they have some new insight. Even more importantly, they felt the presence of God in the session. Yet, upon their return, they may have lost the sense of expectation.

In many cases, they left excited and went home to face all of their problems, yet the homework is still lying undone on the kitchen table. The work of the counsellor is now to help the counsellee understand why they failed.

The response to the question, "How was your week?" is often, "It was even worse than before." I use this answer as an opportunity to do a little teaching on prayer and how to stand against the powers of darkness that do not want your restoration. I explain that the enemy will be working his schemes to block their healing and growth in Jesus Christ.

If the client continually fails to complete their homework, we may have to exercise the love and grace of Christ by telling them that they are wasting their time and finances by not applying what they are being taught. This will often change things. However, there have been a few times over the years that I have refused to carry on with a client, simply because they refused to do their part in applying the homework, or following the instructions I gave them.

Still, do not be hasty in rebuking your client; remember God's grace in your times of lack or sin. Remember the words of Romans 5:20b: *"... but where sin increased, grace increased all the more."* There is usually a way around the problems you have with your client. Whether you're working with the unsaved or the born again, always remember that your words can have a lasting effect on their eternal destiny. If you are working with the born again, which doesn't necessarily make counselling any easier, *always remember how longsuffering Father God has been with you.* Christian counselling is far from easy, but there are huge rewards this side of heaven as we see the captives set free, with families restored and the broken-hearted healed.

Some of us knew, at a very early age, exactly what type of counselling we were to do. Others transition into counselling ministry, often from prayer ministry, just because of their love for people and their desire to minister to others. I need to remind you that your God-given gift makes a way for you. *"A gift opens the way and ushers the giver into the presence of the great"* (Proverbs 18:16).

God enables and drives us to reach out from within ourselves and accomplish that which we were created to do. Many of us—myself included—received our initial training in the very moment of working with and praying for others. Along the way, we attended every seminar and teaching we could find, and our training came primarily through our ongoing experience. Most of us know that there is no better way than to be trained up by experience.

For the most part, I agree with the practice of psychology, as I have been a benefactor of that level of training and expertise. But we need to be cautious, because our training can often get in the way of the spiritual realm. In no way whatsoever do I mean that we should rule out the professionally trained from Christian practice, but depending on the Spirit of God rather than our training would require a radical change in methodology for some. We need to be using what is in our toolbox of experience, as well as our training, in our Christian practice.

Prayer ministry is by nature spiritual; as you look to the Holy Spirit to lead, He will put, the necessary tools into your hand. Personally, after all these years of ministry to others, I am increasingly cognizant of the fact that my God is leading me onward. It should be the desire of every Christian worker to be engaged in the Spirit, and in that, to elevate, to lift up, and to carry our clients on to see great things. The need for Christian workers is escalating at every level. This should pull on the heart of every born-again believer. Step up to the plate and make a difference, whatever your gifting is! This is your opportunity to be obedient to the command of Jesus Christ to make disciples.

The world around us is getting darker and darker, partly because of the sharp increase in occult activities, such as the Harry Potter books, and partly due to the sexual lust that burns like a dry prairie fire circling our world. God has warned us of the consequences: *"In a similar way, Sodom and Gomorrah and the surrounding towns gave themselves up to sexual immorality and perversion. They serve as an example of those who suffer the punishment of eternal fire"* (Jude 1:7).

We are to use our tools of training and experience to help free others from this lifestyle and come to God. Matthew 11:12 says, *"...the kingdom of heaven has been subjected to violence, and violent people have been raiding it."* The Kingdom of God needs the Church to rise up and stand against the increase in outright visible sin.

Rise up, Church of Jesus Christ, and take a stand against the growing darkness that is taking out so many of our children and God's people through sin. I want to provoke you into taking a stand with Jesus against the gates of hell that are unrelentingly pushing against the Bride of Christ.

God has commanded all Christians to be disciple-makers, beyond our unique, individual giftings. Check your giftings by taking that first step of disciple-making, and He will shake heaven and hell to bring about your equipping. Fulfill God's call on your life by accepting the call and moving towards it.

Regardless of your gifting or particular type of ministry, the Bible clearly tells each of us to be burden bearers. In doing so, we find ourselves fulfilling the command to make disciples! *"Carry each other's burdens, and in this way you will fulfill the law of Christ"* (Galatians 6:2)

This will become much clearer as we search the Word for examples of how Jesus and His followers met people's spiritual, emotional and psychological needs. The following quote explain how Jesus interacted with individuals as he worked to meet all their needs.

> Jesus Christ, of course, was the Counselor of counselors. We can all learn from him, because he had perfect insight into human problems and was able to share that insight with others. He was an expert at asking questions, using them to teach, to rebuke irresponsible behavior, and to help others gain insight. He genuinely cared for others, giving them a feeling of self-worth. Because of his warm and personal concern for them, people were able to deal with their problems and not feel threatened. He could be matter-of-fact, rebuking, or friendly, as appropriate.

Jesus Christ could counsel others because of his close relationship with God the Father and because he understood human problems. He not only knew what people needed to do to deal with their problems, but also knew how to motivate people to change. Often he would lay down guidelines or formulate a plan to help individuals deal with their problems.

Christ was a master counselor with perfect balance. He knew when to be directive and when to be suggestive. He knew when to deal with the past and when to deal with the present. He knew the importance of feelings, but he also knew how to effect behavioral changes.[96]

---

96   Meier et al, pp. 339–340.

Chapter Ten

THE PROCESS OF DELIVERANCE

Behold, I give unto you power to tread on serpents and scorpions, and over all the power of the enemy: and nothing shall by any means hurt you.

—Luke 10:19, KJV

10.1. My Testimony

STOP HERE FOR A MINUTE OR TWO. GET STILL IN YOUR HEART AND MIND, and ask God, "Do You have something I am to be doing in ministry, primarily in deliverance?" If you have the slightest bit of curiosity about what you are reading, or feel even slightly drawn into this ministry, then pay attention, for often curiosity is your gifting moving you forward.

Wait on God; He will give you an understanding. But be aware: Satan is always working to hide your call from you! It isn't just about you or me. It's about the whole Church, the Bride of Jesus Christ, which so desperately needs to be informed and then prepared to meet the immediate deliverance needs of our current time.

God called me to carry out deliverance in the early eighties, when there was absolutely nobody I could find practicing such ministry. With the little experience I had in praying for others and seeing demons manifest, I knew that if I were to carry on ministering to others, I first needed deliverance myself.

Eventually, I found a man nine hundred kilometres away who said he had some experience in deliverance and would gladly meet with me at his home. I went and and spent two and a half days receiving ministry from him.

As he prayed, he commanded demons to identify themselves either to him or me. But never once did a demon respond in any form to either one of us. After all this man's praying and effort to bring me some deliverance and freedom, I left for home without any sense of change.

About five hours into my long drive home, I began to sense there was something different in my person, but I couldn't put my finger on what it was. I drove on for some time, then stopped the car and went for a walk down the side of the road praying, asking God to show me what was happening.

I drove on again, but not for long. This time, I was sensing an undeniable and growing excitement, mingled with a growing peace of mind. I was becoming more and more aware that something significant was taking place. I was realizing, little by little, was that the only thoughts in my mind were related to the current situation. This created joy in my heart and peace in my mind, because it was far from normal for me.

Normally, as far back as I could remember, morning, noon and night of every day, my head had been full of constant chatter—accusing, confusing and belittling me. I had believed this was just my brain accusing myself, and had never known anything different. Now here I was, heading off down the road, and driving without any accusations. My mind was so clear, and I was in control of my thoughts. In my excitement, it felt as though my car just flew home that night.

This was not the end of my personal deliverance, but it was a vast step forward that moved me toward accepting my call into deliverance and counselling ministry.

I have included my testimony because it shows some useful principles:

1. For the first time, I received personal deliverance. And now, years later as God has led me, I have seen many individuals set free as I commanded demons to identify their legal ground in a person by speaking into the mind of the host person. And they do!

2. I now believe that in my deliverance session, demons actually were speaking into my mind, as the pastor ministering to me had commanded them to do.

But, because of the ongoing, constant chatter in my mind, which brought nothing but confusion, the demons were able to block anything that may have been helpful for the man ministering to me. This is critical information for those of you involved in deliverance ministry. Confusion is one of Satan's most powerful and successful weapons against mankind.

When the demon was speaking in response to the commands of the man working to set me free, the words were lost, as they just blended with the ongoing chatter in my head. The cure for this common demonic strategy is to use your Jesus-given authority to command the demons to be silent, speaking only to answer your commands for necessary information.

When someone comes into your office for the first time to receive deliverance, they are in usually in a state of fear, and Satan is very happy to add confusion to the mix. You must get control of this before your first session begins. Take whatever time you need to bring the individual into an understanding of the complete process of deliverance, even if it means that you won't get started on deliverance in the first session. It is imperative that the person is able to put his or her full trust in you.

3. This point has to do with discernment. Having seen many set free through deliverance ministry, I believe that the freedom I recognized five hours into my drive home was the result of this man's ability to discern by inquiring into my life and struggles. But even more important was his ability to hear the instruction of the Holy Spirit and to pray accordingly. Don't miss my point! This story demonstrates, *"Is anyone among you in trouble? Let them pray"* (James 5:13). Much deliverance is accomplished as you heed the leadership of the Spirit of God that indwells you.

There will be times when there is simply no response from the demon when you command him to identify himself, although the information from the intake sheet and what you are hearing from the client would indicate there is demonic activity. In times of demonic silence, we must be discerning. Listen carefully for a response from the enemy. More importantly, we must always draw from the person of Jesus, differentiating between the voice of the enemy and the voice of Christ. If you are constantly listening and discerning, you will hear the voice of Jesus.

My own experience of being delivered proves that *"The prayer of a righteous man is powerful and effective"* (James 5:16).

There were no obvious signs of any deliverance happening. This pastor I had driven to see was a praying man, and while he was working to expose the evil one, he was also gathering information about my personal sin issues. We ran out of time; I had to leave for home the evening of the second day.

We closed with him leading me in a prayer of repentance, and then receiving God's forgiveness.

I have no doubt that the pastor carried on in prayer throughout the night, casting out demons relative to the confessed sins for which I had received forgiveness. His fervent prayers were the reason for the freedom and joy that made its way into my soul and spirit man during the long drive home. Never underestimate the power of a righteous praying man or woman!

If the individual you are working with isn't hearing from anything demonic, it could very well be that they have chosen not to believe in the process of deliverance. Also, if your client has brought a friend with them and the friend lacks faith, this too will hinder the process. Their lack of faith—a curse of spiritual deafeness—can strengthen the enemy and enable them to withhold information.

We cannot do deliverance without Jesus. We must always be aware that deliverance is spiritual warfare. As you are working to expose the enemy, he is working to defeat you.

A few months after the incredible change in my life though deliverance, I accidentally came into contact with Mr. Lobdale, a man who lived closer to my home and had been doing deliverance for years.

This man was a gift from God. Finally I had found someone that could meet my need for inner healing and deliverance. He was the second of two pastors that had said they could see the call of God on my life in the that realm. I had several counselling and deliverance sessions with Mr. Lobdale leading.

In one, he said, "Jan, I've been hearing for the past hour or so the words 'heart attack.' Do these words mean anything to you?"

"Yes, they certainly do," I replied. I explained to him that I had an uncle who'd died at the age of fifty-two from a heart attack, and he'd had an older brother who lived much longer but still had many heart problems throughout the years. I also told him that, at the age of forty, I'd had two heart attacks within a twelve-month period. After the second heart attack, I was referred to a heart specialist to see how much damage had been done to my heart. The medical results stated that there was no damage and my heart was healthy and sound!

I told Mr. Lobdale that my doctor at the time had advised me to see a pastor and to have a hard look at my life, saying, "Jan, I was with you both times you had those heart attacks! Amazingly, there is nothing wrong with your heart. There's nothing we can do for you; if you were to have another heart attack, we may very well carry you out in a wooden box."

Mr. Lobdale's response was, "Okay, let's do some digging to determine if there has been any demonic activity regarding your heart problems." A few minutes later, two demons were uncovered, both of their names being Heart Attack. The demons were cast out, and I have never had a single heart problem since that time. In fact, many years later, I still have the same family doctor doing my annual checkup. Recently, he sent me for a stress test on my heart, and the technician that took me through the physical said, "You have the heart of a twenty-year-old!"

There is a message here for everyone reading this: if you're dealing with health issues, in particular those that are unusual or life-threatening, don't turn a blind eye to the fact that there may be demonic activity involved. I am not saying that all health issues have a demonic basis, but rather that you should not discount demonic activity. Satan's strategy has never changed since *"The Lord said to Satan, 'Where have you come from?' Satan answered the Lord, 'From roaming throughout the earth, going back and forth on it'* (Job 1:7).

Satan's strategy of "roaming" has never wavered, and his purpose is the same since Job's day: to steal, kill and destroy. (Again, see 1 Peter 5:8.) I have no doubt that Satan tried to kill me through generational curses of heart problems and heart attacks.

Just recently, I was in contact with Mr. Lobdale, who is still doing deliverance ministry in his old age, and shared with him the circumstances surrounding a young man who had taken his life through suicide. His response to that was, "I don't call a situation like that suicide as we understand suicide today, 'the taking of one's own life.' I call it 'murder' by Satan and his crew."

Now, Satan or his demons cannot go about killing man or woman—not at all. But what they can do is draw a person into sin and then push them into such a deep, dark hole that they cannot see a way out. That person will often give up and take their own life. I know that is true, because I have seen it happen with many. And it absolutely should not be that way.

10.2. Where to Begin?

The New Testament does not give us a platform on which we can build a model for deliverance ministry. I suspect God intended that every disciple of Jesus should be prepared and available at all times to go about healing and casting out demons. In saying that, I, along with many others, conduct deliverance ministry everyday as part of disciple-making. The two should work side by side in every counselling session.

There is a growing need for people to get trained up and specialize in this type of ministry. What I hope to do at the outset of this chapter is to establish a platform that you can easily understand and use as a model for conducting deliverance ministry.

I began working in this area by reading some how-to books on deliverance. Therefore, I started out dealing individually with each and every demon in each person I ministered to. This proved to be a very tedious and time-consuming process. It isn't too hard if the person you are working on has very few demons, maybe four or five, but such a low number is very uncommon. It isn't unusual to be dealing with two or three dozen demons in an individual—and even that might be a low number for some people. But I carried on in this fashion for quite some time.

One day I said to the Lord, "There has to be a better way of doing deliverance." The Lord didn't give me an answer in word, but in my spirit (or person), I felt that if I dealt with the head demons in each person, commonly three or four, it would be much more time efficient. (These numbers vary greatly depending on the ground the enemy has in an individual. Sometimes there are hundreds of demons.) From that time on, I have accomplished deliverance ministry in this way, and over the many years it has proven to work very well for me.

In this process, you don't have to deal with every measly little demon. In fact, I don't deal with the underlings at all.

I will now establish a step-by-step process of tried and proven deliverance ministry.

10.3. Step 1 – Generational Sins

The first thing I do in session one is an intake, getting the information I need from the client relative to their problems. I also get as much information as possible relative to the extended family. I like to find out where their family roots originate. I do this because, as I've learned through experience, many who have roots in countries like Ireland or England have generational sins from hundreds of years back due to family involvement in Druidism, Freemasonry and others.

I have found it very advantageous to deal with all known generational sins before doing any deliverance. So in the first session, I send the client home with a Generational Sin List which you will find in Chapter 5, Generational Sins, as well as in Chapter 13, Toolbox. When the client comes in for the second session, we work through the list together, cutting off all generational curses. This is significant. I watch the client as I pray through this list, and very often it's like a huge weight coming off of them. Their shoulders rise and they sit up straighter in the chair.

In the first session, I also do my best to remove as much fear as possible. Believers frequently anticipate some violence, such as being thrown across the room, as they are going through deliverance. That is based on faulty perceptions. I share with them that the deliverance session will be about as stressful as the conversation we are currently having.

My clients also need to be honest with me about their level of faith. Coupled with mine, it enhances the spiritual force we have against opposing forces. Remember, there were times when even Jesus couldn't do much because of the unbelief of those around him. See Matthew 13:58: *"And he did not do many miracles there because of their lack of faith."* When a client brings in a friend or spouse to sit with them, at times I have had to ask one to leave. Because of their unbelief in this type of ministry, it has made it impossible for me to carry on.

As practitioners, you and I cannot haphazardly go about doing deliverance. We need to establish a well-thought-out means of achieving it, and work within our God-given personalities. For example, I would never conduct deliverance by getting into somebody's face, pushing, hollering, shouting, etc., as that isn't my personality. Many of you, I am sure, have seen this on TV. And I have no doubt many individuals get set free that way. But this isn't the type of deliverance ministry into which God has called me. Neither will it be for most of you who are reading and using this manual. In fact, you will realize that deliverance can be done in a very calm and comfortable manner—for the client as well as for the practitioner.

You will see as you read on that I do not allow demons to speak out at their will and wish. They certainly will speak out, if they can get away with it, grandstanding the session. But it is a disadvantage for us if this is allowed. It actually gives the demons added strength in the session.

10.4. Step 2 – Prayer Covering

Once you've facilitated your client through their first session, the next step is to identify the possibility of demonic activity in the person. When working with a couple, it's good if the husband is the vessel through which deliverance is accomplished, because he is the head over the family and carries a level of authority that complements the authority of the practitioner.

At the same time, it's my experience that deliverance is conducted much more easily through the female rather than through the male. For some reason, the female usually hears in the spiritual realm much more clearly than the male. Most often, if it is acceptable with the couple, I put the wife in the position of being the receiver of the demonic response to my questions and commands. We will call that person "the host," as they are providing the means for the enemy to speak. Once you choose that person, you are moving forward towards engaging the demonic realm.

Before you move in and engage a demon, you must cover the session with prayer. Acknowledge first that without the help of Jesus Christ you cannot do a thing for them. Pray as you see fit, but I always ask Jesus to come and be the very center of all that will take place, asking Him to be our Protector and the One who leads. Pray that God would give peace of heart and mind, especially for the host.

I recommend recording each session. This is because a deliverance session can become very intense, both for the practitioner and the individual receiving deliverance. Recorded information is very valuable, because it is a means of remembering all that has been said, and it is something to go back to once you have finished and have to restart again the following day.

It's very important to have someone else in the room for prayer support throughout the session. This person can also record the questions and answers from the demons.

10.5. Step 3 – Determining Issues

This is a process of coming to an understanding of why a person is demonized, and ensuring that demonic interference has been dealt with properly. Individuals that are demonized are most often deeply wounded, due not only to demonic activity but to lifestyle patterns. This requires you to take your client through the process of inner healing.

Some of their need for healing may be current but some probably lingers on from years of demonization, hurt, or bad relationships, which only makes way for more demonic activity. Prayer is required at this point to restore their soul and their spirit man. This type of healing is not just a one-time prayer. You need to be prepared to bring your client in for healing prayers spread out over months or even a year or two, depending on the depth of the wounding.

10.6. Step 4 – Engaging Demons

When you have completed your opening prayer, it is important to tell the host that when you are commanding the enemy to speak, the command is not directed at them but at the demons. It may seem an unnecessary point, but it is a very common misunderstanding. Also remind them that there is no obligation on their part to make something happen. What happens belongs first to Jesus and then to you as a practitioner. All that the host has to do is say what they hear from the demon.

Sometimes, they will hear nothing. Some people are more prone to seeing things, so the answer from the enemy may very well come in picture form. Sometimes it comes as a thought that enters the mind rather than an obvious word or picture. The host must be keen to pick that up, and it is their responsibility to get the information to the practitioner.

Sometimes the host will hear something that just seems out of place and unnecessary, and make the decision not to share that bit of information. However, it's critical that they do. The enemy does throw things in that are meant to get us off track and confused, but all things must be shared and considered. Record every answer to your questions. You will soon see what is relevant and what is not.

10.7. Establish Parameters

The next step, just before engaging the demonic, is to establish parameters for the demons: what they must do and what they cannot do.

10.7.1. Defeated Foe

I remind the enemy that they are the defeated foe. Jesus Christ has conquered them by His death on the cross and His resurrection. It is we, the redeemed, who have been given all authority over the powers of darkness. I declare to the enemy that they are bound to the chair in which the host is sitting.

10.7.2. Confined Boundaries

It is not uncommon for a demon who has been carried in by the client to attempt to leave the premises, realizing the possibility of exposure. But I always command them at this stage that if any of them have left they must now come back and cannot leave until I command them to.

10.7.3. Truth Confession

I always command the demons to tell the truth and nothing but the truth. Many people laugh at that, saying all demons are liars and there is no truth in them. That is true, but we do have the authority of Jesus to command the truth from them. I always tell demons that if they relate anything short of the truth, they will face the wrath of Jesus Christ. The truth we seek from the enemy is the advantage they have over the client.

I strongly recommend that step-by-step information be recorded. If it is a couple you are dealing with, the one that isn't the host can track what is happening throughout the counselling session. If it is an individual, encourage them to bring along someone that they know and trust who will accurately record what is being said by the enemy.

As a practitioner, it isn't wise to do deliverance on your own. Do your best to have someone with you for prayer covering. If your client has no one to record the session for them, this person can also do that.

At this stage, you need to know what the problem is that you are dealing with. It may be an anger problem, a history of unforgiveness, or some sexual sin issue. There seems to be no end to the ways Satan and his cohorts establish a stronghold within us.

Once you know the issue, address the enemy that is working against the person in that area. However, I won't speak to just any demon. For example, I say, "I command you, demon that has taken my client captive through sexual sin, to separate yourself from the rest of the kingdom of darkness. Stand at attention at the feet of Jesus here in this place and identify yourself. I command the head demon over the situation to respond now." Often, at this time, the speaker will hear the words, "I am here."

Once you make contact, your quest is to determine the root issue that gave this demon ground in the client. If sexual sin is the only ground, it's very simple to deal with. You walk the person through the steps of acknowledging their sin, which gave ground to the enemy. From there you turn them to Jesus, where they repent and receive forgiveness, which closes the door to the area that gave the enemy ground.

Most often, where there is one demon, there are several more which have some legal ground. All the issues have to be worked through, leading them finally to repentance and forgiveness. If you have no idea what they are, you can often find clues by looking at the Generational Sin List. For example, perhaps the client's father and grandfather, plus their eight siblings, were all involved in violence. This gives you the opportunity to address the demon that has been promoting violence down through the years of the family history. You can command the head demon over this type of activity to step up to the plate and identify itself.

While the process of deliverance is relatively straightforward, it isn't easy. The enemy is doing all it can do to deceive you throughout the session, to withhold information and otherwise disrupt or stop the process. Deliverance requires us to take a stand against the schemes of the enemy.

The steps to freedom never change. They are always about acknowledging the sin issue, whether from five hundred years back or from current involvement. You must lead your client to take ownership of their sin and then do what is right before God by putting it behind them.

In an average session, you will be dealing with one head demon at a time, but it isn't uncommon for there to be several of them ruling over dozens of subordinate demons. If you do not manage them well it can get very confusing.

To avoid getting overwhelmed by the numbers, I advise working with one head demon at a time, and only working with four to six issues that come under this head demon. These are the sins that gave the demons ground. If you try to cover too much ground at once, there is the possibility of confusion and leaving some of the sin issues behind.

When dealing with sins that have come down generationally, the client is in the position of standing in for others, past and present. That is to say, they must repent on behalf of those who opened the door for the sin issues in their own life, asking God to forgive them.

Most often this type of ministry takes a session or two. If a session ends with unfinished work, I command the demons that are still there to be locked in a spiritual jailhouse, guarded by the angels of God, until we meet for the next session (see more detail in Section 10.8.1. on "binding and loosing").

One other thing you must do, in bringing closure to sin issues, is to smash and destroy everything that gave leverage to the enemy—everything that enabled them to hold the family members in darkness. Proclaim to the enemy that they have lost their strongholds. Proclaim that the head demon has been defeated, therefore all of the underlings have also been defeated. You are now ready to cast out all these demons. As an example, this is what I say:

I declare that I am heaping on your back, head demon of Anger, all the residue from the strongholds you have lost, as well as all your demonic tools, tricks and schemes. I declare that you are defeated along with all your underlings. I cast you out to the feet of Jesus Christ and you cannot return to those places you once inhabited.

The Word talks about demons going out and coming back, bringing more with them.

When an impure spirit comes out of a man, it goes through arid places seeking rest and does not find it. Then it says, "I will return to the house I left." When it arrives, it finds the house unoccupied, swept clean and put in order. Then it goes and takes with it seven other spirits more wicked than itself, and they go in and live there. And the final condition of that person is worse than the first. That is how it will be with this wicked generation.
—Matthew 12:43–45

To prevent this, I ask Jesus to go into all of those rooms, cleansing and removing even the demonic dust, and then filling those rooms with His very presence.

One other important thing to do is to deal with what I call a "black blanket." I believe that where there are generational iniquities, something hangs over the family members and blocks the light of God from reaching them. Therefore, one of the last things I always do is to take in my spiritual hands that black blanket and thrust it into the fires of hell. I then ask God to penetrate with His light the area that once was covered with darkness.

All the glory for the victory goes to the Father, Son and Holy Spirit. But the joy that we receive is better than the best wine you can buy. There is no greater joy than to see the captives set free.

Because our nation is becoming more international, with individuals coming from every corner of the world, we need to understand clearly that we can command demons to come from any nation of the world to give background information for any client. It will require you to take a strong stand, but you will be successful.

10.8. Other Issues to Be Aware Of

10.8.1. Binding and Loosing

In Chapter 6: Spiritual Warfare, you will find an introduction to the concept of binding and loosing. For this chapter, however, I will expand on that teaching to help you understand how it is relevant for day to day use, and how it may work in a deliverance session.

Binding and loosing is not a long-term strategy. In fact, even Jesus didn't bind up Satan and his cohorts! Rather, He said things like "Go from this person, and never return." As written in Mark 9:25, *"When Jesus saw that a crowd was running to the scene, he rebuked the impure spirit. 'You deaf and mute spirit,' he said, 'I command you, come out of him and never enter him again.'"*

Neither can we bind up Satan and his underlings for any extended period of time. No! They are free to roam as they wish. The simple principle that you and I must live by, relative to the demonic realm, is this: the only means by which Satan and his cohorts can demonize us is our sin. If we choose to live in unforgiveness, the powers of darkness have a legal right to try and attach themselves to us, both outside and inside. If we live a sinless life, or if we quickly go to the Father for forgiving and cleansing after sinning, the enemy has no legal right and, therefore, no ground in our lives.

Accumulated corporate or individual prayer builds a wall of protection which the enemy cannot penetrate. Corporate prayer draws the spirit to us. It is akin to a burning fire against our skin. The enemy can only stand in the presence of prayer for a short time because prayer is the *power of God*.

At one time I was working with a twenty-year-old homosexual male. It had been a hard struggle for this man, but in this session we had finally got a bit of a breakthrough, and I was about to send away three or four homosexual demons. In the midst of doing that, I heard another voice. Right away, to maintain authority over the session, I said, "Whoever you are, I rebuke you and bind you up." Immediately there was a reply with the words, "You can rebuke me but you cannot bind me." When I inquired to whom the voice belonged, the response was, "I am Satan."

In this case, Satan told the truth. We cannot bind him or any of his underlings up for the rest of eternity in some sort of spiritual jailhouse. That doesn't mean we cannot use the concept. It just has to be applied correctly.

I have used binding and loosing at different times in my own home, when the enemy seems to be gaining some advantage over a family member. I have been given authority over my home by God. Therefore, in situations like the above, I bind up the *schemes* of Satan, and loose my family member from his clutches.

In some situations you need to bind and loose continually until the person can get their spiritual feet strongly planted once again.

Often, when doing deliverance, there simply isn't enough time to deal with all the issues in one session. What I often do is put the demons that I am dealing with in a spiritual jailhouse, declaring that they will be held there until such a time as we meet again or until Jesus sees fit to let them go. The reason I bind them up is because demons get pretty aggressive when they start losing massive ground. Sending your client home without the completion of deliverance leaves them facing some very angry demons. Thus, putting the demons in the jailhouse for a week or two is a means of protecting your client from harassment.

I have seen incredible results through binding and loosing. Maybe that success comes from the understanding that its purpose is not for the long term, but for short-term intervention only.

I have a friend who had been battling unsuccessfully with an unfair legal issue for close to two years. I encouraged him to use binding and loosing, which he agreed to do. In less than twenty-four hours, the legal issue was reversed and brought into proper alignment. That was an occasion to praise the Lord!

I encourage you to use binding and loosing, but to do it carefully and prayerfully, giving Jesus the room to lead you.

10.8.2. Freemasonry

Druidism, the Ku Klux Klan, Mormonism, and many other organizations are linked in some way to Freemasonry, which has deep roots that strongly affect us today. Some believe it goes all the way back to Old Testament times, possibly starting around the reign of David.

You may not know anyone in your generation that is practicing Freemasonry or involved in related organizations. But if your family has roots in any of them, the evil ones from those past ages are doing all they can to work against your generation today. You might go back as far as you can in your generational line and still find no indication that there was any involvement in Freemasonry or similar practices. But that doesn't mean they weren't there.

Often in a deliverance session, it is necessary to squeeze the enemy you are dealing with. They won't want you to understand the reason for the ground they have. We put pressure on them by reminding them of their future in hell. This puts fear in them, which is helpful in disabling them. You can also rebuke them, which becomes like a sword or blunt object hitting them if repeated in strength. Some demons cry out as though getting hit by a sword, while others experience the words like a hammer beating on them.

This will eventually cause them to disclose the information you need. They may tell you things like "Yes, there was sacrificing that took place eons of times ago on your mother's side of the family." Regardless of how big or small these sin issues from the past may be, if they aren't dealt with, demons gain access to you in this current generation. Sins build up over time. If there was any sacrificing of children or spilling of blood, or any other sin, at the very least demons will have the ability to harass the family. They will always try to re-create the sin they originally gained ground from.

I worked with a couple once who were going to a Bible school, the husband working towards becoming a pastor. For some time they came in regularly for marriage counselling, and I had gotten to know both of them very well.

One evening after a session, they lingered to socialize. During the conversation, the wife shared that her grandmother was scheduled for surgery for bowel cancer just a few weeks down the road. She also talked about her grandfather, how she loved him and was proud of him because he had made his way up into the higher echelons of Freemasonry.

I eventually said, "Did you know Freemasonry is an occult organization and bowel cancer is often a symptom of being involved with it?" She was utterly shocked! We sat in silence for quite some time.

Eventually I broke the silence and said, "You know how you told me that your son [who was not quite two years old] has been having bowel movements only about once every eight days since birth? Well, your son's problem could very well have roots in Freemasonry."

They asked, "What can we do?"

I responded by saying, "According to my schedule it will be close to three weeks before we can meet again. But tonight I will pray, breaking the power of the curse that has likely produced the cancer in your grandmother and the problem in your son, and we will deal with the rest of the Mason stuff sometime later."

The couple agreed to do that, with me standing in for both her son and her grandmother against the related health problems.

I received a phone call from the wife a few weeks later. She said, "I wanted to call you immediately, but I thought maybe I was just imagining something. On the second day after meeting with you there was a noticeable change in our son's bowel movement, and since the third day, he has had a normal bowel movement every day without fail! My grandmother went in for her operation. In the process of getting her ready, it was determined there was no need for surgery!"

Freemasonry, if not completely exposed and removed by the power of God through prayer, has the power to produce all sorts of things in your life—serious blood disorders, heart pains, chest pains, chronic indigestion, sinus problems, kidney problems, arrogance, anger, mockery, pride, unbelief, secrecy, rebellion, wretchedness, and so much more.

Most Christian bookstores carry some books on Freemasonry. It is worth informing yourself about this area. I regularly consult manuals and reference texts when dealing with people that may have roots in Freemasonry and associated cults.

10.8.3. Levels of Demonic Authority (Principalities and Powers)

The Bible is clear that there is a realm of demonic activity that reigns in the heavenly places, above the realm of normal human life.

> ...We wrestle not against flesh and blood (our foes are not human; however, Satan constantly uses human beings to carry out his dirty work), but against principalities (rulers or beings of the highest

rank and order in Satan's kingdom), against powers (the rank immediately below the "Principalities"), against the rulers of the darkness of this world (those who carry out the instructions of the "Powers"), against spiritual wickedness in high places. (This refers to demon spirits.)[97]

This helps us in the understanding of the upper realm.

God is strong, and he wants you strong. So take everything the Master has set out for you, well-made weapons of the best materials. And put them to use so you will be able to stand up to everything the Devil throws your way. This is no afternoon athletic contest that we'll walk away from and forget about in a couple of hours. This is for keeps, a life-or-death fight to the finish against the Devil and all his angels. Be prepared. You're up against far more than you can handle on your own.
—Ephesians 6:10–13, MSG

As a rule, we aren't dealing with the higher realm of demonic activity, but it is possible to bump into them from time to time. Thus it is incumbent upon us to have a Biblical and practical working knowledge of these upper levels. This will protect us from going where we shouldn't go, but it will give us an understanding should we find that we need to go a little higher than the common demonic foot soldiers that we regularly deal with. We need to be prepared for these higher-level encounters. We get a glimpse into this realm when Daniel says,

A hand touched me and set me trembling on my hands and knees. He said, "Daniel, you who are highly esteemed, consider carefully the words I am about to speak to you, and stand up, for I have now been sent to you." And when he said this to me, I stood up trembling.

Then he continued, "Do not be afraid, Daniel. Since the first day that you set your mind to gain understanding and to humble yourself before your God, your words were heard, and I have come in response

---

97   Swaggart, p. 2071.

*to them. But the prince of the Persian kingdom resisted me twenty-one
days. Then Michael, one of the chief princes, came to help me because I
was detained there with the king of Persia."*

—Daniel 10:10–13

10.9. Levels of Authority over Spiritual Forces

Above the levels where human authority exists, there is a spiritual realm occupied by spiritual forces. There are spirit beings who, through the fall of man
in Eden, have gained a place where they are able to dominate people. When
a person believes in Jesus Christ, by that act, identification with Jesus Christ
in the heavenlies takes place. The believer thus gains in Christ an ascendancy
over the powers.[98]

The following is a snapshot of the levels of authority taken from the
above quote:

1. **Christ**
   *"And God placed all things under his feet and appointed him to be
   head over everything for the church… "* (Ephesians 1:22)

2. **Believers**
   *"And God raised us up with Christ and seated us with him in the
   heavenly realms in Christ Jesus… "* (Ephesians 2:6)

3. **Satan**
   *"As for you, you were dead in your transgressions and sins, in which
   you used to live when you followed the ways of this world and of the
   ruler of the kingdom of the air, the spirit who is now at work in those
   who are disobedient."* (Ephesians 2:1–2)

---

98   Foster & King, pp. 112, 115.

4. Spirits

"... and a woman was there who had been crippled by a spirit for eighteen years. She was bent over and could not straighten up at all." (Luke 13:11)

5. Human Beings

"Then God said, 'Let us make mankind in our image, in our likeness, so that they may rule over the fish in the sea and the birds in the sky, over the livestock and all the wild animals, and over all the creatures that move along the ground.'" (Genesis 1:26)

6. Animals

"You made them rulers over the works of your hands; you put everything under their feet: all flocks and herds, and the animals of the wild, the birds in the sky, and the fish in the sea, all that swim the paths of the seas." (Psalm 8:6–8)

One level of demonic authority is territorial. I discuss this realm of demonic activity briefly in Chapter 8, where I talk about dealing with the demonic power that fills the atmosphere around a church, community, or city. To effectively challenge such power, you and I will have to join together with dozens, if not hundreds, of others in a prayer effort. We pray not singularly, but corporately; not to set a captive free, but to set a territory free. In this type of prayer ministry, the purpose is to determine what strongholds are holding the territory captive.

Once you have that sort of information, you then direct your prayer against the *principalities and powers* that are holding the church or territory in captivity. There can be many different sin issues, and often a principality is assigned to each stronghold over the area. This is a relatively safe environment for those praying because they are joined together in one purpose—to expose the schemes of darkness. In that oneness, mind to mind, heart to heart, there is a corporate shield of protection. But dealing with principalities and powers in the practice of smaller-scale deliverance should not be taken lightly.

Before we move on to the levels of authority, note that the church as a whole generally agrees that demons are the fallen angels who rebelled against the Lord during the insurrection of Lucifer.

10.9.1. Principalities

In a deliverance session, you may find yourself dealing with a principality on your own. *Don't do that! It is too dangerous!*

Always have one or two individuals with you as prayer cover. If you cannot have somebody in your room for some reason, let others know when you are in session and have them pray for you during that time. I've done a great deal of deliverance ministry on my own, but it isn't recommended. *Especially if you are just beginning, don't do it by yourself!*

You definitely need to have prayer support on hand if you know ahead of time you'll be dealing with a principality. In any type of deliverance or inner-healing ministry, if you find yourself in a bad place, you should temporarily close the session until you can get better prayer coverage or help.

The kind of ministry we are dealing with in this book can be performed by most of us. It is normal, everyday deliverance work. But there always is a slim chance of having to deal with a principality or other higher demonic entities. Don't be alarmed! God simply doesn't give us more than we can manage. Let your heart rest in that truth.

There are times—maybe more than I am aware of—when principalities are assigned over a particular family lineage. It's not that common, but you might come across them if you happen to be working with a family unit that has generations of occult involvement or sins like violent rape and sexual abuse down through the ages. I haven't encountered much of this, but the greater the "wickedness" in the person or family lineage, the more powerful the demons involved are.

Our sin issues are like energy bars for demons. The more sin grows, the more ground the enemy acquires, and the more strength they seem to have. I have seen this many times over the years. For example, when I start out working with somebody, the first demon I encounter is usually very angry and strong, very determined to hang onto their ground. But as I move along, dealing with one sin issue after another, the enemy becomes quieter and slower. By the time I get to the last issue, the demon hardly has strength enough to speak. If I ask him to look at himself and tell me what size he is now compared to when we started, many times he can hardly get the words out. He will tell me that there is hardly anything left of him.

This is a good thing to remember when you are facing sin in your own life. If you sin, you feed the demonic; choose righteousness and the enemy fades. You will grow in all areas of your life, because the resident Person of God can now manifest in your person. Where once there was darkness, now there is light.

There are powerful demons that are below the realm of principalities and powers and above the common range of demonic activity. The chance of encountering them is slim, but we must be informed.

I believe the reason Satan assigns demonic entities to particular family lines is to give him territorial access to what is happening in everyday society—in the block I live on or the one you live on, twenty blocks away. This allows him to sustain a measure of darkness in the community in which these families dwell.

The average person is forever unknowingly pushing against the darkness—darkness that keeps us grinding away day by day just to earn a living. And what does that produce? Hopelessness! Hopelessness through which a community today can become like the dark ages of the past!

Drive around a bit and you'll find these places, even in cities and towns in your area. You'll recognize the areas that are occupied by the evil one. They are places that you might drive through in the light of day, but certainly wouldn't walk through at night. This is where you will find dens of demons, feeding on many of our own sons and daughters. *This is a fact!* Think about it. Think about it for awhile! I don't know what it does for you, but there are times when it breaks my heart.

Several times, I have personally encountered principalities that ruled over families. By having these families repent on behalf of their forefathers and decide to stand for Christ, it is possible to strip the principalities of their power over the family units. My instruction isn't to go looking for principalities. *Don't move into that area on your own!* But be open and acknowledge the possibility of them showing up. Then, in prayer, let Jesus give you step-by-step direction.

10.9.2. Powers

Only one time, in all my years of doing deliverance, have I encountered a power. This was accidental. I was working with a couple, dealing with generational poverty for as many generations back as they could remember for all women. The men seemed to do fine, or even prospered, but the female side seemed to live in deep poverty. In dealing with the demon working in that area, I commanded, "Whoever the demon is that goes by the name of Poverty, come forth and identify yourself!"

Of course the demon came forth. But it was very angry and resisted submitting. I recognized right away that it wasn't just an ordinary demon, and I was quite sure it was a principality. So I said, "Okay, you principality, give us the information we need."

I continued commanding it to respond, calling it a principality each time. The demon finally spoke, but with such intense hatred and distaste that you could cut the words with a knife. It said, "I am *not* a principality, I am a *power!*"

I had the impression that this demon was far superior to a principality. You could almost feel its hatred at being confused for what I assume was a lower level of demon. I have never, ever experienced wickedness so potent. There are no words to explain the depth of the darkness in the room.

I addressed the demon again. "Okay, so why did you respond when I called for a principality to come forth?"

"I came because you called my name," it said. This told us that its name was Poverty.

Next I said, "Okay, *you* are here, but who are the demons that work under you in the area of poverty?" After receiving the names of these demons, I said, "Now that I have all the information I need from you, I no longer want to talk to you. So I command you to leave now and to not come back!"

You need to consider that in a situation like this, as we face demonic entities at this high level, we are especially prone to fear. But it is *critical* in that moment that we remain confident in our position in Christ. Anything less can very well give the enemy the advantage.

We do have authority over any level of demon, but I strongly recommend proceeding cautiously when confronted with these higher level demons.

10.9.3. Other Demons (Personality Demons, Jezebel and Ahab Spirits)

Personality Demons: This is another subject we must be aware of. In doing deliverance counselling you will, from time to time, encounter what I call a personality demon. It is more common than we would like to believe.

Personality demons come about when a demon literally embeds into the personality of a person. Once lodged there, it can pretty well rule the life of the person. It does their thinking for them, but even beyond that, it literally speaks on their behalf, using their vocal cords. Sometimes you can detect this if you are listening for it. The demon itself will often have a slighlty different tone of voice than the core person has. Most often it is rough or scratchy.

These types of demons have added strength to resist you in your deliverance attempts, because they have in a sense entered right into the soul of the person. There are times in these kinds of sessions where you have to become a bit more aggressive than you normally would be. *Always remember: you have the God-given authority to trample on snakes and scorpions and overcome all their power* (see Luke 10:19). The process to rid a person of a personality demon is the same as any other counselling session. The difference is that these personality demons normally have generational roots, and it is hard to convince the carrier of these demons that they are actually under demonic control.

This point needs to be made again. Yes, deliverance can be very taxing on the practitioner. It is hard work and requires you to be in prayer, talking to Jesus every moment of the session. But the process that sets the captives free is consistent in absolutely every deliverance session. Neil T. Anderson coined the phrase, "Where the garbage is, there will be rats." In other words, where there is sin, there will be demons—simple as that. The process is to work your client through the identification of all sins in their lives, and deal with them thoroughly with the steps I have given you.

Once the client faces all personal sin issues, there is another step if you are working with a family. Ensure that all members have first received the required level of deliverance and then healing. If the children are young and not involved, there needs to be a cleansing prayer for them also, just to ensure that there is no demonic activity attached to their lives as members of the family.

We need to be aware that the demonic always tries to produce a level of fear within the family. It's a level you generally wouldn't recognize, but it will penetrate the souls of your children. This a scheme of the evil one that can give him leverage throughout the following years.

Lead the family to repentance and ask Jesus to pour His forgiving power over them, setting them free. The enemy may still try to hang on, but in reality, they have nothing left to hang onto. Kick them out, each and every one. And again ask Jesus to move into those areas once occupied by the powers of hell. This will simply, adequately, and absolutely set the captives free, regardless of the level of darkness and sin they have been living in.

Familiar Spirits: A familiar spirit is assigned to family units to harass, kill, and destroy. The familiar spirit is considered by many to be a spirit that follows the family line, and this is my belief also. It works down the generations, doing all it can to direct and abuse family units for its own purpose.

Jezebel and Ahab Spirits: In Chapter 6: Spiritual Warfare, I talked about male headship and mentioned that in the absence of a father to serve as authority in the home, the mother must step into that position.

But I want to point out something else that has turned God's will of male headship upside down. What we are seeing in many cases is that fathers who actually live in the home have been silenced. They may love and care for their children, but have little to say about what is happening in their lives.

There are two obvious reasons for what is happening. First, over the last few decades fathers have abdicated their position of headship over their home. Second, unfortunately, mothers have pushed themselves into the position of headship. Certainly they needed to as the fathers stepped back, but another part of this is the influence of the women's liberation movement, which promoted the idea that the only thing women need from men today is their sperm. So our sons and daughters are watching television programs in which fathers are being portrayed as passive fools or jerks and mothers as the stronger, more intelligent leaders of the family.

This has thrown the doors wide open for wicked Queen Jezebel's spirit to come in like a flood! We get a sense of her works in 1 Kings 21:1–16, where her husband, King Ahab, wanted to buy a particular vineyard but was unable to. Because of that, he went home to bed in a bad mood. See how Jezebel operates:

... [When] Jezebel found her husband vexed and sullen and learned of Naboth's refusal to sell his vineyard, she assured Ahab that the vineyard would soon be his. Two evil men were appointed to charge Naboth with blasphemy against God and the king. Accordingly, Naboth was taken outside the city and stoned to death. The treacherous Jezebel thus framed Naboth so that it would appear he was being executed for breaking the law of Jehovah. Since the property would pass on to Naboth's sons after his death, Jezebel had them murdered as well (2 Kgs. 9:26). The iniquitous queen was as thorough as she was wicked.[99]

That same spirit of wickedness is very much alive and active today in every level of our society. If we are to come against the spirit of Jezebel, we are going to:

Confront a stronghold of immense portions. It is a way of thinking that exists unchecked in most churches.... Jezebel hates the prophets, for the prophets speak out against her. The prophets are her worst enemies. When she wars, it is to stir people against the message of the prophetic church. More than she hates the prophets, she hates the word they speak. Her real enemy is a spoken word of God.[100]

Many authors have written about this infamous woman. In the words of Sampson:

Jezebel is more than the name of a wicked queen who lived at a time of great spiritual decline in the history of God's chosen

99   MacDonald, p. 384.
100 Frangipane, 1991, p. 7.

people. Jezebel is also a spiritual threat to those leaders whose assignments have been to nullify this demonic principality's power in the earth…. Jezebel type controllers are almost always motivated by extreme insecurity. They are usually very wounded people (probably going back to childhood), and they operate in a protective mode of "I am never going to be hurt or rejected again." Because of their insecurity, they seek preeminence, affirmation, and recognition—but in very illegitimate ways.

Jezebel wants to control people, turning them into darkness…. Although not restricted to either sex, Jezebel spirits are often acknowledged as more prevalent in women. Unquestionably, though, Jezebel functions just as proficiently through men.[101]

The Passive Spirit of Adam: The other side of this equation is the *Ahab* spirit, or maybe better said, the individual soul and spirit. The Ahab spirit began with God's first created man, Adam.

In the familiar account of humanity's fall, we see Adam playing the role of a victim. He blamed both Eve and God rather than admitting his own guilt (see Genesis 3). Perhaps this victim role lies at the root of all sin—our pride gets in the way and we refuse responsibility for our actions…. Adam acted passively when he avoided standing up to his wife as she enticed him to disobey God and eat the forbidden fruit. He ate with her in direct disobedience to God's command. Then he responded with passive irresponsibility when confronted by a loving God who asked, "Have you eaten from the tree of which I commanded you that you should not eat?" (Genesis 3:11). Adam's response was drenched with accusation toward God, as Adam declared himself the victim: "The woman whom You gave to be with me, she gave me of the tree, and I ate" (verse 12). In effect, Adam told God, "You're a bad God, and You gave me a bad woman." Passive behavior never wants to deal responsibly with the issue at hand and loves to become the victim. Of course, this is the

---

101 Sampson, 2012, pp. 8, 25, 27, 27.

easy way out—the path of least resistance. Like Adam, passive people declare, "It's not my fault. Somebody else did this to me." Most would rather even blame God then take responsibility for their own actions. Not much has changed since Adam's response in the garden. I am amazed at how many people (including me) blame God for their problems.[102]

These words are a picture of a modern-day Ahab. The Ahab spirit was birthed by Adam because of his passivity, his unwillingness to stand up as the head and say, "Woman, what you want me to do is outright sin against God." This scenario plays out day after day in our society today when the husband, facing conflict with his wife, steps back and finds a comfortable place on the chesterfield. Then the wife takes hold of the situation and deals with it.

Now there is very much that needs to be said about this situation, but I cannot cover it all. There are many books written recently on the Ahab/Jezebel spirit, and I encourage you to inform yourself in this particular area. I merely want to make you aware of the Jezebel and Ahab spirits, and to point out that both are very much at work today in our lives.

As we move closer and closer to the return of Jesus Christ, the Jezebel spirit will only increase in control and wickedness, and its target will be the leaders, the head of the home, the senior pastor of the church, and the leaders of Christian organizations. The goal of the Jezebel spirit will be to indwell as many leaders as possible, which will bring much confusion and unrest within Christian communities.

We live in a time, I believe, when the apostolic is coming into its own. The end times battle will be fought not by the church of today, but by an apostolic church, akin to the church that was raised up by the disciples of Jesus Christ, and the incredible force that was raised up by the apostle Paul. I believe that our days are getting darker, and some of that darkness is Satan, who is beginning to unleash hordes of demons which will bring darkness into our world.

The return of Christ may very well be a long time in coming, but because it is, we are to be prepared. Part of our preparation is to understand

102 Sampson, 2010, pp. 46–47.

our enemy and how we can resist him, with the goal being Satan's defeat. Our battle is not won by facing the enemy and wrestling him to the ground. No, the end times battle will be won by those who have made the decision to stay in step with the Spirit of God that indwells them, to live a life that amplifies the life of Jesus Christ. The Jezebel or Ahab spirit cannot stand "righteous living" or stay in the presence of it, for righteousness is a power of God sent to rebuke all that they stand for.

During a deliverance session, I often come against a disobedient and arrogant demon with the words, "In the authority of Christ given to me I rebuke you." If I get no cooperation, I repeat, "I rebuke you; I rebuke you; I rebuke you; I rebuke you by the authority and power given to me by God in Christ Jesus." It doesn't take many rebukes before the demon cries out, "Stop; stop; you're hurting me," or sometimes, "You're destroying me."

The *Collins Essential Canadian English Dictionary and Thesaurus* defines "rebuke" as to "scold, admonish, castigate, censure, shied, dress down."[103] Rebuking, in spiritual warfare, is like a sword that pierces demons. It is a powerful tool to use against the Jezebel spirit (or any demon you encounter). But you need to be wise when applying the sword of rebuke to the Jezebel spirit.

I previously mentioned a type of situation where the husband steps back and the wife, like Eve, happily steps in and makes the decision. In that moment, she says something to herself like, "Fine, if he's not able to do it, I will." This decision flings the door open for Jezebel to enter.

God has established man to be the head of the home. When the wife usurps his authority, the home's integrity is breached, and evil comes in like a flood. Women, don't do that. It is ungodliness. You may very well have to pick up after your husband for a season. But if in that process, you claim supremacy over the home in your heart, you neuter your husband spiritually, exactly like the Jezebel spirit. The Jezebel and Ahab spirits work hand-in-hand, and you will never win the battle by battling each other. There is only one way to defeat them, and that is by righteous living. I said earlier in this chapter that Jezebel *hates the prophet; she hates the word they speak. Her real enemy is the spoken word of God.*

---

103 Gilmour, p. 673.

10.10. Be Ready for Battle

You may be wondering why the Jezebel spirit is included in this chapter. The reason is that the Jezebel spirit is a top-level principality that targets individuals in positions of authority, such as pastors. Sampson says,

> I cannot emphasize strongly enough that when you deal with a Jezebel, you will be challenged, no matter your approach. Your best debating skills will get you nowhere. When you confront Jezebels with the truth, they will twist it, take no responsibility and blame you. If you take a certain action, they will blame you. If you do not act in a certain way, they will blame you. There is no pleasing them. You cannot please people who are under that demonic influence. Jezebels have a stubborn mindset and do not receive correction. The only thing you can do is draw a line in the sand and refuse to let such a person walk over it—or over you. You must refuse to tolerate Jezebel-like behavior. Following a confrontation, a person with a Jezebel spirit may experience a temporary repentance and acknowledge that a problem exists. As is often the case though, the behavior of Jezebels can be like those air-filled punching dolls that have sand in the bottom. When you knock them down, they bounce right back upright. A Jezebel spirit and the patterns of control it fosters do not let go of someone easily. Do not be fooled into thinking all is well until you have put a trial period in place and the person who had the Jezebel spirit shows consistent change over time. Beyond deliverance from a demon, the person also must allow the Holy Spirit to bring change into his or her personality. Patterns of control often have become deeply entrenched by demonic thoughts that have formed a stronghold over time. Therefore, the person must not only resist the devil, but must continually renounce all thought patterns that formerly led to controlling behaviour. Be ready, because victory over Jezebel will require a battle.[104]

---

104 Sampson, 2012, pp. 110–111.

This battle cannot be fought and won by flesh and blood, but this is the medium for a husband and wife relational struggle. Recognition of a Jezebel or Ahab spirit commonly leads to a major breakdown in a marriage Once the couple realizes what they are dealing with, the accusations begin to fly back and forth.

She accuses the husband for not taking a stand against his passive Ahab lifestyle. He will often rage with words like, "How can I? You're a Jezebel and you have to control everything! You need to have the first and last word in everything that happens in our married life." And on the battle goes.

That sort of activity only empowers the Jezebel spirit, whether it is in the husband or the wife. Many believe Jezebel indwells only women, and that is most common, but if it is to her advantage she will do her work through men also. The ongoing threats and accusations only cause the Ahab spirit to step back more and more from the responsibilities of leadership .

So knowing what you're dealing with can lead to many accusations and make things even worse! If your marital relationship allows you to put aside all of the scrapping and choose forgiveness and righteousness, you can defeat the Jezebel/Ahab spirits by Christ-like living. This requires husband and wife to take control in their own lives, moment by moment and day by day, dealing with whatever spirit indwells them.

Ideally at this point, the husband, who is to be the head, should begin the practice of binding the spirits of Jezebel and Ahab, and loosing himself and his wife from those spirits. If the two of you simply cannot get together on this, go to God alone a few times a day, and bind up the spirits of Ahab and Jezebel for both of you. You don't want to irritate and agitate the spirit of your spouse, which further feeds the spirit's power. Remember that binding won't bring the actions of the enemy to a final halt. No, binding and loosing is more like a lull in the midst of warfare. It allows you to catch your breath and re-establish yourself for the enemy's next bullet.

I have used binding and loosing in my own situation, as well as for clients. I encourage you to use the tool often (several times a day)—when you wake in the morning, when you go to bed at night, and as often as you can in a time of spousal conflict. It takes the wind out of the enemy's sails, and as you loose, you and your spouse can experience a lifting of the darkness. Doing it this way can eliminate the accusations, blaming, and finger-pointing.

I will say it again—you cannot defeat Jezebel or Ahab by accusing each other; only righteous living will put these demons to the run. Here's what you must do to bring an end to Jezebel and Ahab. You are:

> "… to put off your old self, which is being corrupted by its deceitful desires; to be made new in the attitude of your minds; and to put on the new self, created to be like God in true righteousness and holiness. Therefore each of you must put off falsehood and speak truthfully to your neighbour, for we are all members of one body. "In your anger do not sin": Do not let the sun go down while you are still angry, and do not give the devil a foothold."
>
> —Ephesians 4:22–27

See also these instructions later in Ephesians:

> Wives, submit to your own husbands as you do to the Lord. For the husband is the head of the wife as Christ is the head of the church, his body, of which he is the Savior. Now as the church submits to Christ, so also wives should submit to their husbands in everything.
>
> Husbands, love your wives, just as Christ loved the church and gave himself up for her to make her holy, cleansing her by the washing with water through the word, and to present her to himself as a radiant church, without stain or wrinkle or any other blemish, but holy and blameless. In this same way, husbands ought to love their wives as their own bodies. He who loves his wife loves himself. After all, no one ever hated their own body, but they feed and care for their body, just as Christ does the church—for we are members of his body. "For this reason a man will leave his father and mother and be united to his wife, and the two will become one flesh." This is a profound mystery—but I am talking about Christ and the church. However, each one of you also must love his wife as he loves himself, and the wife must respect her husband.
>
> —Ephesians 5:22–33

These Scriptures, when applied, have the potential to remove the Jezebel/Ahab spirits from you and your home. So how to apply them? Remember that righteousness put into action in your life will become a "bomb" against the enemy. Righteousness will remove Jezebel and Ahab, along with their schemes and strongholds.

How do you get to that place? If you are born again, you are righteous in Christ Jesus. That righteousness is a platform from which to live our Christian lives, and it guarantees a place for us in heaven. But there is more! That same righteousness that is *in* us, is also *on* us, and can *go forth* from us.

The Bible says that the Word of God penetrates, dividing soul and spirit, and judging the thoughts and attitudes of our hearts (Hebrews 4:12). As we speak God's words of righteousness, the word goes forth and touches the hearts and souls of others. We also know that Jezebel and Ahab spirits hate the Word, written or spoken, for it is a sword they cannot stand against. We, anchored in Christ through salvation, must go forth in the same way.

I urge you to understand this and then apply it. It is critical for all of us in our Christian life. All righteousness is from God, and there is no righteousness outside of Him. We speak words that can either bless us or curse us. So just as a spoken word goes forth from Jesus, it goes forth from us, with the potential to divide between soul and spirit. In other words, our words spoken in righteousness and truth literally expose sin in others' lives.

My closing thought for this chapter: *are you and I subject to God or to Jezebel?*

While we must have compassion toward those bound with a Jezebel spirit, we must also have compassion toward those who have experienced irreparable damage through the operation of such a spirit. Therefore, we must firmly refuse to go along with any of a Jezebel's ways or controlling tactics. God has called us to victory, and in His victory we each have freedom to make choices under His direction. We are not to be subject to the control of another person—or to a Jezebel spirit operating through him or her. Rather, we are to subject ourselves to God and be led by the Holy Spirit. There is always hope for freedom, even for the person who has come under a Jezebel spirit and is trying to control others. God can restore any damaged life, and He can and will bring deliverance.[105]

Prayer: Father, if there are any areas in which I have subjected myself to someone else's control, I ask for Your forgiveness. Give me the freedom You have purchased for me through Christ's death. I subject myself to the Holy Spirit's leading and guiding. I also ask that You open my eyes to any behaviour through which I may seek to control other people, so that I can choose not to do that. Please remind me that through You, I have everything I need to do what is right, no matter the situation. Please forgive me for any times when I have used or disrespected others, and make my life a blessing to everyone I come into contact with. In Jesus' name, Amen.

---

105 Sampson, 2012, pp. 75–77.

Chapter Eleven

MULTIPLE PERSONALITY DISORDER

THE FOLLOWING IS THE PROVEN METHODOLOGY THAT I HAVE USED IN MY own practice. I put it on paper to help you should you develop your own practice of ministering to the dissociated. I have had the awesome privilege of ministering into hundreds of lives, with a large portion of those being dissociative individuals.

This chapter is my attempt to put in written form some tools by which you can make application for yourself, as well as for your dissociative clients. I strongly urge you to read and even reread the practices and principles laid out in this chapter, learning them until they become a normal part of your counselling practice.

Your response might be, "I could never work with the dissociated!" Let me tell you, you can!

If you like being a part of what God is doing in the lives of the hurting, or mentoring or discipling others, or seeing the broken and devastated healed by a touch from Jesus, then you too can to work with Dissociative Identity Disorder (DID) individuals, simply by using the information in this manual.

Before we go to the next step, we must answer the question, "What qualifies me to minister into the lives of the dissociated?" Simply put, what a dissociated individual needs is for someone who genuinely cares about them and their situation to come alongside them to uncover the dissociated alternate personaities (alter(s)) hidden within.

Many people insist that only those with a doctorate degree in psychology or psychiatry should work with the dissociated because of the possibility of further damaging them. I would agree, if you find yourself dealing with individuals that have been victims of Satanic Ritual Abuse (SRA). But even in SRA cases, there are levels of ministry that can be carried out in a normal counselling session by combining this chapter with Chapter 10: Deliverance.

What you must understand from the outset is that dissociation is not a sickness or a disease that needs a medical doctor to bring healing or a psychiatrist to trace the work of the brain. *Dissociation is a protective means of personal survival facilitated by the brain in times of extreme trauma.* We need to be wise when ministering into the lives of others, ensuring we do not go beyond our own abilities or harm the very ones we are endeavouring to bring into healing and wholeness.

If you care, you can help dissociated individuals. It is that simple.

Many dissociated people have been counselled for months—sometimes years—before their dissociation was discovered. That is the strength of dissociation: it hides the trauma from the host as well as from those who live or work with them. But it need not be that way today, simply because there is so much information available.

However as simple as the concept may be, treating dissociation is far from easy, primarily because we are dealing with deeply traumatized individuals. The majority of clients that have come into my office for ministry didn't come because of dissociation. No! They came in knowing that their lives were totally out of control and their family was about to about to explode. At that point, DID wasn't a part of their vocabulary.

At times, the host, realizing for the first time that they are dealing with dissociated entities, may become irrational and try to get the "alters" out of their person. Take your time; use the first and even second session to earn the trust of the host . It is our job to teach the host that the entities have been their salvation, and this often is very hard to receive.

Remember, when these individuals arrive in your office, they most often have no idea that they have ever dissociated.

Don't just barge into their lives, but build trust with the host; get to know them a bit before setting into the business side of things. Remember always: trust is a premium! The priority is to build a genuine relationship with the host person. Again, this is critical and sometimes very hard to do.

Once you have earned the trust of the host, then over time earn the trust of other alters one by one before you move on to uncover yet-unidentified alters. Again, this is critical; treat them just as you know Jesus would. There may be times when an alter, for whatever reason, turns against you, or maybe against a new alter that was just uncovered.

This can very well have you and the inner child (within the host) in a state of confusion, a place of disarray. This isn't a problem if you are working with only one or two alters, but most often you will be working with many more. This can be somewhat disconcerting for you, as well as any dissociated alters.

Remember, again, the importance of trust. If an alter thinks you don't care for them or you don't have the means to look after them, they may go into hiding. This is why you need to nurture relationship within the system (the family of alters) first. When things turn sour, they will know they have an advocate in you.

And yes, things will turn sour while working with the dissociated. But some of the greatest experiences I have had in ministry have been ministering into the lives of these people, seeing them healed and functioning in society, healthy in soul and spirit.

DID is not a curse that we should run from, but a blessing. DID is the brain's ability to set aside extreme personal trauma and place it in designated pockets within the brain, enabling the trauma victim to live out somewhat of a normal life with no cognizant memories of the trauma.

For example, take a five-year-old girl being abused every night at home. If she is able to dissociate the horror that she experiences every night, then she able to turn off this trauma, at least to some degree. This allows her to function in somewhat of a normal state throughout her day.

11.1. The Unregenerate Client and Demonic Interference

At times you will encounter individuals coming in for ministry who aren't born-again believers; you need to counsel them accordingly. Such individuals can be very hard to counsel. This isn't because they are hard and resistant—not at all.

In fact, in my experience unbelievers are often easier to mentor or counsel than believers. However, because their spirit man is not regenerated, the evil ones have free reign to work against them, hindering what you're endeavouring to do. We must always be aware that Satan and his crew are working hard against us, every step of the way.

For example, child molestation is literally driven by the powers of darkness. Once I get a client to a point where they have confidence and we are beginning to move forward, I explain the dynamics of demonic interference and how it may be interfering with their ongoing healing.

Deliverance is really quite simple once you understand the process; it becomes a tool in your hand as you minister to the dissociated. I have many memories of trying to get information from an alter, when the alter responds by saying, "I can't give you the information that you are asking for because something dark and angry is beating on me, and it says it will kill me if I tell you." This is clearly demonic interference.

Drawing from my experience, it can be very confusing when you're ministering to an alter and another one steps in. At times, it might shut your session down altogether.

Dissociated alters may or may not know of Jesus as Saviour. While ministering into the alter system, I try to bring Jesus into what is taking place. For example, if a particular alter is having a hard time and doesn't really want to move on, I try to connect them with Jesus. I do what I can by praying out loud, asking Jesus to do what He can do for the alter just uncovered.

The alter may be fearful and afraid, so I ask Jesus to take the fear from them. Some time later when you ask the same alter how things are, they may respond by saying, "Jesus told me not to be afraid because He will look after me." Similar things can be done on the way to integration so that, when the time comes, the alters know Him and are happy to go home with Him. That is good news for the alter(s). For the host, the work of rebuilding their person begins.

This is a great opportunity to explain to them the work of the cross and salvation, and to give them opportunity to invite Christ into their heart, without being intrusive and pushy.

11.2. Levels of Disorder

I have found this system to be of practical use in determining a client's level of dissociation.

There are three levels of DID within this chapter. They are laid out in such a way to help you as you minister to DID individuals. I am presenting the following in a three-level format of my own making.

- Level One: Silent Zone
- Level Two: Dissociative Identity Disorder (DID)
- Level Three: Multiple Personality Disorder (MPD)

I have included some of my experiences to help you understand these levels. These experiences of mine are to be tools in your hands as you minister into the lives of others.

11.3. Level One: Silent Zone

In the Silent Zone, there are no words, thoughts, or memories available from your client. This contrasts with Levels Two and Three, where you will encounter another voice (or two) once you begin to uncover dissociated parts.

For me, this level is the hardest to work with of the three. In this level, information that can be useful clinically is very hard to retrieve from the client. This is because although the individual comes in deeply hurt, he has absolutely no memories whatsoever of the trauma in his life that would explain the current situation.

It is the least encountered level.

At this level, people can be horrifically traumatized through various types of abuse, yet have no memories of their past trauma. This traumatization does not develop dissociation; traumatized individuals in this first level have no capacity or are unable to successfully dissociate. They seem to have the capacity to block out the trauma from the incident(s).

These individuals have no memories and no alters that would carry the horror from the night before, and they cannot figure out the reason why they are bound up. Therefore, they live in constant fear and anxiety.

An example of the Silent Zone would be a middle-aged woman, Jane, who had been coming into my office for some time. She was married to a man who loved her dearly, but they were having serious marital problems.

The husband said his wife wouldn't trust him in any area of life, and thus they were unable to grow together as a team or unit.

After having exhausted all my tools, I suggested that we meet with her parents to see if their daughter had trauma of any kind with a man in the distant past. As far as they knew, there was none.

However, while I was at their home, an uncle arrived at the house unexpectedly to visit, and upon being told of the purpose of the meeting, he was able to shed some light on the situation. The day of Jane's birth, the uncle had arrived at the hospital before her dad, who made it very clear upon his arrival that the last thing he wanted was a baby girl. He then had immediately stormed out of the hospital room, angrily slamming the door behind him. This is an example of the sort of wounding that can take place as far back as birth—or even before.

Some will find it hard to believe that a child can actually be wounded psychologically while still in the womb or newly born. But this is more common than any of us would want to believe. Jane had absolutely no knowledge of the psychological wounding in her soul that had taken place the day she was born and rejected by her father. In this particular case, we were able to reconcile the daughter, through the process of forgiveness, first with her father and then with her husband. With just a few counselling sessions, Jane, through prayer and inner healing, was freed from her inability to trust her husband.

Many have the same problem as Jane, with no memories to attach to the inner fears. They face the frustration of not being able to live a normal life in work or in personal relationships. They tend to live in a state of hopelessness, which some are aware of, although they do their best to mask it. I have counselled such individuals.

Because there seems to be no evidence or memories of the past that would indicate previous trauma had occurred, Level One, the Silent Zone, is particularly hard for counsellors. It is akin to trying to pull teeth from a hen.

As you attempt to draw information from those at Level One, you can at times detect a heart that silently aches, a soul which knows only slumber and has withdrawn from life. Level One individuals will really tax your time and abilities, as they come in week after week and year after year.

But don't ever give up on them; they need our help every bit as much as other DID individuals do. As daunting as the task is, we must push onward. This is our opportunity to apply the law of love—a law that has come down to us through the ages, found particularly in the story of the Good Samaritan. It is as relevant now as it was in the time of Jesus (Luke 10:30–37).

Be careful not to rush into these peoples' lives. Yes, you see the hopelessness in their eyes, and you know that hopelessness for a Christian is a sin. But don't judge them. This is your opportunity to get to know them. Take a session or two in your office; build a bit of a relationship before you start in with counselling and the business side of your office. We are all created in the image of God, and that mentality will make it easier for you to counsel them.

11.3.1. Traumatized and Unable to Dissociate

Some traumatized individuals are unable to dissociate, and these individuals may be unable to get to the root of their pain.

They seem to have the capacity to block out trauma, depending on their age and personality. They have no memories and no alters that would carry their horror stories from the past. They cannot understand why they are bound up and live in constant fear and anxiety.

Many of the individuals that come to you for ministry will come for a few weeks, some for months, and others for years. Some of these long-term individuals have gone through the same horror as the dissociated (Level Two), have but have no capacity to dissociate.

Professionals have determined that 70% of the population can dissociate in times of extreme trauma, with the remaining 30% having to carry that trauma, with it always on their minds.

But for some, you will never get to the root of the problem. Take the example of an eighteen-year-old woman who had left home to live on her own. Occasionally, she sought male friendship, but this just seemed to increase her level of fear.

We met weekly for an hour, opening every session with unobtrusive prayer. At times when discussing her situation, she would feel something emotional, but she could never explain her feelings. She had been coming to my office for over a year, and there was no notable growth. Therefore, I suggested a female counsellor that I had thought would be a better fit. But she simply wasn't interested in trying a different counsellor. We carried on week after week for the better part of another year, yet she still seemed frozen, emotionally and relationally.

She eventually left our city, and I lost contact with her.

One day, many years later, she unexpectedly dropped into my office, looking radiant and beautiful. She explained to me how my prayers, along with my teaching on prayer, changed her over the years and brought healing to her whole person.

I never understood the root cause of her problem. Nonetheless, it certainly bore the marks of sexual molestation at a very young age. Unable to dissociate, she would have unconsciously buried the abuse somewhere in her brain, and as a counsellor, I wasn't able to access the horror of sexual abuse in her very early years.

For some clients, you will never get to the bottom of a situation. We must accept that we cannot bring healing to everyone. One option is to refer "stuck" clients to someone else. But Jesus wouldn't leave these individuals behind, and neither should we.

What you must do in these situations is to counsel your clients to leave behind what they don't know, teaching them how to walk in step with Jesus every day of their lives while applying and praying the Word. Their hope lies in the future. Our God is a God of past, present, and future.

It is exciting for the practitioner when a client finally leaves the past behind, looking onward and upward, hand in hand with Jesus. Never, ever give up on these individuals. As my eighteen-year-old client shows, you should never underestimate the power of persistent and targeted prayer in the mighty name of Jesus.

In that case, I opened up each session with prayer, modeling in a non-intrusive manner the need to be in continuous contact with the Father, Son, and Holy Spirit. By doing this, we give our clients the most basic and yet essential tool.

I knew a psychologist who was working with MPD individuals. As part of their treatment, he would send them to a Christian counsellor for the healing of their spirit man, their soul and their mind. As believers, we have something so powerful in bringing healing and wholeness that the unbeliever does not have. We have Jesus, our Creator and the Healer of the soul, who takes away our sins. He takes us into places and situations relative to inner healing and being set free, where the unbeliever and even Christian doubters cannot go.

We have the arsenal of prayer. Always remember, it is incumbent upon us to open every session in prayer. Throughout the session, remain hand-in-hand with the third person of the Trinity, who is our Counsellor. Close in the same way, abiding in Jesus, the Vine (see other sections dealing with prayer in the Index).

We must never forget that we have a powerful advantage over the unbeliever when it comes to setting the hurting free. As James 5:16 (AMP) says,

Therefore, confess your sins to one another [your false steps, your offenses], and pray for one another, that you may be healed and restored. The heartfelt and persistent prayer of a righteous man (believer) can accomplish much [when put into action and made effective by God—it is dynamic and can have tremendous power].

While this type of ministry can be extremely taxing, God will make a way.

Looking back to the angry father in the hospital at the time of Jane's birth, Jane would never have received freedom from the fear of man had I not gone the extra mile to let God use me. There are many similar situations. And, one by one, those clients will make their way into your home or office. Let the Spirit of God lead you to show your care for them, and you will see relationships healed and restored.

11.3.2. Sexual Child Abuse

Another topic we will cover in this first level is the sexual abuse of a child—for example, child molestation. It is literally driven by the powers of darkness.

Molestation may not be done with any type of force, verbal or physical. Nonetheless, if there is no proper intervention early on, it can leave a child wounded for life.

If this takes place within the family unit it is incest. But wherever the sexual activity has come from, it is a blatant violation at all levels, spiritually, psychologically, and physically. If there is no intervention to bring exposure of the sexual abuse and forgiveness, these hurting individuals may very well carry the pain of abuse into their old age.

I have listened to many who have been victims of this kind of abuse. The perpetrator could very well be the boy next door or a brother, but from my experience, it is usually the father, or occasionally the mother.

In some cases the sexual abuse is premeditated; in other cases, it is a father's love gone astray. This abuse can begin at a very young age, sometimes even within the first or second year of the child's life.

The father will begin by doing whatever he has to do to draw his daughter in and under his care. He takes her to places where other family members don't go. All the while, he is impressing upon her mind that she is Daddy's Little Girl. Later, she becomes his Princess, and wherever Daddy goes, so goes his Princess. She grows accustomed to her father's hugs and rubs and kisses.

Suppose the girl turns three years old without knowing that the rubs were inappropriate. She is now accustomed to her daddy's affection and time. She wants it to carry on because in her understanding, Daddy is showing her his love. It was all done with such seeming tenderness and care.

But there comes a time when the father, fearful of being found out, has to bring this activity to a stop. And the only option is to turn his back on his daughter. This sudden withdrawal can cause low-level dissociation within the child. Later on in her teens or twenties, she might uncover foggy memories that indicate sexual abuse. This is an unimaginable betrayal of the father's love.

I have worked with quite a few clients with similar situations as this one, where memories of sexual abuse surface around eighteen to thirty years. With this information, we need to facilitate the process of reconciliation between the perpetrator and the victim. In a situation like this, often the truth has already made its way out, and the mom has come to realize the child is being abused by the father.

If a situation like this arrives in your office, it's up to you, the practitioner, to take time to reconcile the family if it is possible. This is the work of forgiveness.

This is just some of what you will encounter in this first level, the Silent Zone, where usable feedback is very hard to find.

There comes a time for some individuals—often after many months or sometimes years—when they reach a place of extreme overload. For survival, the brain moves to dissociate. But those that fall into this first level are unable to do so successfully. This leaves them with a kind of partial dissociation, with scattered and blurry memories that for the most part are unusable. This type of trauma is called Borderline Personality Disorder (BPD).

11.3.3. Probing Questions

Many times over the years, after spending many hours over a period of months and exhausting all my tools, my clients have provided only negative feedback. Some report, "I'm not getting better; I'm still very anxious and afraid when I see my grandfather." Or, perhaps the boy next door sexually violated the little neighbour girl, who is now twenty-eight years old. In this situation, if I am unable to gather any helpful information, I ask, "Is there a child, a little girl, on the inside?"

In this first level, you may get the occasional response. But in Levels Two and Three, you will find this tool to be more fruitful. There, the host will hear the answer to your question on the inside (from one of the alters), and she in turn will relay the words spoken to you.

Again, for me this first level has been the hardest level of the three covered in this chapter. Fortunately, it is also the least encountered.

Healing begins as you make your way into the life of an alter. But I must stress once again, because of the fragility produced by you, the counsellor, and an alter that is trying hard to hide, you will never reach these individuals until you have built a strong level of trust.

On average, I would say that most dissociation is birthed by ongoing situations in a home or relationship, situations that are wrong and sinful, with an unwilling participant who has no control over the situation. If this carries on, it only increases the hurt and pain that produce dissociation.

(A reminder: for the 30% who are unable to dissociate, they really have no alternative but to hide themselves from society when faced with overwhelming memories of extreme sexual abuse.)

11.4. Level 2: Dissociative Identity Disorder (DID)

When working with hurting people, we must always be proactive in uncovering the dissociated alters. This system works to hide the unbearable, the painful, the shameful—and hide them it will!

I have worked with some individuals for months, and had gotten nowhere before asking the question, "Is there a little girl on the inside, maybe crying and afraid?"

Almost instantly, the host person heard in her mind, "I am hiding in the closet." I took some time to explain to the alter that now she was in a safe place. In a few minutes, she identified herself to the host, and in a very short time, she was being held by Jesus.

My point is, we must ask probing questions. Often these dissociated parts are uncovered throughout the course of ministry, even more so if you are incorporating a deliverance type of ministry.

As I have already said in many different ways, it is my experience that the demonic realm is more often than not involved in the processes that lead to DID and MPD. The demonic knows exactly how, when, and where to apply the pressure needed to beak us down spiritually and psychologically.

They aren't interested in taking our lives. Their main focus is to splinter personalities to bring confusion and disarray, ending all peace. From there, they have the upper hand as they work from the inside, manipulating and hiding some dissociated parts while creating others, promoting an inner environment of fear, anger, and pain through which they can control the core person by harassing the inner family.

All the while the core person has no understanding why her sleep time is so troubled and her days so confusing, filled with anger and hatred along with strange pictures that speed thorough her mind, unattached to any of her memories or knowledge.

Often while I've ministered to DID and MPD individuals, while receiving information from an inner child it has cried out in pain, "Help me, I'm being beat up!" That is a signal for us to bind up any demon trying to disrupt the session. At that point, I command the demon to stop and then ask the inner child why she was being beat up.

More often than not the answer is, "Because he said he would beat me up if I talked to you!" The inner child seldom has the word "demon" in their vocabulary, but they are usually familiar with ugly and mean creatures that have names like Hate, Abuse or Rape—the list of names is endless.

Through their power over the inner child, the demons force the core person to do whatever evil they want. If the inner child resists, they are beaten by the demons.

This seems like something right out of a horror movie, but it is real life. It can be horrifying for the host person upon first realizing that she had dissociated and is now dealing with dissociated parts. Often, she very strongly rejects the alter state(s), and blames them for all the problems she has had in the past—decades' worth in some cases. Once or twice, I've even seen a client begin pounding on her tummy, trying to get these things (alters) out of her.

In this case, it will be a long time before you can reconcile the alter system with the host person. A situation like this is as fragile as paper in the wind, and you and I are the ones that have to bring these situations back into some sort of normality. This must be done by working with the host person and the alter(s) together.

I believe that God, foreseeing the depth of depravity mankind would fall into, built into the brain the ability to dissociate. Removing trauma from conscious memory allows for the abused to live out their days with a semblance of normalcy.

As for you and me, we can never—*must* never—do ministry without prayer, seeking the wisdom of Holy Spirit and following Jesus in every session.

When I started bumping into these situations, I cried out many times to God, "Where were You? Why did You let this carry on?"

One time, I was working with a five-year-old inner child. As a child, the woman who had dissociated had done everything she could to hide from her father one night. But she failed to get herself totally hidden. Because her father had to hunt her down, he was very angry and beat her before raping her. When I heard this information, I could I literally feel her pain. I asked Jesus, "Where were you?" The little dissociate said from inside the woman, "Jesus showed me how he wrapped his body around me to take the pain from my father's beating."

This is much more common than we would think. Some of what takes place with little girls is so vile that I shudder while putting it on paper.

It usually takes a session or two to get a response from an alter, but it's worth it, because alters can sense the level of trust within the host person. Trust allows alters to join in the dialogue with the host and the counsellor.

By talking softly, in a genuine, caring tone, and with a little coaxing, you can help bring them into a place of trusting you. Alters have the ability to pick up whether you care. If you don't remember their response or the client's response to questions, they will quickly doubt your sincerity.

You will talk directly to the alters, and then the host will relay to you whatever has been said on the inside of her brain. At this point, you don't know how many alters are within the host. There could be one, or many. You want to start with one alter. However, if there is one alter uncovered, there probably are more. The counsellor is the caregiver, and must stay on top of everything going on in the host person.

Get to know an alter, and through dialogue, win its trust. That will give you an ally to work with, along with the host person who is kept in tune with what is happening. There is one alter that you must try hard to access, whom I call the head alter; this is the one you will work with in the process of healing, wholeness, and (eventually) integration.

Be careful to ensure that each alter has the opportunity to share their situation. Alters are sensitive to what you say, and if they think you aren't being completely honest with them, or if you promise them something and don't follow through, they will go back into hiding. You will need to earn their trust again before they allow you access and answers.

At times the level of the care required becomes very intense. For instance, I have experienced at times with different clients a voice that is not the client's own. This is sometimes called an alter state or alternate personality. This type of ministry can be somewhat unpredictable, and requires caution.

I'm not saying that there is a danger of physical violence. What I am saying is that alters are ultra sensitive. You cannot pull the wool over their eyes. If they sense that you are upset with them, they will disappear. And then you find yourself still working weeks later in an attempt to provide a safe place for all involved, including you.

You must also be aware of something I call "layers." While you won't use this in the first level, you likely will in Levels Two and Three. Often in ministry, we remove a layer of heartache and pain, only to find another layer hidden underneath. There may be a multitude of layers such as shame, psychological pain, betrayal, and hatred.

We must always be aware that demons will hide the alters. Demons commonly try to silence the alters by laying on them. This is not unusual demonic behaviour and cannot be overlooked, because it is often very successful scheme for them. Remember the story I told in chapter 3 about the man whose spirit had been pushed down and silenced so that he could not respond to the truth of God's Word? In the same way, demons will try to silence and repress alters.

Let's return to the topic of gathering information from alters. The first action is to establish the host's psychological and emotional platform. This helps alters to feel safe since it establishes the host as point person. This is critical. At times, I didn't know the number of the alter states present in the host—naturally this depends on the severity of the dissociation. There may be as few as five, or as many as a dozen. Once you get this platform in place, you begin the work of engaging the alters. It is vital for the process of integration that you gather information about the state of each alter.

Some alters will be overcome with fear of being exposed. This may cause them to go into hiding for some time. Other times, as a good level of trust is built between the practitioner and the client, they will realize that integration is the best for all, and eventually each one of the alters will step into total integration with the host person. All this is done with you as the middle man or woman, along with the host person, who receives answers or questions from the alters.

There are many obstacles that get in the way of the alters becoming one with the host person. In one such case, I worked with Mary, whose alters thought that she was working against what they wished to do. In such a case, more time needs to be given to bring the host and the alter system together. Even once the alters are on your side and want to integrate, there may be more alters that none of them are aware of.

As much as you can, try to eliminate any situation that would promote anxiety, fear, and uncertainty. If you do, there can be reconciliation between the host and the dissociated. At this point, you can begin to understand the complexity of the alter system, as you guide the host person in questioning the alters about their origins.

If there is still animosity between the host and the alter system, this isn't going to work. Once the alters trust me, I draw information from them one at a time, speaking directly into the alter system.

To get individual names and information from each alter, have them tell their story, with you leading and asking questions. Whether they are past or current, the host relays the information to the practitioner. Since the dissociated and the host use the same brain and usually hear each other, the host person is enabled to share the whole dialogue.

11.5. Level 3: Multiple Personality Disorder (MPD)

Level Three, Multiple Personality Disorder (MPD), produces multiple personalities. Up until recently, this particular level was considered to be a dissociative disorder. For our purposes, we will analyze it as the third level of dissociation.

This level has the capacity to create an alter that can speak outwardly, just as you and I do. We know that Satanic Ritual Abuse prolifically creates alters. Generally this kind of disorder is birthed out of more extreme levels of trauma and dissociation.

At times during the process of counselling, the alters speak out directly to the counsellor. It isn't necessary to work at gathering information from the host person once we know for certain that we are dealing with Level Three alters. Instead of conversations being mediated through the host, they take place directly between the alter and the ones leading the session. This is much easier for the counsellor, but it is also much easier for the host person, who now isn't in the middle of the situation. However, it is absolutely necessary to keep the host person involved in all that is taking place. It is she who carries within her all that has taken place and what will come. She holds the pivotal role, and she should always say "yes" or "no" to any decisions being made, with the counsellor guiding the full faculty of the host person.

Within MPD, there are different levels of control over the host. Some alters will be able to take control entirely—to go for a drive, shopping, or even out to meet someone, without the host person having any idea of what has taken place.

Most commonly, MPD alters can speak out at their own whim, having access to the whole person at will. The host won't know what has happened until later, when she looks in her purse to find her cash is all gone, replaced with jeans in a teenager's size. Other alters can speak out but seem unable to access the whole (host) person. Before we move on, I must reiterate that trust alone is the key into the dark and hidden places of the host's alters.

In one sense, the dissociated will cause us to earn our right to enter their space. I have had to spend weeks and sometimes months to win or earn an alter's trust, only to lose it soon after because I inadvertently misunderstood some information the alter had given me. In one case, as I brought an alter out in a session, she felt I was being accusatory towards her, and it was several weeks before she would trust me again.

If you are a male working with a victim of sexual abuse, this can open a door for temptation that you have to continually guard against. This is why it is incumbent on us to take and keep good notes, which is simply good working practice. Documentation protects you and client. If your client is of the opposite sex, it is especially important for them to bring a support person or prayer warrior whom they trust. Above all, you want to create an environment that allows the client to feel safe.

If your client comes weekly for a period of months, then in all likelihood you will need to go to your earlier notes for reference. Don't rely on the host person for information gathered throughout your sessions—that would overload your client and their alter states, who carry within them the memory of every second of the rape, beating, or whatever the trauma may have been.

Documentation will help you create a clear picture of the events. The partial pieces you learn can be fit together to make a complete picture, so you don't need to retraumatize the client by making them relive the trauma over and over again. Some clients may have some vague mind pictures, along with psychological confusion. The dissociated parts themselves carry always the hellish memories of the rape or beating, which remain as though they are happening right now within the brain. As a result, they seem constantly on the lookout for danger.

All it takes for a dissociate to manifest is to see the perpetrator or someone that looks like them, or anything that reminds them of the traumatic situation, and they slip instantly into protection mode.

This has happened a few times in sessions with my clients. In one case, I was about halfway through a morning session when my secretary knocked on my door, saying there was very anxious lady that needed to meet with me and would wait until I was available. The waiting room chairs were placed in such a way that there was a good view of Main Street. The client had been waiting for about a half hour when she suddenly stood up, toppling over her chair.

She then went running down the stairs and out onto Main Street. Seconds later, her husband caught up to her with his car and brought her back. There was no ministry then, but she came back the next day and explained what had happened. As she had been looking out the window in my waiting room, she thought she saw a man who had sexually violated her over a long period, starting in her kindergarten years.

The client had originally come in due to marital problems. Dissociation wasn't part of her vocabulary. But she was an MPD with six alters, and I worked with her off and on for about two years. It was only dissociation that allowed the core person to carry on in some sort of a normal fashion, such as going to work and tending to the children. All the while, the alters carried the pain and shame of the abuse.

Once again, if you have not earned their perceived level of trust, you will have no access to the inner child in the dissociated individual.

Relative to befriending alters,

Every alter is a real personality with real problems. Each has real feelings to work through and real needs that must be attended to. Multiples have become adept at picking up subtle indications about people's feelings—they can tell immediately if they are being treated condescendingly, and they will not put up with it. There are alters in every system who have been traumatized and who will be alert for the earliest sign of danger.[106]

I had no knowledge base when I accidentally encountered my first client with MPD, which was very much a shocker. I had read about the topic in the occasional reference in books on deliverance. However, one day I was plunged into it when a new client arrived at my office door, brought in by a layperson from a church we both attended.

The woman came in to deal with an issue of anger, especially at the mention of her father's name. As it turned out, she had been sexually violated by her father for a long, long time, and was refusing to forgive him. I explained the personal ramifications of not forgiving her father. She agreed to forgive him, but when we started the actual process of forgiving her father (who was not present), she went ballistic. She was up and out of her chair, running around the room.

I was unable to stop her. I wondered if this level of energy was driven by the powers of darkness, so I spoke out and said, "Satan, if you or any of your demons are making this woman run, in the name of Jesus I bind up every demonic entity fuelling this behaviour." She immediately stopped, dropped into a chair, and then out of her mouth came the voice of young girl. She cried out, "Help me, help me, my daddy is beating on Mommy's tummy, trying to kill me." These words came from an exposed and fearful alter.

It took an hour just to get things settled enough to have a conversation with the host. In the original situation, the father was very angry because his wife was pregnant again, and he was literally trying to kill the child within the mother's womb. Later, I talked with the father; he left angry, and I never saw him again. But I did spend years with the mother, his wife, who had actually dissociated five different times.

Throughout the years, the alter that cried out, "Help me, help me!" literally took charge of the alter system, including the host. This alter was twelve years old, but when she came into my office something must have triggered the memory of her father beating on her mother's tummy with her in the womb.

---

106 Friesen, p. 164.

The alter was very strong, and as the mother drove her daughter into town for counselling sessions, the child's alter would try to take over the steering wheel of the car. No doubt this left the mother absolutely drained from trying to keep the vehicle in the centre of the road. This isn't a fairytale! I myself saw her exhaustion from fighting with the alter.

My prayer is that many of you will feel and heed the call of God on your life to work with the dissociated, at least at this lower level of dissociation. I will say it again—some of the greatest joy I have experienced in ministry has been working with the dissociated.

In this chapter I have given you some basic tools and information, primarily from my own experience. One thing you can count on: if you decide to practice the type of ministry advocated in this manual, you will find yourself dealing with different levels of DID and MPD. If you purposely stay away from the realm of deliverance it won't occur as much, but I wouldn't encourage that, simply because so many dissociated people are in desperate need of healing.

11.6. Satanic Ritual Abuse (SRA) and MPD

If you've chosen to work with the dissociated, if you've chosen to follow God's calling to minister into the lives of others, you must also be aware of Satanic Ritual Abuse (SRA). You will certainly encounter it, especially if you live in a bigger city. Most of what we find at the lower levels of SRA is very easily managed by using the chapter on deliverance in this manual.

SRA is a tool of Satan to *enlarge* his kingdom with his wicked ways and means. For the sake of this manual, I will discuss two levels of SRA, a lower level and a higher level.

11.6.1. Lower Level SRA
SRA can take mankind right into the bedroom of hell with Satan himself. Dealing with the lower levels of SRA is akin to doing deliverance.

I have worked with a few adults who have been victims of what I will call low level SRA, each one coming at different times and from different locations. None of them are connected in any way, which suggests this issue goes beyond any one geographical area or family line. Some of the clients experienced lower levels of dissociation, and all had similar stories.

Fear was a major theme—fear of dark cellars, and dark and scary wooded areas. Many remembered sexual stuff happening at a very young age. They recognized occult activities and paraphernalia in their fireside or basement memories.

The ministry required for these individuals was very much the same as dealing with anyone with DID or MPD. I would say the activities were only borderline SRA. But there was still damage done, which primarily required forgiving the parents and neighbours involved. This lower level of SRA is something that you or I can bring healing into.

Satanic Ritual Abuse is practiced in the heavily wooded areas of our nation, in farming areas unseen by those who drive by.

The sites themselves often have a large metal barrel, like a used oildrum, on the premises to facilitate burning. Any number of families come together, and their sacrifice to Satan may be something as small as a barn cat. They will strip the cat and burn it in the fire for the glory of Satan. A father will at times impregnate his daughter and later abort the fetus for a sacrifice.

It is the powerful influence of Satan in this setting that drives the father to rape his daughter. Wife swapping is also frequently involved in satanic work. You already have the tools necessary to treat this situations in this manual, but I would really encourage you to carefully study demonic activity and the concept of forgiveness as you work on bringing these clients back into society.

These situations are also extremely tough on the counsellor personally. Just think of the daughter being raped by her father, not old enough to know what was going on, and then having her fetus burnt. She will be deeply traumatized and there needs to be a means of reconciliation. Forgiveness is necessary, but will be difficult.

It is hard and exhausting working with these individuals. Unwilling wives who have been swapped in the midst of all this hell will also feel a strong sense of betrayal and anger. Prayer and forgiveness are sorely needed.

If their experience was much worse than these examples, I would certainly ask them to find a professional. Even after all these years in ministry, there are some things I can't deal with, and it would be in the best interests of the individual to get them the help they need.

As I've said before, if we are unable to meet the need of the one we are ministering to, we can do them harm by trying to hang on to them. Simply said, this is doing them a disservice. Do all you can, and from there release them to someone who can take them the next mile.

11.6.2. Higher Level SRA

The second level is found in the deepest, darkest places in our nations, and sometimes in the bowels of big cities. This is where Satan worshippers do their deadly work, raping and pillaging, and burning women and girls for Satan's glory.

In all likelihood you will never encounter such evilness, but you will find people in your office that have been traumatized and raped by Satan—the cruellest things you can imagine.

I have encountered individuals who have been burned on an altar or witnessed such activity. They come in wounded and disillusioned. It is a horror story, but it takes place.

To close this topic, if someone were come to me for help after being involved in SRA, either as victim or practitioner, I would get some solid background information.

11.7. Integration

Integration is the progress of alters becoming one with Jesus. This is a very fragile process, and it takes a bit of coaxing to bring the dissociated to a place where they can accept the invitation.

Occasionally, I've seen fusion take place spontaneously, as forgiveness and healing make a way for integration. But this isn't my preference. The reason is because rushing or forcing integration may not give time for a solid connection with Jesus, which can be very disconcerting for the client, and just produce further fear and confusion.

If you send your client home after a one-hour session that closed with the host person and the dissociated becoming one, only for the client to wake the next morning in a dissociated state, you can expect to see the alter's trust level drop to zero.

A time or two in my ministry, the process of fusion had to be put on hold because of the alter's fear that fusion may never work for him.

As I bring an alter towards integration, I do my best to insure all issues relative to that alter have been looked after, such as unforgiveness towards the host or other alters. Most importantly, all issues relating to the perpetrator must have been dealt with. Seldom do we work with the perpetrator—and in fact, this is not in any way necessary. The alter can make a way for successful integration by granting forgiveness to the perpetrator for all they did to the alter.

I am going to issue a caution. Some believe that those who have been raped or sexually violated in some way will eventually require a confrontation with their perpetrator as part of their healing. There may indeed need to be a confrontation, but never until the victim has grown into a place of real strength in his own person. The reason: when confronted with accusations of abuse, most perpetrators deny having had anything to do with it.

Can you even imagine what that would do an alter? The thought of having to confront the abuser would likely be traumatic enough to bring about a whole new level of dissociation. Any healing that had taken place could very well be lost. As you are moving towards fusing, ensure that the alter is 100% on board. This is a very critical time.

Should the alter have a change of heart partway into the process of integration, it could be a long time before they are ready again.

The secret to success is to take your time, getting all available information and alternatives into the hands of the host person, as well as those of the alter wishing to integrate. Encourage the inner child to make the decision, reminding him that integration and wholeness are the will of Jesus.

Once they agree, I ask Jesus to come and take the hands of the host person and the alter together, and He does. Most often, the host will be able to visualize the alter becoming one with Jesus, and she will often inform me of each step as it takes place. It is always an exciting and holy time.

Remember that while we need Jesus as we minister to others, we never need Him more than when dealing with the dissociated. It can be a very hard sell to bring an alter to the place of knowing and accepting Jesus Christ as their Saviour. Satan has actually named many of his demons "Jesus," and he uses them to confuse the alter system. The demonic will move alters around for their advantage. In such cases, you will need to uncover the demons that are masquerading in the name of Jesus.

Another roadblock that gets in the way of integrating is the male figure. It is the male that beats and rapes, and for some alters, Jesus is seen as just another dangerous man. I have sometimes spent days earning an alter's trust before they would allow Jesus to speak to them, even from a distance. It really is akin to the salvation walk—they move towards Jesus without saying "yes" until they are convinced He really is who He says He is. Once they make that decision, Jesus will make a way for the alter to become one with the host.

1. I always do my best for the core person; they need good support from someone they can trust. It can be a disadvantage to have too many helpers present, as the message to the core person and the alter system can get convoluted, and the process can come to a stop. However, there is a real advantage to having at least one helper with you in the sessions, as this helps give continuity for the sake of the alter person. They can also take notes for you, which helps to keep you on track.

2. It's imperative to be alert to a voice that isn't human. While it's often easy to recognize demonic voices, we must be alert to the enemy's schemes. Listen as they respond to you. Demonic voices tend to be cold, scratchy, and cranky, with lack of relational capability. Pay attention to the voice.

3. Mapping can be very helpful, both for you and the alter system. Even if you are only dealing with one or two alters, it helps you to build a profile of their personalities. Often, having their names recorded for the purpose of wholeness builds hope in the alters.

At every opportunity, it is our responsibility to promote hope. Alters were created in a place of hellish pain by no doing of their own, and left with no possible means of escape. The only consistent they have is hopelessness. In saying that, I do not want to trivialize the mental and emotional capacity of each alter. They are able, after all, to build a complex psychological protective stronghold, which requires our help to untangle it. This process cannot be rushed—a key principle we must adhere to in all ministry to the dissociated.

While dissociated, the host person is basically tied to the whims of the alter states. After healing, the host must learn what normal life is. You may bring them to a place of reconciliation with the perpetrator that caused the dissociation—a husband, father, family member, or acquaintance. Yet again I caution that reparation with the individuals who caused the trauma may not be possible. Be sensitive and do not proceed unless both parties are at a place where this can happen.

I have taken many people through the steps from the beginning to the end. What a joy it is been for me and for them! And it will be so for you too, as you use this chapter to work with the dissociated.

> *"For I know the plans I have for you," declares the* LORD, *"plans to prosper you and not to harm you, plans to give you hope and a future. Then you will call on me and come and pray to me, and I will listen to you. You will seek me and find me when you seek me with all your heart. I will be found by you," declares the* LORD, *"and will bring you back from captivity."*
>
> —Jeremiah 29:11–14

TOOLBOX

Part V

Chapter Twelve

PRAYERS AND PRAISE

THIS CHAPTER IS ARRANGED SO THAT YOU CAN WRITE IN YOUR experiences and revelations from God, keeping in mind to write in the date, place, and lesson learned from each one. This chapter will help you in your growing prayer life, along with various other matters brought into play as you move onwards and upward in the Lord Jesus Christ. It is also intended to challenge and equip you, as you learn who God would have you be and grow toward that goal. Jot down any notes as you see fit.

> *And pray in the Spirit on all occasions with all kinds of prayers and requests. With this in mind, be alert and always keep on praying for all the Lord's people.*
>
> —Ephesians 6:18

Prayer

Prayer is, without a doubt, the most important and critical practice in our Christian lives. And it happens to be the shortest chapter in this book. Why? Because if I were to include everything that needs to be said about the kind of prayer you will need to work out all the principles and concepts of this book, it would require another volume. In this chapter, you will find simple and practical examples from the Bible and other sources for your everyday prayer life.

John 10:14 says, *"I am the good shepherd; I know my sheep and my sheep know me…"* Hughes expands on the concept of knowing God's voice:

> *Men and women who have spent much time listening to God claim that they can distinguish between their own imagination and the quiet voice of the Spirit within their hearts…. I stress that it only comes after*

practice. It is an art that has to be cultivated. It is essential to set aside time specifically for this purpose. In today's world… where time seems to be something most people do not have, is it any wonder that the practice of listening to God is a lost art?[107]

1. Prayer is the meat and honey of our spiritual life. Waiting on God is part of the art of receiving. It isn't only the Holy Spirit that speaks into our heart and mind. In my own personal and ministry experience, I daily speak to Jesus, both in the early morning hours and throughout the day; He, in turn, speaks back to me. As believers, we should all learn to discern who we are hearing from, whether Father, Son, or Holy Spirit.

_____

_____

_____

_____

_____

_____

2. Hughes also says,

There is communion with God, that asks for nothing yet asks for everything… when we pray in His name, we receive that what He knows is right for us to receive.[108]

And further,

---

107 Hughes & Brooks, September 24, 2015.
108 Hughes & Brooks, September 18, 2015.

It is always helpful to have a notebook and pen with you during your times with God so that you can write anything that occurs to you or that He may say to you. The notebook and pen are signs of faith since they show that you expect some message to come to you. Once you have read the Word you will find your thinking and aspirations start moving in the right direction. And you will then pray prayers that are in harmony with the will of God.[109]

So get out your pen and paper and wait. Waiting upon Jesus becomes an art unto itself. Jesus has told us, *"Ask and it will be given to you; seek and you will find; knock and the door will be opened to you"* (Matthew 7:7).

_____

_____

_____

_____

_____

_____

3. Hughes says of a great historical prayer warrior,

George Muller, a man who established a great ministry among the orphaned children… told how beginning prayer time by reading a portion of scripture transformed his devotional life. The Word is very relevant in our morning and evening devotional times.[110]

109 Hughes & Brooks, October 3, 2015.
110 Hughes & Brooks, September 21, 2015.

If you are just beginning a prayer life or haven't disciplined yourself yet, start out with a reasonable amount of time, such as fifteen minutes: five minutes in praise and worship, five minutes in prayer, and five minutes reading the Bible. It won't be long before you find yourself hungry for more time with the Lord.

_____

_____

_____

_____

_____

_____

4. As Billy Graham once said, "If you are too busy to spend a little time with God each day in personal prayer, and the reading of His Word, then you are busier than God intends you to be." I believe this to be true.

_____

_____

_____

_____

_____

_____

5. Richard Newton has said, "Prayer and patience and faith are never disappointed. I have long since learned, if ever I was to be a minister, faith and prayer must make me one."[111] Make this quote your daily agreement with the Father, Son and Holy Spirit.

_____

_____

_____

_____

_____

_____

6. My friend had a vision of Father God, the Son, and the Holy Spirit: Father God was seated on the throne, with Jesus sitting in front of Him; they were talking back and forth, intently and purposefully. Meanwhile, the Holy Spirit was standing on God's left side, facing them both. There was a sense that Jesus' conversation with God was His intercession for us. When Jesus and Father God were done speaking, Jesus gave the Holy Spirit the approval to go and tell my friend what He and Father God were talking about, bringing her His own interceding prayers. This vision brought to life the following passage:

> But when he, the Spirit of truth, comes, he will guide you into all the truth. He will not speak on his own; he will speak only what he hears, and he will tell you what is yet to come. He will glorify me because it is from me that he will receive what he will make known to you. All that belongs to the Father is mine. That is why I said the Spirit will receive from me what he will make known to you.
>
> —John 16:13–15

111 Bounds, p. 45.

_____

_____

_____

_____

_____

_____

7. There is one baptism, but there are many fillings. We receive one Spirit, but there are many fillings of the Holy Spirit. It is incumbent upon us to seek God continually, spending time daily with the Godhead. This is a means of keeping your soul person topped up with the Spirit of the living God.

Acts 2:4 says, *"All of them were filled with the Holy Spirit and began to speak in other tongues as the Spirit enabled them."* This was not a one-time event; it was something God wanted to keep doing in the lives of those early believers—and for us today.

"Do not get drunk on wine, which leads to debauchery. Instead, be filled with the Spirit…" (Ephesians 5:18). You are children of light, so live continually in that way, being filled continually with the Light, and drawing continually from the Godhead. Literally, we are to "Keep on being filled with the Holy Spirit." Because we will run dry otherwise, we need to spend time in His presence daily, asking for a fresh infilling.

_____

_____

_____

_____

---

8. Warfare: In the process of praying, we may find ourselves wrestling with the demonic.

For though we live in the world, we do not wage war as the world does. The weapons we fight with are not the weapons of the world. On the contrary, they have divine power to demolish strongholds. We demolish arguments and every pretension that sets itself up against the knowledge of God, and we take captive every thought to make it obedient to Christ.
—2 Corinthians 10:3–5

Psalm 27:13–14 says, *"I remain confident of this: I will see the goodness of the Lord in the land of the living. Wait for the Lord; be strong and take heart and wait for the Lord."*

Therefore, dear friends, since you have been forewarned, be on your guard so that you may not be carried away by the error of the lawless and fall from your secure position. But grow in the grace and knowledge of our Lord and Savior Jesus Christ. To him be glory both now and forever! Amen.
—2 Peter 3:17–18

Knowledge of the Word is also critical to our success in overcoming the power of darkness. The knowledge of the Word of God and its purposes is absolutely critical in your day-to-day prayer life as well.

_____

_____

_____

9. *"Though my father and mother forsake me, the Lord will receive me"* (Psalm 27:10). Yes! God's promises are true, and we can stand on them knowing He will do what He says. Although I have said it again and again, I remind you that if we are living with unforgiveness in our hearts, no matter how small and regardless of who it is towards, God cannot hear our prayers. Our prayers cannot be answered with unforgiveness in our heart.

_____

_____

_____

_____

_____

_____

10. Murray says,

In olden times believers met God, knew Him, walked with Him, had the clear and full consciousness that they had dealings with the God of heaven, and through faith had the assurance they and their lives were well-pleasing to Him. When the son of God came to earth revealing the Father, it was so that fellowship with God and the assurance of His favor might become clearer and be the abiding portion of every child of God.[112]

Jesus is calling to us! *"Here I am! I stand at the door and knock. If anyone hears my voice and opens the door, I will come in and eat with that person, and they with me"* (Revelation 3:20).

_____

_____

_____

_____

_____

_____

11. The Bible isn't open to private interpretation. As God breathed His Word into man for the creation of the Bible, in the same way He uncovers the brilliance of the written Word for us today. God has miraculously preserved His written Word as a perfect picture of Him and His righteous ways.

_____

_____

_____

_____

_____

112 Murray, p. 5.

12. I read an article about a woman who opened up a Hebrew Bible. When she did so, the style of the letters and language suddenly came to life. The Hebrew print looked to her like living tongues of fire. This profound image helped her to see the truth of Hebrews 4:12: *"For the word of God is alive and active. Sharper than any double-edged sword, it penetrates even to dividing soul and spirit, joints and marrow; it judges the thoughts and attitudes of the heart."*

Acts 2:3–4 says, *"They saw what seemed to be tongues of fire that separated and came to rest on each of them. All of them were filled with the Holy Spirit and began to speak in other tongues as the Spirit enabled them."*

_____

_____

_____

_____

_____

_____

13. Our prayer is perfumed with praise. Max Lucado says,

Prayer is the recognition that if God had not engaged himself in our problems, we would still be lost in the blackness. It is by his mercy that we have been lifted up. Prayer is that whole process that reminds us of who God is and who we are.

I believe there is great power in prayer. I believe God heals the wounded, and that he can raise the dead. But I don't believe we tell God what to do and when to do it. You see, there's a difference between faith and presumption. There's a difference between be-lieving he's the almighty God and demanding he become our di-vine servant.[113]

Praise is to lift up the mighty name of God, to boast in the name of God.

This is what the Lord says: "Let not the wise boast of their wisdom or the strong boast of their strength or the rich boast of their riches, but let the one who boasts boast about this: that they have the understanding to know me, that I am the Lord, who exercises kindness, justice and righteousness on earth, for in these I delight," declares the Lord.

—Jeremiah 9:23–24

_____

_____

_____

_____

_____

_____

14. A.W. Tozer says,

There is not in the world a kind of life more sweet and delightful than that of a continual conversation with God. Those only can comprehend it who practice and experience it, yet I do not advise you to do it from that motive. It is not pleasure which we ought to

---

113 Lucado, p. 1391.

seek in this exercise, but let us do it from a principle of love, and because God would have us.[114]

_____

_____

_____

_____

_____

15. Hughes says, "The goal of all Christian development and the whole purpose of thriving spiritually is that we might reflect the beauty and character of Jesus. As I said earlier, God is so excited about Jesus that He wants to make everyone like Him."[115]

_____

_____

_____

_____

_____

_____

---

114 Bell, p. 241.

115 Hughes & Brooks, February 29, 2016.

16. Prayer is a place where we can celebrate Jesus.

The most important event in human history is an event planned even before the creation of the world. It is the keeping of a promise made to Abraham over 2000 years earlier. It is the fulfilment of a host of prophesies regarding a Messiah who would come to establish his Kingdom.[116]

Jesus is worth celebrating for what He has done for us! As He said, *"I am the way and the truth and the life. No one comes to the Father except through me"* (John 14:6).

_____

_____

_____

_____

_____

_____

17. You are children of light, so live that way. The age that we live in is becoming darker and darker.

All these are the beginning of birth pains. Then you will be handed over to be persecuted and put to death, and you will be hated by all nations because of me. At that time many will turn away from the faith and will betray and hate each other, and many false prophets will appear and

---

116 Smith, p. 1349.

deceive many people. Because of the increase of wickedness, the love of most will grow cold, but the one who stands firm to the end will be saved.
—Matthew 14:8–13

What you have just read was written approximately two thousand years ago. We live now in a world that is much darker than those days.

Revelation warns us about the darkness of our time, and the importance of standing firm in the faith.

The revelation from Jesus Christ, which God gave him to show his servants what must soon take place. He made it known by sending his angel to his servant John, who testifies to everything he saw—that is, the word of God and the testimony of Jesus Christ. Blessed is the one who reads aloud the words of this prophecy, and blessed are those who hear it and take to heart what is written in it, because the time is near.
—Revelation 1:1–3

Jesus will return soon, and He calls us to faithfulness.

"Look, I am coming soon! Blessed is the one who keeps the words of the prophecy written in this scroll."

...

"Look, I am coming soon! My reward is with me, and I will give to each person according to what they have done. I am the Alpha and the Omega, the First and the Last, the Beginning and the End.

"Blessed are those who wash their robes, that they may have the right to the tree of life and may go through the gates into the city. Outside are the dogs, those who practice magic arts, the sexually immoral, the murderers, the idolaters and everyone who loves and practices falsehood.

"I, Jesus, have sent my angel to give you this testimony for the churches. I am the Root and the Offspring of David, and the bright Morning Star."

The Spirit and the bride say, "Come!" And let the one who hears say, "Come!" Let the one who is thirsty come; and let the one who wishes take the free gift of the water of life.

I warn everyone who hears the words of the prophecy of this scroll: If anyone adds anything to them, God will add to that person the plagues described in this scroll. And if anyone takes words away from this scroll of prophecy, God will take away from that person any share in the tree of life and in the Holy City, which are described in this scroll.

He who testifies to these things says, "Yes, I am coming soon."

Amen. Come, Lord Jesus.

The grace of the Lord Jesus be with God's people. Amen.

—Revelation 22:7, 12–21

I have chosen parts of the book of Revelation to get your attention, but I encourage you to read through the whole book. Revelation can radically change the way you are living out your Christian life. This book itself promises a blessing if you read it through. But more than that, we are living in the last days. Are you and your family going to rise up out of the darkness and shine in those last days? That is what Isaiah 60:1–2 calls us to: *"Arise, shine, for your light has come, and the glory of the Lord rises upon you. See, darkness covers the earth and thick darkness is over the peoples, but the Lord rises upon you and his glory appears over you."*

_____

_____

_____

_____

_____

_____

18. Over the years, my soul has been sorrowful with how casual we can become when referring to the high and holy God. His name is Father. He is our Papa God, yet we must never forget that He is holy, high, and mighty—the Omnipotent One.

We desperately need to come face to face with His holiness, to be humbled under His mighty hand, and draw closer to Him in His beauty and majesty. The following passages will remind us of these truths.

Ascribe to the Lord the glory due his name; worship the Lord in the splendor of his holiness.

—Psalm 29:2

For this is what the high and exalted One says—he who lives forever, whose name is holy: "I live in a high and holy place, but also with the one who is contrite and lowly in spirit, to revive the spirit of the lowly and to revive the heart of the contrite.

—Isaiah 57:15

If we have never had the experience of taking our commonplace religious shoes off our commonplace religious feet and getting rid of all the undue familiarity with which we approach God, it is questionable whether we have ever stood in His presence. The people who are flippant and familiar are those who have never yet been introduced to Jesus Christ. After the amazing delight and liberty of realizing what Jesus Christ does, comes the impenetrable darkness of realizing Who He is.[117]

The Lord reigns, let the earth be glad; let the distant shores rejoice. Clouds and thick darkness surround him; righteousness and justice are the foundation of his throne. Fire goes before him and consumes his foes on every side. His lightning lights up the world; the earth sees and trembles. The mountains melt like wax before the Lord, before the Lord of

---

117 Chambers, pp. 2–3.

all the earth. The heavens proclaim his righteousness, and all peoples see his glory.

All who worship images are put to shame, those who boast in idols—worship him, all you gods!

Zion hears and rejoices and the villages of Judah are glad because of your judgments, Lord. For you, Lord, are the Most High over all the earth; you are exalted far above all gods. Let those who love the Lord hate evil, for he guards the lives of his faithful ones and delivers them from the hand of the wicked. Light shines on the righteous and joy on the upright in heart. Rejoice in the Lord, you who are righteous, and praise his holy name.

—Psalm 97:1–12

_____

_____

_____

_____

_____

_____

_____

_____

_____

Look, I am coming soon! My reward is with me, and I will give to each person according to what they have done. I am the Alpha and the Omega, the First and the Last, the Beginning and the End.

—Revelation 22:12

What good will it be for someone to gain the whole world, yet forfeit their soul?

—Matthew 16:26

Chapter Thirteen

TOOLBOX

IT IS MY PURPOSE TO HELP YOU ACQUIRE MANY TOOLS AND PRINCIPLES as possible that will assist you in ministering to others. As you minister, no matter the situation, your first question should always be "What does the Word say"?

This chapter is for your own personal information, so you can look up topics as they become relevant. I have dropped interesting and helpful nuggets throughout this Toolbox.

How does God guide us? Gumbel has this to say:

> We all have to make decisions in life. We are faced with decisions about relationships, marriage, children, use of time, jobs, money, holidays, possessions, giving and so on. Some of these are very big decisions; some smaller. In many cases, it is of the utmost importance that we make the right decision—for instance in our choice of a marriage partner. We need God's help.
>
> Guidance springs out of relationship with God. He promises to guide those who are walking with him. He says: "I will instruct you and teach you in the way you should go" (Psalm 32:8). Jesus promises to lead and guide his followers: "he calls his own sheep by name and leads them out... his sheep follow because they know his voice" (John 10:3–4).[118]

If we are going to make a difference in the lives of those that look to us for help, it is imperative we have a toolbox full of up-to-date, sharpened, sanitized, usable tools. We can all pray for healing, or wisdom, or ask "Oh God, deliver my sister." But if He has called us to come alongside our brothers and sisters to

---

118 Gumbel, p. 7.

help carry their burden, it is also imperative for us to understand their burden, which will eventually help in the removal of the specific problem.

I remember very well one of my first clients. It was in the mid-80s. Everyone was talking about the "inner child," and I thought this whole topic was crazy. I had done everything I knew to do with this client. She'd had some very good ministry, and was happy with where she was at. However, there seemed to be some sort of obstacle that still held her back in some areas.

She came back for another session, with no change. As the session began, I had just started to pray for wisdom when the Lord said, "Jan, pray for the inner child." I don't recall the level of my faith at that time, but I knew the voice of God—and so I prayed. I had only begun with my prayer directed at the inner child when my client began to cry uncontrollably. We were finally able to deal with the issue, hidden from her and those who'd known her all those years.

When we finished that day, she was free. Yes, she came in for a few more sessions, but the point is, she never would have received her freedom without the child within being uncovered. We must have a full toolbox. This was the first of many, many people I've encountered with Dissociative Identity Disorder (Chapter 11).

One time in prayer, as the Lord was speaking to me about His call on my life, He led me to the following verses, Isaiah 57:14–16. The caption inserted by the NIV writers just before verse 14 reads "Comfort for the Contrite," which is the essence or heart of the passage.

> And it will be said: "Build up, build up, prepare the road! Remove the obstacles out of the way of my people." For this is what the high and exalted One says—he who lives forever, whose name is holy: "I live in a high and holy place, but also with the one who is contrite and lowly in spirit, to revive the spirit of the lowly and to revive the heart of the contrite. I will not accuse them forever, nor will I always be angry, for then they would faint away because of me—the very people I have created."

We simply will not get into the deeper, hidden issues of clients' lives without training, hands on ministry, and the leading of the Holy Spirit. As I said at the outset of the book, I started with very little training but was compelled by the Spirit to move into ministry. We are all called to be ready at any time to lend a shoulder to someone in need. The Bible makes it clear that where there are gifts, there is a calling, and where there is a calling, there is also a God-given anointing.

Over the years, I have seen many receive giftings without ever unwrapping the parcel. Sometimes they feel a sense of calling but become discouraged, seemingly unable to move on. Note this: the gifting is ignited little by little as we work the Gift. The anointing is released according to our ability to steward the gift. Our gifting grows with use, but a gift unused becomes like a dry and dusty land. The life-producing water of God's Word just runs off the uncultivated, hardened ground.

The area of our giftedness is akin to a well-planned, cultivated and watered garden, a garden with all kinds of vegetables, fruits and flowers—some for life-giving nourishment, others for healing of all kinds. As we use it, a gift grows and puts down roots in the soil of our soul.

It is imperative that we have a good, solid foundational understanding of the Word of God. In the Word, we will acquire many tools and principles that will assist us in ministering. Remember, as we begin to minister to others, in every situation we encounter our first question should always be, "What does the Word say?"

A

Anger—Be aware that anger does not only display itself in active forms such as hitting, pinching, throwing things, or slamming doors. It also takes more subtle forms like silence, irritation, resentment, malice, bitterness, and hatred. Did you know also that exceeding the speed limit can also be a form of anger—anger towards authority? Chronic forgetfulness, frigidity, and impotence also display anger.

Anorexia nervosa—I have worked with many individuals afflicted with this disorder, and have experienced great success. Notably, every one of those cases involved demonic activity in some way or other.

B

Bitter root—*"See to it that no one falls short of the grace of God and that no bitter root grows up to cause trouble and defile many"* (Hebrews 12:15). Bitter roots are wounds, and they result in angry responses (i.e. judgements made on us as little children and adults, consciously or unconsciously, that are forgotten, but remain alive and active in the unconscious). As roots, they feed life with matter upon which to act. As bitterness in the heart, they infect the mind with negative psychological expectancies.

As judgements, they necessitate the reaping of seeds that have been sown. Law is inflexible and relentless, but for the grace of God. To the law of sowing and reaping (Galatians 6:7), we must add the law of increase (Genesis 1:28; 1 Thessalonians 3:12 and 4:10; Colossians 2:19). We never sow one seed and get one back. The seed we sow may be tiny—an angry impression, a resentment held against some family member as a child—and forgotten. The longer it remains undetected or neglected, the longer it grows; the law of sowing and reaping guarantees that no one ever gets away with anything at any time or place.

Burden bearing—*"Brothers and sisters, if someone is caught in a sin, you who live by the Spirit should restore that person gently. But watch yourselves, or you also may be tempted. Carry each other's burdens, and in this way you will fulfill the law of Christ"* (Galatians 6:1–2). We can celebrate that our God is a God who cares. Every one of us, in some way or another, is called to live out the law of caring.

If God has called us to come alongside our brothers and sisters to help carry their burdens, it is imperative for us to have some ability to understand their burden. This will eventually help them to remove the burden. To speak to the deeper, hidden issues of individuals' lives, we need training and hands on ministry, along with the leading of the Holy Spirit. As beginners, our initial training often provides us only with head knowledge, which we draw upon along with our personal life experiences. This is fine; it is a good start. Your training comes as you begin to help those that come to you for ministry.

As I have previously said, I started with very little training, but was led and compelled by the Spirit to move into this type of ministry. I do believe we are all called to be ready at any time to lend a shoulder to someone in need. The Bible makes it clear there are gifts; if there is a calling, there is also a God who calls or does the callling.

C

Captive Spirit—A condition that begins when an individual flees or turns away from life or is in rebellion. This is often because of early woundings or child-hood traumas. Individuals can be aware of something wrong or missing, like a prisoner in a tower might look out of his barred window to view life. These individuals are locked into fleshly strongholds where demons can take advantage of them (John 10:10). The spirit can go to sleep, or it can be tormented, traumatized, withered, emaciated, or in agony.

There are many common symptoms, but some important markers to aid in recognizing a captive spirit are the degree of seriousness of the indicators given below, or an inability to function (such as slumbering).

Asking the following questions will help to discern a captive spirit. Pay attention to the response of the client as you ask these questions. Observe the body language and facial expressions, and listen to the voice inflections and pauses to help you confirm the presence of a captive spirit.

1. Do you feel hollow, empty or vacant, as though something is missing? (Lamentations 3:6–9) yes____ no____
2. Do you feel alone, lonely, or separate, even when with compan-ions? (Psalm 88:18) yes____ no____
3. Do you feel persecuted, afflicted, or tormented, even when no one is bothering or hurting you? yes____ no____
4. Do you sense you have talents, powers and energies inside you can't reach, as though they are locked away? (Psalm 88:1–8) yes____ no____
5. Is marital sex glorious and joyful (as opposed to something you just do)? yes____ no____
6. Do you ever have inner rage, when there is nothing on the sur-face to be angry about (like captives raging at their prison bars)? yes____ no____

7. Do you sense there is a film, a mist, a fog over life? Is everything (colours, sounds) dimmed, muted, hidden? yes____ no____

8. In the presence of anointed worship or teaching, do you suffer overpowering sleepiness (narcolepsy)? yes____ no____

9. When in the presence of an anointed service, or servant, do you sometimes suffer vertigo (dizziness)? yes____ no____

10. Have you ever suffered from dyslexia? (This is common in captives, as both dyslexia and captivity have spiritual withdrawal or rebellion at the root) yes____ no____

A Prayer to End Captivity

Lord, we thank You for the gift of our spirits, breathed into us by You at conception. Now we ask You to lead us to the place where _____'s spirit is.

(Wait on the Lord, and describe what He reveals to you.)

Father, we ask that You move into this place with _____, and lead the way out. Carry her if walking is too difficult.

Lord, I ask You to minister to the wounded spirit and withered "limbs." Massage them, causing the blood to flow again. Pour Your strength in. Pour the oil of Your Holy Spirit over the wounds to bring relief. Wrap _____ in Your robes of righteousness; cause Your healing to radiate all around through her spirit and body. I ask You to declare the boundaries beyond which the enemy may not come. Cause Your brilliance and holiness to shine forth from _____ so that the enemy cannot see. Sweep away her footprints so the enemy cannot follow.

Lord, walk with _____ for a while so she can lean on You when her legs and will give out. Provide enough time for her to gain the strength of body and spirit necessary to choose life. At a place that is right for _____, I ask that You also release the gifts, talents, and energies You gave her as an inheritance for living a full life.

Return _____'s stolen birthright.

Now, Father, together we dismiss the enemy. We ask that Your angels be commissioned to deal with the powers of darkness as You see fit. We ask You to bring other guarding angels to protect _____. We ask that in Your kindness You seal or destroy the prison (be specific) and blow away all evidence of it with the mighty wind of Your Holy Spirit.

Christian counsellor—A therapist/helper who accepts the Bible as the final standard of authority. One individual seeking to help another recognize, understand and solve their problem(s) according to the standard of the Bible. The key point: the Bible holds the answer to every need and question.

Correction—Just because someone corrects us, it doesn't mean that they have rejected us. This misunderstanding often contributed to marital breakdown, but it can be found in any sort of relationship. We must consider carefully what people say to us, and not immediately assume rejection.

Covenant—A divine promise.

Crossroad—I have used the example of the crossroad several times throughout this manual. I see it as a flashing red road sign, saying *stop!* It is meant to get the reader's attention. The crossroad serves as a place to stop, a place to reconsider, an opportunity to turn back to God in repentance. The concept of the crossroad dates back to Jeremiah's time. There God calls us to *"Stand at the crossroads and look; ask for the ancient paths, ask where the good way is, and walk in it, and you will find rest for your souls"* (Jeremiah 6:16). This crossroad is not only a gift from God. It is a meeting place with Him for all who seek His will and ways. It is a place we can run to in times of confusion, hardship, or trouble. The crossroad is a place of reflection, regaining perspective, and seeking God for the best way forward.

Curses—A curse can be defined as "a prayer that harm will come to someone." Curses are words spoken against us to bring harm; they work in our mind to produce a stronghold, and can alight through witchcraft, legalism, and superstition. Important note: they all work the same way.

D

Deception—Almost without exception, deception begins with a claim to some special revelation outside and beyond the Bible. This may be as sophisticated as the Book of Mormon or as simple as the unique teachings of a religious group's leader. These teachings or groups may be even quasi-Christian, with a belief system based on the group leader's or organization's understanding. Be aware of the information that enters into your soul and mind

Depression—Because I have ministered to many living in perpetual depression, I know the remedy is found in Philippians 4:8: *"Finally, brothers and sisters, whatever is true, whatever is noble, whatever is right, whatever is pure, whatever is lovely, whatever is admirable—if anything is excellent or praiseworthy—think about such things."*

G

Generational/family sins—Here is a list of common problems in homes and families.

Abandonment
Abuse: physical/sexual/emotional
Addictions: sex/food/alcohol/drugs
Adultery
Allergies
Alzheimer's
Anger
Anti-Christian
Arthritis
Barrenness
Bestiality

Betrayal

Blame

Blind: Spiritual/physical

Blood disorders/circulation issues

Bitterness

Cancer

Co-dependency

Compulsive behaviour

Conception out of wedlock

Constant feeling of guilt

Controlling

Critical spirit

Deafness

Deceitfulness

Depression

Destruction, dying out of family

Diabetes

Dishonouring parents

Divorce

Dyslexia/aphasia

Eating disorder

Epilepsy

Failure

Fear and paranoia

Fornication

Frigidity

Gambling

Hatred

Heart problems

Homosexuality/lesbianism

Hypocrisy

Idolatry

Illegitimate child

Imprisonment

Incest

Infirmity/sickness/disease

Insanity/breakdown

Insecurity

Insomnia

Jealousy/envy

Kidney problems

Laziness

Legalism

Lying/falseness

Manipulation

Materialism

Migraines/headache

Miscarriages/abortion

Multiple Sclerosis

Murder

Nervousness

Obesity/anorexia/bulimia

Obsessions/masturbation

Overprotectiveness

Perversion

Phobias

Pornography

Poverty

Prejudice

Premature death

Pride (can be high or low opinion of oneself)

Prostitution

Rape

Rebellion

Rejection

Robbery

Schizophrenia

Selfishness

Self-righteousness
Scoliosis (or back problems)
Shame
Silent treatment
Suicide
Tragedies
Unforgiveness
Feeling of unworthiness
Violence
Witchcraft/occult involvement
Workaholism

Tracing Your Roots (a worksheet to accompany "Generational sins")
Go through the list of people below and note any possible generational sins connected with each individual.

Father
Father's Father –   Father's Father's Father
                    Father's Father's Mother
Father's Mother –   Father's Mother's Father
                    Father's Mother's Mother
Mother
Mother's Father –   Mother's Father's Father
                    Mother's Father's Mother
Mother's Mother – Mother's Mother's Father
                    Mother's Mother's Mother

Forgiveness Prayers (for family and others whose sins have affected you)

Lord, I don't know how to make forgiveness happen! I can't cleanse my own heart or change my feelings! I don't know how to trust, and I'm afraid to hold my heart open. But today, I'm making a choice to forgive. I know for some of these hurts, I will have to choose again and again until You make forgiveness real and complete in me. Please God, give me the willingness and strength to persevere in choosing forgiveness until it is accomplished in me by Your power. Lord, I forgive all offences and painful experiences connected with (each name) because it made me feel

I choose to forgive my father for _____

I choose to forgive my mother for _____

I choose to forgive (name) for _____

I choose to forgive (name) for _____

I choose to forgive (name) for _____

I choose to forgive (name) for _____

Forgive me, Heavenly Father, for all my sinful responses. Amen.

Today I choose to forgive all these people, not because I feel forgiveness or because they are right, but because I choose to be obedient to you, Father. I realize Your ways are higher than my ways, and I release these people, whom I have named, from my hurt, my disappointment, my resentment, my anger, my hatred, my unforgiveness, and my bitterness, especially my parents and family or anyone I have made a bitter root of judgement against. Thank you Lord, that I will no longer reap from those bitter roots that I have sown. Father, I let go of all resentments and bitterness stored in my heart. Wash me clean, Lord Jesus.

Here are the people I have hurt and the ones who have hurt me. I release them to you, and I forgive those who have despitefully used me. I pray for my enemies (those who have hurt me) as You have commanded, and I ask you to bless them and save them. Forgive me for the things I have done against them.

You tell me to give You my problems because You care for me. Thank you, Lord, that these people are no longer my problem; they are Yours. Thank you, Lord, for setting me free. Please heal me of my hurts in regards to these people. Please change my heart about them as only You can do. Forgive me for all condemning judgements I have made. Give me a new and right spirit that will enable me to hate sin but look with compassion and love upon the sinner. Heal the wounded heart of the child within me. Bring my childish ways and expectations to righteous maturity.

Fill me now, Father, in all the areas we have dealt with today and make them Yours forevermore. Lord, set a guard around my heart that I might function in love. Pour Your love in. Let Your light shine into all the hidden places of my heart. Enlighten the eyes of my heart, Lord, to see You and love You as You really are, and to walk in Your way. Amen.

H

Healing through deliverance—Remember, very much of sickness and disease is demonically conceived.

Jesus still heals today. He no longer personally lays hands on or physically touches people as He did before His death. But today, He works through people who will allow the same anointing that was upon Him to flow through them in manifestations of the Holy Spirit and through prayers of faith.

O

Open your mouth—We all have enemies or giants in our lives that need to be defeated. You cannot defeat Goliath with your mouth shut.

He looked David over and saw that he was little more than a boy, glowing with health and handsome, and he despised him. He said to David, "Am I a dog, that you come at me with sticks?" And the Philistine cursed David by his gods. "Come here," he said, "and I'll give your flesh to the birds and the wild animals!"

David said to the Philistine, "You come against me with sword and spear and javelin, but I come against you in the name of the Lord Almighty, the God of the armies of Israel, whom you have defied. This day the Lord will deliver you into my hands, and I'll strike you down and cut off your head. This very day I will give the carcasses of the Philistine army to the birds and the wild animals, and the whole world will know that there is a God in Israel. All those gathered here will know that it is not by sword or spear that the Lord saves; for the battle is the Lord's, and he will give all of you into our hands."

As the Philistine moved closer to attack him, David ran quickly toward the battle line to meet him.

—1 Samuel 17:42 – 48

P

Parenting—Feminist leader Gloria Steinem has declared: "By the year 2000 we will, I hope, raise our children to believe in human potential, not God." Do you know who is teaching your children and what they are being taught in school, at church, and at other social functions?

Be aware of the epidemic of sexual activity that is assaulting our younger generations. The Bible says, *"Start children off on the way they should go, and even when they are old they will not turn from it"* (Proverbs 22:6). Therefore, the responsibility for your children growing up with a Biblical understanding of God's gift of sexuality belongs to you, the parent(s). You are responsible and will answer to God for the lack of early teaching in this realm. Sanford says,

> Affection feeds the personal spirit with strength and builds habits of normal healthy intimacy. It constructs channels for wholesome physical touching. Such appropriate practices tend to ward off and make repulsive whatever is inappropriate. Consistent parental nurture enables a true working conscience, which acts to keep the person from sin rather than merely to convict after the event.... A lack of discipline basically leaves the passions in control of the person rather than the other way around.[119]

---

119 Sandford, 2006, pp. 120–121.

Perception—This is often a key element in marital breakdown. Dr. James Dobson says the following:

> It has been my observation that lust for forbidden fruit is often incidental to the real cause of marital decay.... The critical element is the way one spouse begins to perceive the other and their lives together. It is a subtle thing at first, often occurring without either partner being aware of the slippage. But as time passes, one individual begins to feel trapped. That's the key word, *trapped*. In its more advanced stages, a man considers his wife (gender is interchangeable throughout these discussions) and thinks these kinds of thoughts: "Look at Joan. She used to be rather pretty. Now with those fifteen extra pounds she doesn't even attract me anymore. Her lack of discipline bothers me in other areas, too—the house is a perpetual mess and she always seems totally disorganized. I hate to admit it, but I made an enormous mistake back there in my youth when I decided to marry her. Now I have to spend the rest of my life—can you believe it—all these years I have left—tied up with someone I'm disinterested in.... When married persons find themselves hurtling relentlessly toward a divorce, they sometimes turn to marriage counselors, ministers, psychologists and psychiatrists to stem the tide. The counsel they are subsequently given often involves changes in the way the two partners relate to one another from day to day. It may be proposed that they reserve an evening each week as "date night," or that they alter their sex habits or workaholic lifestyles. Such advice can be helpful in reestablishing communication and understanding between two wounded and disappointed people, but it may be inadequate to save a dying marriage. Why? Because the counsel is directed at the *surface* issues.
>
> In most troubled marriages, a basic problem lies ominiously below these relatively minor irritants. It involves the way one party has begun to perceive the other, as we have described. When expressed in materialistic terms, it is the value ascribed to one human being by another. That perceived worth is incorporated in the

word *respect* and is absolutely basic to all human relationships. The way we behave from day to day is largely a function of how we respect or disrespect the people around us... the way husbands and wives relate is a function of their mutual respect and admiration. That's why marital discord almost always emanates from seeming disrespect somewhere in the relationship! That is the bottom line of romantic confrontation.

What I've been trying to describe are those gradual changes in perception—that subtle deterioration in attitude that precedes marital conflict.... If there is hope for the dying marriage... it is likely to be found in the reconstruction of respect between warring husbands and wives.[120]

The key word in what have just read is the word "perception." Our perception determines how we respond to or receive our spouses, or really anyone we interact with along the road of life. My dictionary says of the word "perception": consciousness feeling, grasp, idea, impression...[121] None of these are established truths or facts. The problem here is that we argue against one another using only perceptions, not established truths.

Many marriages and families are torn apart because either the husband or the wife took their stand according to skewed perception. I draw attention to this area because making decisions according to an unproven truth is very common among people coming in for counselling. One of the first things I usually do with a couple is to establish the husband's and wife's perceptions of their marital problem. Again, while we are talking about husband and wife, this problem reaches into every relational experience we have.

This, in my opinion, has the ability to distance us from God, little by little. We are dealing now not with truths, but with untruths and half-truths, which of course are against the teachings of the Word of God. This puts us in a place of unforgiveness. If we carry on, the next step is the jailhouse. I know of many marriages that have fallen apart, simply because one or the other is taking a stand on the half-truth because of a wrong perception.

---

120 Dobson, pp. 49–50; emphasis in original.
121 Gilmour, p. 599.

What are your beliefs and attitudes about the state of your marriage (or other relationship) today?

_____

_____

_____

_____

How do you feel about the state of your marriage/relationship today?

_____

_____

_____

_____

What is your perception of your thoughts and beliefs? Do you think they need to be changed? Do you think they can be changed?

_____

_____

_____

_____

If you think anything about your thoughts and beliefs should be changed, what measureable plans could you make to increase the success of your marriage?

Prayer—Our prayers of faith are the vehicles that cause God's Word to be manifested upon the earth.

Pride—Dealing with pride is always tough, but we are to be strong in the Lord and in the strength of His might. To prepare us for the application, let's pray this prayer together.

> Dear Heavenly Father, I confess that I haven't been humble in all things, even though I know that pride goes before destruction, and my arrogant spirit will stumble. I have given territory to Satan through my pride, believing I could rely on my own strength and resources to be successful. I now confess my sin of pride. I have centred my life on me, instead of you. I renounce my self-centredness and ask you to guide me in all that I do. Help me to be humble and to regard others more highly than myself. Show me, Lord, where I need to work in this area of pride. Amen.

Some Possible Attitudes of Pride to Contemplate
1. A stronger desire to do my will than God's.
2. Sometimes thinking that my ideas are better than others (attitude).
3. Thinking of myself as more or less important than I should.
4. Thinking that I have no needs.
5. Often thinking I am more humble than others.
6. Finding it difficult to admit I was wrong.
7. Unexpressed thoughts; judgements through the use of silence (i.e. being silent because those talking are not as good or self-controlled as I am).

Take some time, and list those you know need to be dealt with.

_____

_____

_____

_____

Lord, I admit that I have been proud in the following areas:

_____

_____

_____

_____

Lord Jesus, I ask that you bring to mind any other way I have been deceived into building strongholds of pride:

_____

_____

_____

_____

Father, forgive me for all of these sins of pride. I choose to humble myself and place all my confidence in you. Forgive me where I have given ground to the enemy and allowed him to build strongholds in these areas. I choose to let your word be a lamp unto my feet as Satan tries to deceive me in the future. Amen.

S

Slumbering spirit—For those of you who will be ministering into the lives of others, there is a very good chance that you will bump into a slumbering spirit. It is created by different means, but more often than not because the child in the womb, or just birthed, realizes that she or he isn't wanted. These individuals thus grow up withdrawn and in a place of slumber, disengaged from life. This is very common. Healing comes only as this individual is received by his or her parents and those around him or her. As the mentor or counsellor, you can do much for these individuals just by loving and caring for them, drawing them out of the darkness.

Spiritual immune system—Where did your client's sickness come from? Again, illnesses are often birthed by the powers of darkness.

Superstition—Tools that the enemy uses to gain access to the mind so that the truth cannot penetrate it.

W

Warfare—Here is a prayer for a friend—an act of spiritual warfare.

> Heavenly Father, I bring before You and the Lord Jesus Christ one who is very dear to you and to me, _____. I have come to see that Satan is blinding and binding (him/her) in bondage. (He/she) is in such a condition that (he/she) cannot or will not come to You for help on (his/her) own. I stand in for (him/her) in intercessory prayer before Your throne. I draw upon the Holy Spirit, that He may guide me to pray in wisdom, power, and understanding.
>
> In the name of the Lord Jesus Christ, I loose _____ from the bondage the powers of darkness are putting upon (him/her). I bind them in the name of the Lord

Jesus Christ and forbid them to work. I bind all powers of depression that are seeking to cut _____ off and imprison (him/her) in a tomb of despondency. I pray that You would loose (him/her) from the powers of darkness, and that the Holy Spirit would apply all of the mighty work of the Lord Jesus Christ directly against any forces of darkness seeking to destroy _____.
In Jesus' name. Amen.

Worship—Always improves your outlook. There is nothing better than a powerful encounter with God that reminds us to be thankful. Make a list of all the things you are thankful for and give God the praise and worship for bringing them into your life.

_____

_____

_____

_____

_____

_____

_____

_____

_____

_____

_____

_____

_____

_____

_____

_____

_____

_____

_____

_____

_____

_____

_____

_____

_____

_____

BIBLIOGRAPHY

Abanes, Richard. 2001. *Harry Potter and the Bible*. Camp Hill, PA: Horizon Books.

Ankerberg, John, and John Weldon. 1996. *The Facts on Halloween*. Eugene, OR: Harvest House Publishers.

Augsburger, David. 1998. *The Freedom of Forgiveness: Revised and Expanded*. Chicago: Moody Press.

———. 2000. *The New Freedom of Forgiveness*. 3rd ed. Chicago: Moody Press.

Bell, James R. 2010. *Practicing the Presence of God*. Xulon Press.

Bounds, E.M. 2013. *Power through Prayer*. Merchant Books.

Burdick, Donald W. 1976. *The Expositor's Bible Commentary with the New International Version of the Holy Bible, Volume 12, James*. Frank E. Gaebelein, ed. Grand Rapids, MI: Zondervan.

Carter, Tom. 1998. *2200 Quotations from the Writings of Charles H. Spurgeon: Arranged Topically or Textually and Indexed by Subject, Scripture, and People*. Grand Rapids, MI: Baker.

Cedar, Paul. 1998. *A Life of Prayer*. Nashville, TN: Word Publishing.

Chambers, Oswald. 1935. *The Golden Book of Oswald Chambers: My Utmost for His Highest*. New York: Dodd, Mead, & Co.

Collins, Gary R. 1980. *The Rebuilding of Psychology*. Wheaton, IL: Tyndale House Publishers.

Crabb, Lawrence J., and Dan Allender. 1984. *Encouragement: The Key to Caring*. Grand Rapids, MI: Zondervan.

Cramer, Dennis. 2007. *Breaking Christian Curses: Finding Freedom from Destructive Prayers*. Cedar Rapids, IA: Arrow Publications.

Deere, Jack S. 1986. *The Bible Knowledge Commentary: Old Testament, Deuteronomy.* John F. Walvoord & Roy B. Zuck, eds. Wheaton, IL: Victor Books.

Dobson, James. 2007. *Love Must be Tough: New Hope for Marriages in Crisis.* Tyndale Momentum.

Dyer, Charles H. 1986. *The Bible Knowledge Commentary: Old Testament, Ezekiel.* John F. Walvoord & Roy B. Zuck, eds. Wheaton, IL: Victor Books.

Foster, K. Neill, and Paul L. King. 1998. *Binding and Loosing: How to Exercise Authority over the Dark Powers.* Camp Hill, PA: Christian Publications.

Frangipane, Francis. 1991. *The Jezebel Spirit.* Cedar Rapids, IA: Arrow Publications.

———. 1998. *The Stronghold of God.* Orlando, FL: Creation House.

Friesen, James G. 1997. *Uncovering the Mystery of MPD.* Eugene, OR: Wipf and Stock Publishers.

Gilmour, Laura (ed). 2006. *Collins Essential Canadian English Dictionary and Thesaurus.* Glasgow, UK: Harper Collins.

Graham, Billy. 1997. *Just As I Am: The Autobiography of Billy Graham.* San Francisco: HarperSanFrancisco.

Gumbel, Nicky. 2003. *How Does God Guide Us?* Alpha Christian Resources.

Gurnall, William. 2002. *The Christian in Complete Armour: Volume 1, Abridged Version.* Edinburgh: Banner of Truth.

Harris, Murray J. 1976. *The Expositor's Bible Commentary with the New International Version of the Holy Bible, Volume 10, 2nd Corinthians.* Frank E. Gaebelein, ed. Grand Rapids, MI: Zondervan.

Hayford, Jack W. (ed). 1995. *Hayford's Bible Handbook.* Nashville, TN: Thomas Nelson.

Hayford, Jack W. 2002. *Prayer is Invading the Impossible.* Gainseville, FL: Bridge-Logos Publishers.

Hendricks, Howard G., and William D. Hendricks. *Living by the Book.* Chicago: Moody Press.

Hickey, Marilyn. 2000. *Breaking Generational Curses.* Tulsa, OK: Harrison House.

Hill, Craig. 1992. *The Ancient Paths.* Littleton, CO: Family Foundations International.

Hoover, David W. 1997. *How to Respond to...the Occult.* St. Louis, MO: Concordia Publishing House.

Hughes, Selwyn. 1995. *Every Day with Jesus: Overcoming "Giants."* November 12. Farnham, UK: CWR.

———. 2001. *Christ Empowered Living: Celebrating your Significance in God.* Nashville, TN: Broadman & Holman Publishers.

Hughes, Selwyn, and Mick Brooks. 2011. *Every Day with Jesus, Know it - Do It.* April 12. Farnham, UK: CWR.

———. 2012a. *Christ Empowered Living: Celebrating your Significance in God.* Farnham, UK: CWR.

———. 2012b. *Every Day with Jesus.* April 18. Farnham, UK: CWR.

———. 2015. *Every Day with Jesus.* September 18, September 21, September 24, October 3. Farnham, UK: CWR.

———. 2016. *Every Day with Jesus.* February 29. Farnham, UK: CWR.

Jeremiah, David. 2011. *I Never Thought I Would See the Day!* New York: FaithWords Publishing.

Kendall, R.T. 2007. *How to Forgive Ourselves Totally.* Lake Mary, FL: Charisma House.

Kinnaman, Gary D. 1990. *Overcoming the Dominion of Darkness: Personal Strategies for Spiritual Warfare.* Old Tappan, NJ: Chosen Books.

Kraft, Charles H., and Mark White (eds). 1994. *Behind Enemy Lines: An Advanced Guide to Spiritual Warfare.* Ann Arbor, MI: Servant Publications.

Lochhaas, Phillip H. 1995. *The New Age Movement.* St. Louis, MO: Concordia Publishing House.

Logan, Jim. 1995. *Reclaiming Surrendered Ground.* Chicago: Moody Press.

Lucado, Max. 1995. *The Inspirational Study Bible: Life Lessons from the Inspired Word of God.* Nashville, TN: Thomas Nelson.

MacDonald, William. 1995. *Believer's Bible Commentary : Old and New Testaments.* Nashville, TN: Thomas Nelson.

Meier, Paul D., Frank B. Minirth, Frank B. Wichern, and Donald E. Ratcliff. 1996. *Introduction to Psychology and Counseling: Christian Perspectives and Applications.* 2nd ed. Grand Rapids: Baker Books.

Michaelsen, Johanna. 1989. *Like Lambs to the Slaughter.* Eugene, OR: Harvest House Publishers.

Milligan, Ira. 2010. *The Scorpion Within: Revealing the Eight Demonic Roots of Sin*. Shippensburg, PA: Destiny Image Publishing.

Murphy, Ed. 1996. *The Handbook for Spiritual Warfare: Revised and Updated*. Nashville, TN: Thomas Nelson.

Nori, Don. 2005. *Breaking Generational Curses: Releasing God's Power in Us, Our Children, and Our Destiny*. Shippensburg, PA: Destiny Image Publishers.

Penn-Lewis, Jessie, and Evan Roberts. 1985. *War on the Saints*. Fort Washington, PA: The Christian Literature Crusade.

QuickVerse. October 21, 2011. "Experiencing God Day by Day."

Rice, D.T. 2011. *Psychology: A Christian Perspective*. High school ed. Epworth, GA: Rocking R Ventures.

Sampson, Steve. 2010. *Discerning and Defeating the Ahab Spirit: The Key to Breaking Free from Jezebel*. Bloomington, MN: Chosen Books.

———. 2012. *Confronting Jezebel: Discerning and Defeating the Spirit of Control*. Grand Rapids, MI: Chosen Books.

Sandford, John L. 2006. *Why Some Christians Commit Adultery: Causes and Cures*. Lake Mary, FL: Charisma House.

Sandford, John L., and Mark Sandford. 1992. *A Comprehensive Guide to Deliverance and Inner Healing*. Grand Rapids, MI: Chosen Books.

Sheets, Dutch. 2012. *Dream: Discovering God's Purpose for Your Life*. Bloomington, MN: Bethany House Publishers.

Silvoso, Ed. 1994. *That None Should Perish: How to Reach Entire Cities for Christ through Prayer Evangelism*. Ventura, CA: Regal Books.

Simpson, A.B. 1996. *Hard Places: Stepping Stones to Spiritual Growth*. Camp Hill, PA: Christian Publications.

Smith, F. LaGard. 1984. *Jesus the Christ: The Daily Bible in Chronological Order in 365 Daily Readings*. Eugene, OR: Harvest House Publishers.

Steer, Roger. 1995. *Hudson Taylor: Lessons in Discipleship*. Crowborough, UK. Monarch Publications.

Strong, James. 1984. *The New Strong's Exhaustive Concordance of the Bible*. Nashville, TN: Thomas Nelson.

Sumrall, Lester. 2002. *Spirit Soul and Body: United in Oneness with God*. Whitaker House.

Swaggart, Jimmy. 2005. *The Expositor's Study Bible KJV/Concordance.* Jimmy Swaggart Ministries.

VanGemeren, Willem A. 1991. *The Expositor's Bible Commentary with the New International Version of the Holy Bible, Volume 5, Psalms.* Frank E. Gaebelein, ed. Grand Rapids, MI: Zondervan.

Wagner, C. Peter. 2009. *Warfare Prayer: What the Bible Says About Spiritual Warfare.* Shippensburg, PA: Destiny Image Publishers.

Wagner, Doris M. 2005. *How to Minister Freedom.* Ventura, CA: Regal Books.

Walvoord, John F. 1983. *The Bible Knowledge Commentary: New Testament, Revelation.* John F. Walvoord & Roy B. Zuck, eds. Wheaton, IL: Victor Books.

White, Thomas B. 2001. *The Believer's Guide to Spiritual Warfare: Wising Up to Satan's Influence in Your World.* Ventura, CA: Regal Books.

Wright, H. Norman. 1977. *Training Christians to Counsel.* Eugene, OR: Harvest House Publishers.

Zodhiates, Spiros. 1992. *The Complete Word Study Dictionary: New Testament.* Chattanooga, TN: AMG Publishers.